First Japanese Reader for Business

Miku Ono

First Japanese Reader for Business

Bilingual for Speakers of English

Beginner and Elementary (A1 A2)

Audio tracks inclusive

LANGUAGE
PRACTICE
PUBLISHING

First Japanese Reader for Business
by Miku Ono

Series Title: Graded Japanese Readers, Volume 12

Audio tracks: www.lppbooks.com/Japanese/FJRB/En

Homepage: www.audiolego.com

Design: Audiolego Design
Images: Canstockphoto

Copyright © 2017 2021 Language Practice Publishing
Copyright © 2017 2020 2021 Audiolego
This book is in copyright. Subject to statutory exception and to the provisions of relevant collective licensing agreements, no reproduction of any part may take place without the written permission of Language Practice Publishing.

目次
Table of contents

Pronunciation 7

How to control the playing speed 10

Beginner level 11

Chapter 1 How are you? 12

Chapter 2 What is her position? 23

Chapter 3 Can you tell me about your company? 34

Chapter 4 How much time do you need to process my order? 44

Chapter 5 Can I help you with something? 53

Chapter 6 Do you know how to process order forms? 61

Chapter 7 Can you help me to figure it out? 70

Chapter 8 Whose are these responsibilities? 78

Chapter 9 Can you accept a fax for me? 86

Chapter 10 At what time will the conference start? 96

Chapter 11 Do you think Michael is more responsible? 108

Chapter 12 How should I introduce you? 120

Elementary level 131

Chapter 13 アンチウィルスソフトウェア 132

Chapter 14 卸売り会社 141

Chapter 15 経営陣が決断を下しました 152

Chapter 16 どの割引を当てにすることができますか？ 162

Chapter 17 カスタムされたプログラム 171

Chapter 18 有利な条件 178

Chapter 19 代表の中国への出張 187

Chapter 20 プログラムブロックの試験 196

Chapter 21 北京 205

Chapter 22 交渉 216

Chapter 23 インストール 225

Chapter 24 品質と値段は正しいレートです 235

Chapter 25 取締役会の会議 244

日英辞書 Japanese-English dictionary 251

英日辞書 English-Japanese dictionary 269

Recommended books 287

Pronunciation

Hiragana	Katakana	Romaji	Hiragana	Katakana	Romaji
あ	ア	a	そ	ソ	so
い	イ	i	しゃ	シャ	sha / sya
う	ウ	u	しゅ	シュ	shu / syu
え	エ	e	しょ	ショ	sho / syo
お	オ	o	た	タ	ta
や	ヤ	ya	ち	チ	chi / ti
ゆ	ユ	yu	つ	ツ	tsu / tu
よ	ヨ	yo	て	テ	te
か	カ	ka	と	ト	to
き	キ	ki	ちゃ	チャ	cha / tya
く	ク	ku	ちゅ	チュ	chu / tyu
け	ケ	ke	ちょ	チョ	cho / tyo
こ	コ	ko	な	ナ	na
きゃ	キャ	kya	に	ニ	ni
きゅ	キュ	kyu	ぬ	ヌ	nu
きょ	キョ	kyo	ね	ネ	ne
さ	サ	sa	の	ノ	no
し	シ	shi / si	にゃ	ニャ	nya
す	ス	su	にゅ	ニュ	nyu
せ	セ	se	にょ	ニョ	nyo

Hiragana	Katakana	Romaji	Hiragana	Katakana	Romaji
は	ハ	ha	れ	レ	re
ひ	ヒ	hi	ろ	ロ	ro
ふ	フ	fu / hu	りゃ	リャ	rya
へ	ヘ	he	りゅ	リュ	ryu
ほ	ホ	ho	りょ	リョ	ryo
ひゃ	ヒャ	hya	わ	ワ	wa
ひゅ	ヒュ	hyu	ゐ	ヰ	i / wi / i
ひょ	ヒョ	hyo	ゑ	ヱ	e / we / e
ま	マ	ma	を	ヲ	o / wo / o
み	ミ	mi	ん	ン	n-n'(-m) / n-n'
む	ム	mu	が	ガ	ga
め	メ	me	ぎ	ギ	gi
も	モ	mo	ぐ	グ	gu
みゃ	ミャ	mya	げ	ゲ	ge
みゅ	ミュ	myu	ご	ゴ	go
みょ	ミョ	myo	ぎゃ	ギャ	gya
や	ヤ	ya	ぎゅ	ギュ	gyu
ゆ	ユ	yu	ぎょ	ギョ	gyo
よ	ヨ	yo	ざ	ザ	za
ら	ラ	ra	じ	ジ	ji / zi
り	リ	ri	ず	ズ	zu
る	ル	ru	ぜ	ゼ	ze

Hiragana	Katakana	Romaji	Hiragana	Katakana	Romaji
ぞ	ゾ	zo	ぶ	ブ	bu
じゃ	ジャ	ja / zya	べ	ベ	be
じゅ	ジュ	ju / zyu	ぼ	ボ	bo
じょ	ジョ	jo / zyo	びゃ	ビャ	bya
だ	ダ	da	びゅ	ビュ	byu
ぢ	ヂ	ji / di / zi	びょ	ビョ	byo
づ	ヅ	zu / du / zu	ぱ	パ	pa
で	デ	de	ぴ	ピ	pi
ど	ド	do	ぷ	プ	pu
ぢゃ	ヂャ	ja / dya / zya	ぺ	ペ	pe
ぢゅ	ヂュ	ju / dyu / zyu	ぽ	ポ	po
ぢょ	ヂョ	jo / dyo / zyo	ぴゃ	ピャ	pya
ば	バ	ba	ぴゅ	ピュ	pyu
び	ビ	bi	ぴょ	ピョ	pyo

How to control the playing speed

The book is equipped with the audio tracks. The address of the home page of the book on the Internet, where audio files are available for listening and downloading, is listed at the beginning of the book on the bibliographic description page before the copyright notice. With the help of QR codes, you can call up an audio file in no time, without typing a web address manually. Simply hold your smartphone with camera app on over the QR code. Your smartphone will scan the code and will offer you to follow the scanned audio file link.

We recommend using free **VLC media player** to control the playing speed. You can control the playing speed by decreasing or increasing the speed value on the button of the VLC media player's interface.

Beginner Course

1

Audio

氷を砕く
Break the ice

"ママ、今日ぼくは勇敢だったんだ！"と幼い男の子はお母さんに言いました。"大きな、生きてる虫を見てたんだけど逃げ出さなかったんだ！"

mama, kyō boku wa yūkan datta n da! to osanai otokonoko wa okāsan ni iimashita. ōkina, ikiteru mushi o miteta n da kedo nigedasanakatta n da!

"Mom, I was brave today!" a little boy says to his mom. "I was looking at a big, live bug and I did not run away!"

元気ですか？
How are you?

単語
Words

1. 10、十 [juu] - ten
2. 〜の中 [〜 no naka] - in
3. 〜と／〜で [〜to / 〜de] - with / at
4. 〜なる(動詞) [〜naru (doushi)] - be *(Verb)*
5. 〜の上 [〜no ue] - on
6. あなた [anata] - you
7. ありがとうございます [arigatougozaimasu] - thank you
8. いくら(いくつ) [ikutsu (ikura)] - how much (many)
9. お願い、どうぞ [onegai,douzo] - please
10. これ [kore] - this
11. これは〜です [kore ha 〜 desu.] - here is
12. こんにちは！[konnichiha!] - Hello!
13. そして、と [soshite, to] - and
14. それ [sore] - it
15. とても [totemo] - very
16. どうやって [douyatte] - how
17. どこ [doko] - where
18. はい [hai] - yes

19. アイデア [aidea] - idea
20. アメ [ame] - candy
21. イギリス人、英国人 [igirisujin, eikokujin] - Englishman, British
22. オフィス、事務所 [ofisu, jimusho] - office
23. カード [ka-do] - card
24. カタログ [katarogu] - catalog
25. テーブル [te-buru] - table
26. パートナー、仲間、協力者 [pa-tona-, nakama, kyouryokusha] - partner
27. プロジェクト、企画 [purojekuto, kikaku] - project
28. マネージャー、支配人 [mane-ja-, shihainin] - manager
29. 安心 [anshin] - glad
30. 位置する、〜にある [ichisuru, 〜ni aru] - located, is
31. 何/あれ [nani / are] - what / that
32. 何、どれ [nani, dore] - what, which
33. 会社 [kisha] - firm
34. 会社、企業 [kaisha, kigyou] - company, enterprise
35. 企業 [kigyou] - enterprise
36. 喜び、楽しみ [yorokobi, tanoshimi] - pleasure
37. 機材、設備 [kizai, setsubi] - equipment
38. 急ぐ(動詞) [isogu (doushi)] - hurry (Verb), to rush
39. 協力、提携 [kyouryoku, teikyou] - collaboration, cooperation
40. 興味深い [kyoumibukai] - interesting
41. 近所の [kinjyono] - neighboring
42. 契約 [keiyaku] - contract
43. 月曜日 [getsuyoubi] - Monday ['mʌndei]
44. 建物 [tatemono] - building
45. 効率的、効力 [kouritsuteki, kouryoku] - efficient, effective
46. 広い、広々とした [hiroi, hirobirotoshita] - spacious, roomy
47. 紅茶 [koucha] - tea
48. 考える(動詞)、熟考する [kangaeru (doushi), jyukkosuru] - think (Verb), to contemplate
49. 高価、(値段が) 高い [kouka, (nedan ga) takai] - expensive
50. 今 [ima] - now
51. 今日 [kyou] - today
52. 砂糖 [satou] - sugar
53. 仕事、取引 [bijinesu, torihiki] - business, deal
54. 私 [watashi] - I
55. 私の [watashi no] - mine, my
56. 時間 [jikan] - hour, time
57. 質、品質、クオリティ [shitsu, hinshitsu, kuoriti-] - quality
58. 書類、文書 [shoryi, bunsho] - document
59. 商品、製品 [shouhinn, seihin] - goods, products
60. 上手に、うまく [jyouzuni, umaku] - well
61. 心地が良い [kokochi ga ii] - comfortable
62. 新しい、目新しい [atarashii, metarashii] - new, novel
63. 親切、良い [shinsetsu, yoi] - kind, good
64. 成功した [seikoushita] - successful
65. 製造設備、製造ライン [seizousetsubi, seizourain] - manufacturing facilities, production lines
66. 製品 [seihin] - products
67. 責任、責務 [sekinin, sekimu] - responsibility, duty

68. 責任のある [sekinin no aru] - responsible, liable
69. 専門家 [senmonka] - specialist
70. 大きい、巨大 [ookii, kyodai] - big, large
71. 題名、名前 [daimei, namae] - title, name
72. 沢山、多くの [takusan, ookuno] - many, a lot of
73. 誰 [dare] - who
74. 男性 [dansei] - man
75. 値段表、値段のリスト [nedanhyou, nedan no risuto] - price list
76. 地方、地域 [chihou, chiiki] - district
77. 中央 [chuuou] - center
78. 中心、主要な [chuushin, shuyou na] - main, major
79. 長い [nagai] - long
80. 提供する、申し出る [teikyousuru, moushideru] - offer
81. 同僚、従業員 [douryou, jyuugyouin] - coworker, employee
82. 特別 [tokubetsu] - special
83. 日 [hi] - day
84. 彼 [kare] - he
85. 彼ら、彼女ら、それら [karera, kanojyora, sorera] - they
86. 彼女 [kanojyo] - she
87. 秘書 [hisho] - secretary
88. 費用 [hiyou] - expense
89. 美しい [utsukushii] - beautiful
90. 必要、必須 [hitsuyou, hissu] - necessary
91. 複雑 [fukuzatsu] - complex
92. 訪ねる [tazumeru] - visit
93. 忙しい [isogashii] - busy
94. 役職、地位 [yakushoku , chii] - position, post
95. 約束された、有望な、期待できる、考え方 [yakusokusareta, yuunouna, kangaekata] - promising, perspective
96. 優れた、良い、元気 [sugureta, yoi, genki] - good
97. 有益な、有利な、もうかる [yuuekia, yurina, moukaru] - profitable, advantageous, lucrative
98. 予定、計画 [yotei, keikaku] - plan
99. 欲しい(動詞) [hoshii (doushi)] - want *(Verb)*
100. 離す [hanasu] - separate
101. 良い、素敵 [yoi, suteki] - nice
102. 緑 [midori] - green

B

1

-こんにちは！
-konnichiha!
-いい天気ですね！
-iitennki desune!
-それは何ですか？
-sore ha nan desuka?
-これは私のびじねすかーどです。

1

- Hello!

- Good day!

- What is that?

- This is my business card.

-kore ha watashi no bijinesuka-do desu.

-ありがとうございます。これは何ですか？
-arigatougozaimasu. kore ha nandesuka?

-これは私たちの会社の名前です。それは成功したものです。
-kore ha watashitachi no kaisha no namae desu. sore ha seikoushita mono desu.

-あれは何ですか？
-are ha nandesuka?

-これは私の役職です。私はまねーじゃーです。
-kore ha watashi no yakushokudesu. watashi ha mane-ja- desu.

-とても良いですね。
-totemo ii desune.

2

-今日は月曜日ですか？
-kyou ha getsuyoubi desuka?

-はい、今日は月曜日です。
-hai, kyou ha getsuyoubi desu.

-何時ですか？
-nanjidesuka?

-10時です。
-juujidesu.

-元気ですか？
-genkidesuka?

-元気です。ありがとうございます。
-genki desu. Arigatougozaimasu.

-あなたは時間はありますか？
-anata ha jikan ha arimasuka?

-はい、あります。
-hai, arimasu.

- Thank you. What's this?

- This is the name of our company. It is a successful one.

- What is that?

- This is my position. I am a manager.

- Very nice.

2

- Is today Monday?

- Yes, today is Monday.

- What time is it?

- It's ten o'clock.

- How are you?

- Good, thank you.

- Do you have some time?

- Yes, I do.

3

- あなたは紅茶はいりますか？
- anata ha koucha ha irimasuka?
- はい、喜んで。それは緑茶ですか？
- hai, yorokonde. sore ha ryokucha desuka?
- はい、お願いします。これはあめといくつかの砂糖です。
- hai, onegaishimasu. kore ha ame to ikutsuka no satoudesu.
- あなたの予定は何ですか？
- anata no yotei ha nandesuka?
- 今日私は沢山やることがあります。
- kyou watashi ha takusan yarukoto ga arimasu.

4

- あなたは私たちの会社に興味ありますか？
- anata ha watashitachi no kaisha ni kyoumi arimasuka?
- はい、私は興味があります。
- hai, watashi ha kyoumi ga arimasu.
- あなたは何か企画を持っていますか？
- anata ha nanika kikaku wo motteimasuka?
- 私たちは企画をいくつか持っています。それらは新しいです。
- watashitachi ha kikaku wo ikutsuka motteimasu. sorera ha atarashii desu.
- それらは期待でますか？
- sorera ha kitai dekimasuka?
- はい、それらは期待できます。
- hai, sorera ha kitai dekimasu.
- あなたは何か新しいあいであを持っていますか？
- anata ha nanika atarashii aidea wo motteimasuka?
- はい、もちろんです。
- hai, mochiron desu.

3

- Would you like some tea?
- Yes, with pleasure. Is it green tea?
- Yes, please. Here are candies and some sugar.
- What are your plans?
- Today I have a lot to do.

4

- Are you interested in our company?
- Yes, it interests me.
- Do you have any projects?
- We have some projects. They're new.
- Are they promising?
- Yes, they are promising.
- Do you have any new ideas?
- Yes, of course.

5

-あなたのカタログはどこですか？
-anata no katarogu ha doko desuka?
-私たちのかたろぐはてーぶるの上にあります。これが私たちの新しいかたろぐです。
-watashitachi no katarogu ha te-buru no ue ni arimasu. kore ga watashitachi no atarashi katarogu desu.
-このかたろぐの中には何がのっていますか？
-kono katarogu no naka niha nani ga notte imasuka?
-これは私たちの新しい製品のかたろぐです。それらは高品質です。
-kore ha watashitachi no atarashii seihin no katarogu desu. sorera ha kouhinshitsudesu.
-これは何ですか？
-kore ha nandesuka?
-これらは私たちの製品です。それらは高品質です。
-korera ha watashitachi no seihin desu. sorera ha kouhinshitsudesu.

6

-あなたは申し出はありますか？
-anata ha moushide ha arimasuka?
-はい、あります。私たちの申し出は有益です。あなたはそれに興味がありますか？
-hai, arimasu. watashitachi no moushide ha yuuekidesu. anata ha soreni kyoumi ga arimasuka?
-はい、それは良いですね。これは興味深い申し出です。
-hai, sore ha iidesune. kore ha kyoumibukai moushide desu.
-これは何ですか？
-kore ha nandesuka?

5

- Where is your catalog?

- Our catalog is on the table. Here is our new catalog.

- What's in this catalog?

- This is a catalog of our new products. They are high quality.

- What is this?

- These are our products. They are of good quality.

6

- Do you have an offer?

- Yes, I do. Our offer is profitable. Are you interested in it?

- Yes, it's nice. This is an interesting offer.

- What is this?

-これは 私たちの値段のりすとです。それは長いです。
-kore ha watashitachi no nedan no lisuto desu. sore ha nagai desu.

7

-あなたの事務所はどこですか？
-anata no jimusho ha doko desuka?
-事務所は中央に位置します。それは心地が良く大きいです。
-jimusho ha chuuou ni ichishimasu. sore ha kokochigayoku ookiidesu.
-それは離れた建物ですか？
-sore ha hanareta tatemonodesuka?
-はい、それは離れた建物です。それは美しいです。-はい、それは離れた建物です。それは美しいです。
-hai, sore ha hanareta tatemonodesu. sore ha utsukushii desu.

8

-これらの人々は誰ですか？
-korera no hitobito ha daredesuka?
-これらは私たちの従業員です。彼らはすぐ優れた専門家です。
-korera ha watashitachi no juugyouindesu. karera ha sugureta senmonka desu.
-これは誰ですか？
-kore ha daredesuka?
-これは私たちの秘書です。彼女は責任があります。
-kore ha watashitachi no hisho desu. kanojo ha sekinin ga arimasu.
-これらの人々は誰ですか？

- This is our price list. It is long.

7

- Where is your office?
- The office is located in the center. It's comfortable and large.
- Is that a separate building?
- Yes, it is a separate building. It is beautiful.

8

- Who are these people?
- These are our employees. They are good specialists.
- Who is this?
- This is our secretary. She is responsible.
- Who are these men?
- They are managers.

-korera no hitobito ha daredesuka?
- 彼らは支配人です。彼らは成功しています。
-karera ha shihainin desu. karera ha seikou shiteimasu.
- 彼らには沢山責務がありますか？
-karera niha takusan sekimu ga arimasuka?
-はい、彼らはとても忙しいです。
-hai, karera ha totemo isogashii desu.

9
-あなた達の製造設備はどこですか？
-anatatachi no seizousetsubi ha doko desuka?
- 私たちの製造設備は近くのえりあに位置します。
-watashitachi no seizousetsubi ha chikaku no eria ni ichishimasu.
-それらは効率的ですか？
-sorera ha kouritsuteki desuka?
-はい、私たちの製造らいんは大きくて効率的です。
-hai, watashitachi no seizourain ha ookikute kouritsuteki desu.
-あなたは沢山費用を持っていますか？
-anata ha takusan hiyou wo motteimasuka?
-はい、その企業は沢山費用を持っています。
-hai, sonokigyou ha takusan hiyou wo motteimasu.

10
-これは何ですか？
-kore ha nandesuka?
-これは私たちの企業の計画です。
-kore ha watashitachi no kigyou no keikaku desu.
-それは新しいですか？
-sore ha atarashiidesuka?

They are successful.
- Do they have many responsibilities?
- Yes, they are very busy.

9
- Where are your manufacturing facilities?
- Our manufacturing facilities are located in a nearby area.
- Are they effective?
- Yes, our production lines are large and effective.
- Do you have a lot of expenses?
- Yes, the enterprise has a lot of expenses.

10
- What is this?
- This is the plan of our company.
- Is it new?

-はい、その建物は新しいです。それは広いです。
-hai, sonotatemono ha atarashii desu. sore ha hiroi desu.
-これは何ですか？
-kore ha nandesuka?
-それは機材です。それは複雑で高価です。
-sore ha kizai desu. sore ha fukuzatsude kouka desu.

11

-あれは誰ですか？
-are ha daredesuka?
-これらは私たちのぱーとなーです。彼らは英国人です。
-korera ha watashitachi no pa-tona- desu. karera ha eikokujin desu.
-それはあなた達の契約書ですか？
-sore ha anatatachi no keiyakusho desuka?
-はい、これは私たちの契約書です。
-hai, kore ha watashitachi no keiyakusho desu.
-あなた達は書類を持っていますか？
-anatatachi ha shorui wo motteimasuka?
-はい、私たちは必要な書類を持っています。
-hai, watashitachi ha hitsuyouna shorui wo motteimasu.
-あれは何ですか？
-are ha nandesuka?
-これは特別な申し出です。それは有益です。
-kore ha tokubetsuna moushide desu. sore ha yuueki desu.

- Yes, the building is new. It is spacious.
- What is this?
- That is equipment. It is complicated and expensive.

11

- Who is that?
- These are our partners. They are British.
- Is this your contract?
- Yes, this is our contract.
- Do you have documents?
- Yes, we have the necessary documents.
- What is that?
- This is a special offer. It is advantageous.

-あなたは 私たちの 主要 ぱーとなーです。
-anata ha watashitachi no shuyou pa-tona- desu.
-私はとても嬉しいです。
-watashi ha totemo ureshii desu.
-私たちの申し出を考えてください。ゆっくりでいいです。
-watashitachi no moushide wo kangaetekudasai. yukkurude ii desu.
-私はあなたと協力できて良かったです。
-watashi ha anata to kyouryokudekite yokatta desu.

- You are our main partner.
- I am very pleased.
- Consider our offer. Take your time.
- I'm glad to collaborate with you.

2

Audio

氷(こおり)を砕(くだ)く
Break the ice

幼(おさな)い二人(ににん)の少年(しょうねん)が話(はな)しています。
"弟(おとうと)の名前(なまえ)どうやって決(き)めた?"と一人(いちにん)の男(おとこ)の子(こ)が聞(き)きます。
"僕(ぼく)はばっとまんって名前(なまえ)が良(よ)かったんだけど、ぱぱとままがとむって名前(なまえ)にしたんだ。"と深(ふか)くため息(いき)をつきながら答(こた)えました。

Two little boys are talking.
"How did you name your younger brother?" one of them asks the other.
"I wanted to name him Batman," the boy answered and sighed deeply, "but my parents named him Tom."

osanai ni nin no shōnen ga hanashiteimasu. otōto no namae dō yatte kimeta? to ichi nin no otokonoko ga kikimasu. boku wa Battoman tte namae ga yokatta n da kedo, papa to mama ga Tomu tte namae ni shita n da. to fukaku tameiki o tsuki nagara kotaemashita.

彼女の役職は何ですか？
What is her position?

単語
Words

1. 12、十二 [juuni] - twelve
2. 〜から [〜kara] - from
3. 〜だった [〜datta] - was
4. 〜のため [〜no tame] - for
5. いいえ [iie] - no
6. いくつか、何個か [ikutsuka, nankoka] - a few, several
7. ここ [koko] - here
8. これ [kore] - this
9. さようなら！[sayounara!] - Goodbye!
10. しかし、けれども [shikashi, keredomo] - but
11. すでに [sudeni] - already
12. そこ [soko] - there
13. どこ/どこから [doko/doko kara] - where / from where
14. エンジニア [enjinia] - engineer
15. オーダー、注文 [o-da-, chuumon] - order
16. カフェ [kafe] - cafe
17. モダン、現代の [modan, gendaino] - modern
18. モデル [moderu] - model
19. リーダー、社長 [ri-da-, shachou] - leader, head
20. 火曜日 [kayoubi] - Tuesday
21. 学ぶ(動詞)、勉強する [manabu (doushi), benkyousuru] - learn *(Verb)*, to study
22. 客、ゲスト [kyaku, gesuto] - guest
23. 勤勉な、熱心な、勉強好きな [kinbenna, nesshinna, benkyouzukina] - diligent, studious

24. 金曜日 [kinyoubi] - Friday
25. 契約、契約書 [keiyaku, keiyakusho] - contract
26. 見る (動詞)、会う [miru (doushi), aru] - see (Verb), look (Verb)
27. 厳しい [kibishii] - strict
28. 更に、より [sarani, yori] - more
29. 最後 [saigo] - last
30. 私たち [watashitachi] - we
31. 私たちの [watashitachi no] - our
32. 状況、状態、期間 [joukyou, joutai, kikan] - condition, term
33. 人々 [hitobito] - people
34. 数字、番号 [suuji, bangou] - number
35. 素晴らしい、優秀な、大変良い [subarashii, yuushuuna, taihen yoi] - excellent
36. 総支配人、取締役、指導者 [soushihainin, torishimariyaku, shidousha] - general manager, director
37. 他の [hoka no] - other
38. 大きい [ookii] - large
39. 暖かい [atatakai] - warm
40. 値段 [nedan] - price
41. 昼食、夕食 [chuushoku, yuushoku] - lunch, dinner
42. 朝 [asa] - morning
43. 町 [machi] - city
44. 天気 [tenki] - weather
45. 電話 [denwa] - phone
46. 働く (動詞) [hataraku (doushi)] - work (Verb)
47. 道、道路、外 [michi, douro, soto] - street, outside
48. 背の高い、高い [se no takai, takai] - tall, high
49. 満足して、喜んで [manzokushite, yorokonde] - pleased
50. 有益な [yuuekina] - profitable
51. 頼りになる [tayorininaru] - reliable
52. 良く知られた、有名な [yokushirareta, yuumeina] - wellknown, famous

B

1

-おはようございます！お会いできて嬉しいです。今日は調子がいいですね！
-ohayougozaimasu! oaidekite ureshii desu. kyou ha choushi ga iidesune!
-こんにちは！ありがとうございます。
-konnnichiha! arigatougozaimasu.
- 調子はどうですか？
-choushi ha doudesuka?
- 大変良いです。
-taihen yoi desu.

1

- Good morning! Glad to see you. Looking good today!

- Hello! Thank you very much.

- How are you?

- Excellent.

きょう　そと　あたた
-今日は 外は 暖かいですね。
-kyou ha soto ha atatakai desune.
　　　よ　てんき
-はい、良い天気です。
-hai, ii tennki desu.

2

きょう　　かようび
-今日は火曜日ですか？
-kyou ha kayoubi desuka?
　　　きょう　かようび
-はい、今日は火曜日です。
-hai, kyou ha kayoubi desu.
なんじ
-何時ですか？
-nanji desuka?
　　じ
-12時です。
-juniji desu.
ちゅうしょく　た
-昼　食　を食べましたか？
-chushoku wo tabemashitaka?
　　　　わたし　ちゅうしょく　た
-いいえ、私は昼食を食べていません。
こうちゃ
紅茶はいかがですか？
-iie, watashi ha chuushoku wo tabeteimasen. koucha ha ikaga desuka?
　　　よろこ　　わたし　　　いっしょ　こうちゃ
-はい、喜んで。私はあめと一緒に紅茶が
ほ
欲しいです。
-hai, yorokonde. watashi ha ame to issho ni koucha ga hoshii desu.
-カフェはどこですか？
-kafe ha doko desuka?
　　　　　ちか　　とお　　　　　　　　よ
-かふぇは近くの通りにあります。それは良いかふぇです。
-kafe ha chikaku no toorini arimasu. sore ha ii kafe desu.
　　　　さわさんじん
-そこには沢山人はいますか？
-soko niha takusan hito ha imasuka?

- Today's warm outside.
- Yes, the weather is nice.

2

- Is today Tuesday?
- Yes, today is Tuesday.
- What time is it?
- It's twelve o'clock.
- Have you had lunch?
- No, I have not had lunch. Do you want some tea?
- Yes, with pleasure. I want tea with candies.
- Where is the cafe?
- The cafe is on the nearby street. It is a nice cafe.
- Are there a lot of people?

-いいえ、そこには 人は沢山いません。
-iie, soko niha hito ha takusan imasen.

3

-あなたの役職は何ですか？
-anata no yakushoku ha nandesuka?

-私はまねーじゃーです。これは私のびじねすかーどです。
-watashi ha mane-ja- desu. kore ha watshi no bijinesuka-do desu.

-あれは何ですか？
-are ha nandesuka?

-あれは私たちの会社の名前です。それは成功しています。
-are ha watashitachi no kaisha no namae desu. sore ha seikou shiteimasu.

-この数字は何ですか？
-kono suuji ha nandesuka?

-これは私たちの会社の電話番号です。
-kore ha watashitachi no kaisha no denwabangou desu.

-会社は大きいです。
-kaisha ha ookii desu.

4

-あなたはどこで働いていますか？
-anata ha dokode hataraite imasuka?

-私は事務所で働きます。それは私たちの会社の事務所です。私はとても忙しいです。
-watashi ha jimusho de hatarakimasu. sore ha watashitachi no kaisha no jimusho desu. watashi ha totemo isogashii desu.

-あなたの事務所はどこですか？
-anata no jimusho ha doko desuka?

- No, there are not a lot of people.

3

- What is your position?

- I am a manager. This is my business card.

- What is that?

- That is the name of our company. It is successful.

- What is this number?

- This is our company phone number.

The company is large.

4

- Where do you work?

- I work in the office. It is our company office. I'm very busy.

- Where is your office?

- Our office is in the

27

- 私たちの事務所は中央にあります。
-watashitachi no jimusho ha chuuou ni arimasu.
-それは大きな建物ですか？
-sore ha ookina tatemono desuka?
-この建物は大きくて背が高いです。
-kono tatemono ha ookikute se ga takai desu.
-事務所に働いている人は沢山いますか？
-jimusho ni hataraiteiru hito ha takusan imasuka?
-はい、事務所には働いている人は沢山います。彼らは責任感があります。彼らはよく働きます。
-hai, jimusho niha hataraiteiru hito ha takusan imasu. karera ha sekininkan ga arimasu. karera ha yoku hatarakimasu.

5

-これは誰ですか？
-kore ha dare desuka?
-これは私たちの秘書です。彼女は沢山働きます。
-kore ha watashitachi no hisho desu. kanojo ha takusan hatarakimasu.
-これは誰ですか？
-kore ha dare desuka?
-これはみかえるです。彼はまねーじゃーです。彼はここでは新しいです。彼は勤勉で責任感があります。
-kore ha mikaeru desu. kare ha mane-ja- desu. kare ha kokode ha atarashii desu. kare ha kinben de sekininkan ga arimasu.
-彼はどこから来ましたか？
-kare ha dokokara kimashitaka?

- center.
- Is it a large building?
- This building is large and tall.
- Are there many workers in the office?
- Yes, there are a lot of workers in the office. They are responsible. They work well.

5

- Who is this?
- This is our secretary. She works a lot.
- Who is this?
- This is Michael. He is a manager. He's new here. He is diligent and responsible.
- Where is he from?
- He's from another town.
- Who are these

- 彼は別の町から来ました。
- kare ha betsu no machi kara kimashita.

- これらの人々は誰ですか？
- krera no hitobito ha dare desuka?

- これらは私たちのえんじにあです。彼らは優れた専門家です。
- korera ha watashitachi no enjinia desu. Karera ha sugureta senmonka desu.

- これは誰ですか？
- kore ha dare desuka?

- これは私たちの客です。彼は支配人です。彼はよく知られた会社から来ました。
- kore ha watashitachi no kyaku desu. kare ha shihainin desu. kare ha yokushirareta kaisha kara kimashita.

- あなたの部長はどこですか？
- anata no buchou ha doko desuka?

- 私たちの部長は事務所にいます。彼は厳しいです。彼は良いりーだーです。彼は忙しいです。
- watashitachi no buchou ha jimusho ni imasu. kare ha kibishii desu. kare ha ii ri-da- desu. kare ha isogashii desu.

6

- あなたはおーだーはありますか？
- anata ha o-da- ha arimasuka?

- はい、私たちはおーだーが沢山あります。私たちは沢山仕事があります。
- hai, watashitachi ha o-da- ga takusan arimasu. watashitachi ha takusan shigoto ga arimasu.

- あなたの製造設備は大きいですか？
- anata no seizousetsubi ha ookii desuka?

people?

- These are our engineers. They are good specialists.

- Who is this?

- This is our guest. He is a manager. He is from a well-known company.

- Where is your general manager?

- Our general manager is in the office. He is strict. He's a good leader. He's busy.

6

- Do you have any orders?

- Yes, we have a lot of orders. We have a lot of work.

- Is your production

-はい、私たちの製造設備は大きいです。それはもだんです。
-hai, watashitachi no seizousetsubi ha ookiI desu. sore ha modan desu.
- Yes, our production facility is large. It is modern.

-そこに機材はありますか？
-sokoni kizai ha arimasuka?
- Is there equipment?

-はい、そこには沢山機材があります。それはもだんです。
-hai, sokoni ha takusan kizai ga arimasu. sore ha modan desu.
- Yeah, there's a lot of equipment. It is modern.

7

-あれは何ですか？
-are ha nandesuka?
- What is that?

-これらは私たちの製品です。それらは良い品質です。
-korera ha watashitachi no seihin desu. sorera ha ii hinnshitsu desu.
- These are our products. They are of good quality.

-あなたはかたろぐを持っていますか？
-anata ha katarogu wo motteimasuka?
- Do you have a catalog?

-はい、私たちのかたろぐは新しいです。
-hai, watashitachi no katarogu ha atarashii desu.
- Yes, our catalog is new.

-それはどこですか？
-sore ha doko desuka?
- Where is it?

-それはてーぶるの上にあります。
-sore ha te-buru no ue ni arimasu.
- It is on the table.

-あなたはかたろぐを沢山持っていますか？
-anata ha katarogu wo takusan motteimasuka?
- Do you have many catalogs?

-はい、私たちは沢山の興味深いかたろぐを持っています。私たちの製品はそこにあります。
-hai, watashitachi ha takusan no kyoumibukai katarogu wo motteimasu. watashitachi no seihin ha sokoniarimasu.
- Yes, we have a lot of interesting catalogs. Our products are there.

-あなたは新しいもでるは持っていますか？
- Do you have a new

-anata ha atarashii moderu ha motteimasuka?
-はい、私たちは新しくて面白いもでるを沢山持っています。
-hai, watashitachi ha atarashikute omoshiroi moderu wo takusan motte imasu.

8

-あなたは契約を持っていますか？
-anata ha keiyaku wo motteimasuka?
-はい、私たちは他の会社との契約を持っています。
-hai, watashitachi ha hoka no kaisha tono keiyaku wo motteimasu.
-あなたは契約の新しい条件に満足していますか？
-anata ha keiyaku no atarashii jouken ni manzoku shiteimasuka?
-はい、契約の条件は良いです。
-hai, keiyaku no jouken ha ii desu.
-それは有益ですか？
-sore ha yuueki desuka?
-はい、この契約は有利で有益です。
-hai, kono keiyaku ha yuuri de yuueki desu.

9

-あなたの企画は何ですか？
-anata no kikaku ha nandesuka?
-私たちはいくつかの新しい企画を持っています。それらは成功しています。
-watashitachi ha ikutsuka no atarashii kikaku wo motteimasu. sorera ha seikou shiteimasu.
-あなたの企画は計画の段階ですか？
-anata no kikaku ha keikaku no dankai desuka?

model?
- Yes, we have a lot of interesting new models.

8

- Do you have a contract?
- Yes, we have a contract with another firm.
- Are you satisfied with the new terms of the contract?
- Yes, the terms of the contract are good.
- Is it profitable?
- Yes, this contract is lucrative and profitable.

9

- What are your projects?
- We have several new projects. They are successful.
- Are your projects in

-いいえ、私たちの企画はすでに製造されています。
-iie, watashitachi no kikaku ha sudeni seizou sareteimasu.

10

-あれは何ですか？
-are ha nandesuka?

-これは私たちの最新の値段表です。新しい値段はそこです。
-kore ha watashitachi no saishin no nedanhyou desu. atarashii nedan ha soko desu.

-あなたの値段は高いですか？
-anata no nedan ha takai desuka?

-はい、それらは高い方です。
-hai, sorera ha takaihou desu.

-これらはあなたの新しい条件ですか？
-korera ha anata no atarashii jouken desuka?

-はい、これらは私たちの新しい条件です。しかしあなたにとってはそれらは更に有益です。
-hai, korera ha watashitachi no atarashii jouken desu. shikashi anatanitotte ha sorera ha sarani yuueki desu.

11

-あなたにはぱーとなーはいますか？
-anata niha pa-tona- ha imasuka?

-はい、私たちは沢山ぱーとなーがいます。彼らは頼りになります。
-hai, watashitachi ha takusan pa-tona- ga imasu. karera ha tayorini narimasu.

-彼らは新しいかたろぐを持っていますか？
-karera ha atarashii katarogu wo motteimasuka?

-いいえ、彼らは新しいかたろぐを持っていません。
-iie, karera ha atarashii katarogu wo motteimasen.

the planning stage?

- No, our projects are already in production.

10

- What is that?

- This is our latest price list. The new prices are there.

- Are your prices high?

- Yes, they are higher.

- Are these your new terms?

- Yes, these are our new terms. But for you, they are more profitable.

11

- Do you have partners?

- Yes, we have many partners. They are reliable.

- Do they have new catalogs?

- No, they do not have new catalogs.

-あなたは 私たちの 新しい 申し出に 興味がありますか？
-anata ha watashitachi no atarashii moushide ni kyoumi ha arimasuka?
-はい、これらの 申し出は 興味深いです。
-hai, korera no moushide ha kyoumibukai desu.
-あなたは 私たちの 新しい 条件を 調査したいですか？
-anata ha watashitachi no atarashii jouken wo chousa shitai desuka?
-はい、これらの 条件は 有利です。
-hai, korera no jouken ha yuuri desu.
-金曜日に 会いましょう。
-kinyoubi ni aimashou.
-さようなら！
-sayounara!

- Are you interested in our new offers?

- Yes, these offers are interesting.

- Do you want to explore our new terms?

- Yes, these terms are advantageous.

- See you on Friday.

- Goodbye!

3

Audio

<small>こおり　くだ</small>
氷 を 砕く
Break the ice

<small>いちにん　　かあ　　　むすこ ようす かくにん</small>
一 人 のお 母 さんが息 子の様 子を 確 認 しよう
<small>むすこ　しんしつ　はい　　　　　　　かれ　ゆか</small>
と息 子の寝 室 に 入 っていきました。彼 は 床 に
<small>ねころ</small>
寝 転 がっています。

A mom comes into the bedroom and sees her little son lying on the floor.

34

"ぽーる、寝ているの？"とお母さんはぽーるに聞きます。

"違うよ、遊んでるんだ"とぽーるは答えました。

それを聞いたお母さんは寝室を後にしました。10分後、様子を見に息子の寝室に戻ってきたのです。彼はまだ、同じ場所に寝転がったままです。

"どんなお遊びをしているの？"とお母さんは息子に聞きました。

"壊れたろぼっとの真似げーむをしているんだ"と彼は言いました。

"Paul, are you sleeping?" the mom asks.

"No. I am playing," the son answers.

The mom goes away. She returns to the bedroom ten minutes later. Her son is lying on the floor in the same place.

"What game are you playing?" she asks.

"I am playing a robot. A broken robot."

ichi nin no okāsan ga musuko no yōsu o kakuninshiyou to musuko no shinshitsu ni haitteikimashita. kare wa yuka ni nekorogatteimasu. Po-Ru, neteiru no? to okāsan wa po-ru ni kikimasu. chigau yo, asonderu n da to po-ru wa kotaemashita. sore o kiita okāsan wa shinshitsu ogo ni shimashita. 10 fungo, yōsu o mi ni musuko no shinshitsu ni modottekita no desu. kare wa mada, onaji basho ni nekorogatta mama desu. donna o asobi o shiteiru no? to okāsan wa musuko ni kikimashita. kowareta robotto no mane ge-mu o shiteiru n da to kare wa iimashita.

あなたの会社について教えてくれませんか？
Can you tell me about your company?

単語
Words

1. ～する必要がある、～しなければならない [～suru hitsuyou ga aru, ～shinakereba naranai] - must, to have to
2. ～だけ [～dake] - only
3. ～でない [～de nai] - not
4. ～によって [～ni yotte] - by
5. ～に適している(期間や状況に) [～ni tekishiteiru (kikan ya joukyouni] - be suitable (about terms or conditions)
6. あなたの [anatano] - your
7. してもよい [～shitemoyoi] - may, can
8. する(動詞)、行う、作る [～suru (doushi), okonau, tsukuru] - do (Verb), to perform, to make
9. まだ [mada] - yet
10. もちろん [mochiron] - of course
11. よく [yoku] - often
12. よく考え抜いた [yoku kangaenui ta] - thoughtful
13. アプローチ(動詞) [apuro-chi (doushi)] - approach (Verb)

14. クライアント、顧客 [kuraianto, kokyaku] - client, customer
15. スタッフ、社員 [sutaffu, shainn] - staff, personnel
16. マネージャー、管理者 [mane-jya-, kanrisha] - manager
17. 違う [chigau] - different
18. 可能である、もしかしたら [kanou dearu, moshikashitara] - possible, perhaps
19. 解決策 [kaiketsusaku] - solution
20. 確かである [tashika dearu] - sure
21. 感謝する(動詞) [kansha suru (doushi)] - thank *(Verb)*
22. 管理する(動詞)、リードする [kanrisuru (doushi), ri-dosuru] - manage *(Verb)*, to lead
23. 関係、フィードバック [kankei, fi-dobakk] - relation, feedback
24. 疑問 [gimon] - question
25. 協力する(動詞) [kyouroku suru (doushi)] - cooperate *(Verb)*
26. 携わる(動詞) [tazusawaru (doushi)] - engage *(Verb)* (in an activity)
27. 経験 [keiken] - experience
28. 決定する(動詞) [kettei suru (doushi)] - decide *(Verb)*
29. 言う(動詞)、教える [iu (doushi), oshieru] - tell *(Verb)*
30. 後に残る(動詞)、遅くなる [ato ni nokoru (doushi), osokunaru] - linger *(Verb)*, to be late
31. 更に、より [sarani, yori] - more
32. 時間に正確な [jikan ni seikakuna] - punctual
33. 時間通りに、時間内に [jikandoorini, jikannai ni] - in time
34. 取る(動詞) [toru (doushi)] - take *(Verb)*
35. 十分 [juubun] - enough
36. 重要 [juuyou] - important
37. 助ける(動詞)、役立つ [tasukeru (doushi), yakudatsu] - help *(Verb)*
38. 詳細 / じっくり、徹底的に [shousai / jikkuri, tetteitekini] - detail / thoroughly
39. 象徴する(動詞)、代表する [shouchou suru, daihyou suru] - represent *(Verb)*
40. 常に、いつも [tsuneni, itsumo] - always
41. 慎重に [shinchouni] - carefully
42. 人間 / 人 [ningen / hito] - human / man
43. 説得する(動詞) [settoku suru (doushi)] - persuade *(Verb)*
44. 全て [subete] - all
45. 待つ(動詞) [matsu (doushi)] - wait *(Verb)*
46. 提供する(動詞) teikyou suru(doushi) - provide *(Verb)*
47. 電話する(動詞) [denwa suru (doushi)] - call *(Verb)*
48. 渡す、あげる(動詞) [watasu, ageru (doushi)] - give *(Verb)*
49. 答える(動詞) [kotaeru (doushi)] - answer *(Verb)*
50. 動機付ける(動詞)、やる気になる [doukizukeru (doushi), yarukininaru] - motivate *(Verb)*
51. 導く、リードする [michibiiku, ri-dosuru] - lead
52. 売る [uru] - sale
53. 発行する(動詞)、置く [hakkousuru (doushi), oku] - issue *(Verb)*, to place
54. 発展 [hatten] - development
55. 反対にする [hantai ni suru] - reverse
56. 反対意見、意見の不一致 [hantai iken, iken no fuicchi] - disagreement
57. 用意、準備 [youi, jyunnbi] - ready
58. 来る(動詞) [kuru (doushi)] - come *(Verb)*, to arrive

B

1

-いい天気ですね！
-iitenki desune!
-こんにちは！私たちの事務所であなたに会えて嬉しいです。
-konnichiha! watashitachi no jimusho de anatani aete ureshii desu.
-あなたは私のために時間はありますか？
-anata ha watashi no tameni jikan ha arimasuka?
-もちろん、私はあなたの質問に全て答えられます。
-mochiron, watashi ha anata no shitsumon ni subete kotaeraremasu.
-まねーじゃーと会ってもいいですか？
-mane-ja- to attemo ii desuka?
-彼は忙しいです。あなたは待てますか？
-kare ha isogashii desu. anata ha matemasuka?
-はい、もちろん待てます。
-hai, mochiron matemasu.

2

-あなたの会社について教えてくれませんか？
-anata no kaishani tsuite oshiete kuremasenka?
-はい、私はあなたを会社に紹介したいです。
-hai, watashi ha anata wo kaishani shoukai shitai desu.
-それは大きな会社ですか？
-sore ha ookina kaishadesuka?
-はい、私たちの会社は大きいです。私たちは一生懸命働かないといけません。

1

- Good day!
- Hello! Glad to see you in our office.
- Do you have some time for me?
- Of course, I can answer all your questions.
- Can I see the manager?
- He's busy. Can you wait?
- Yes, of course I can.

2

- Can you tell me about your company?
- Yes, I want to introduce you to our company.
- Is this a large company?
- Yes, our company is large. We have to work hard.

-hai, watashitachi no kaisha ha ookii desu. watashitachi ha isshoukenmei hatarakanaito ikemasen.

3

- 注文してもいいですか？
-chumonshitemo ii desuka?

- はい、もちろん、あなたはいま注文することができます。
-hai, mochiron, anata ha ima chumonsurukoto ga dekimasu.

- この注文は私の会社にとって重要ですか？
-kono chuumon ha watashi no kaishani totte juuyou desuka?

- もちろん、あなたの注文は慎重に、そして徹底的に処理しなければなりません。
-mochiron, anata no chumon ha shinchou ni, soshite tetteitekini shorishinakereba narimasen.

4

- もしかしてあなたにはぱーとなーがいますか？
-moshikashite anata niha pa-tona- ga imasuka?

- はい、私たちには沢山ぱーとなーがいます。
-hai, watashitachi niha takusan pa-tona- ga imasu.

- あなたの会社は彼らと協力していますか？
-anata no kaisha ha karera to kyouryoku shiteimasuka?

- はい、私たちは彼らと協力しています。いくつかの大きな会社が私たちのぱーとなーです。
-hai, watashitachi ha karera to kyouryoku shiteimasu. Ikutsuka no ookina kaisha ga watashitachi no pa-tona- desu.

5

- 値段表をどこで見ることができますか？
-nedanhyou wo dokode mirukoto ga dekimasuka?

- 秘書が持っているかもしれません。私たちはかたろ

3

- Can I place an order?

- Yes, of course, you can place an order now.

- Is this order important for my company?

- Of course, your order must be carefully and thoroughly processed.

4

- Perhaps you have partners?

- Yes, we have many partners.

- Is your company collaborating with them?

- Yes, we are collaborating with them. Several large companies are our partners.

5

- Where can I see the price list?

- The secretary may

ぐを持っています。
-hisho ga motteiru kamoshiremasen. watashitachi ha katarogu wo motteimasu.

- 遠慮します。私は値段を見なければなりません。
-enryo shimasu. watashi ha nedan wo minakereba narimasen.

-では、秘書からそれをもらえますよ。
-deha, hishokara sore wo moraemasuyo.

have it. We have a catalog.

- No, thanks. I have to see the prices.

- Well, you can get it from the secretary.

6

-これは誰ですか？
-kore ha daredesuka?

-これは私たちのリードセールスマネージャーです。
-kore ha watashitachi no ri-do se-rusu mane-ja- desu.

- 彼は何ができますか？
-kare ha nani ga dekimasuka?

- 彼は効率的に他の人を説得できます。
-kare ha kouritsutekini hokanohito wo settokudekimasu.

- 彼はどのような人ですか？
-kare ha donoyouna hito desuka?

- 彼は自信に満ちています。
-kare ha jishinni michiteimasu.

6

- Who is this?

- This is our lead sales manager.

- What can he do?

- He can effectively convince others.

- What kind of man is he?

- He's confident.

7

-これはあなたの秘書ですか？
-kore ha anata no hishodesuka?

-いいえ、あれはPRまねーじゃーです。
-iie, are ha pi-a-ru mane-ja- desu.

- 彼女は経験がありますか？
-kanojo ha keiken ga arimasuka?

-はい、彼女は経験があります。彼女は優れた専門家です。

7

- Is this your secretary?

- No, that is the PR-manager.

- Does she have experience?

- Yes, she has experience. She's a

-hai, kanojo ha keiken ga arimasu. kanojo ha sugureta senmonka desu.

- 彼女の任務は何ですか？
-kanojo no ninmu ha nandesuka?

- 彼女の任務は顧客にふぃーどばっくを提供することです。
-kanojo no ninmu ha kokyaku ni fi-dobakku wo teikyousuru koto desu.

- これらがPRまねーじゃーの責任の全てですか？
-korera ga pi-a-ru mane-ja- no sekinin no subete desuka?

- いいえ、これらはPRまねーじゃーの責任の全てではありません。
-iie, korera ha pi-a-ru mane-ja- no sekinin no subete deha arimasen.

- 他は何ですか？
-hoka ha nandesuka?

- 彼女は私たちの会社を代表してくらいあんとに会わないといけません。
-kanojo ha watashitachi no kaisha wo daihyoushite kuraianto ni awanaito ikemasen.

8

- あなたの会社にはひゅーまんりそーすまねーじゃーはいますか？
-anata no kaisha ni ha hyu-man riso-su mane-ja- ha imasuka?

- はい、私たちにはひゅーまんりそーすまねーじゃーがいます。彼女は優れた専門家です。
-hai, watashitachi niha hyu-man riso-su mane-ja- ga imasu. kanojo ha sugureta senmonka desu.

- 彼女の任務は何ですか？
-kanojo no ninmu ha nandesuka?

- 彼女の任務は他の人にやる気を与え、そして

- good specialist.

- What are her duties?

- Her duties are to provide feedback to customers.

- Are these all the PR-manager's responsibilities?

- No, these are not all the PR-manager's responsibilities.

- What are the others?

- She has to represent our company to clients.

8

- Does your company have an HR (human resource) manager?

- Yes, we have an HR manager. She's a good specialist.

- What are her duties?

- Her duties are to

争いを解決します。
-kanojo no ninmu ha hokanohito ni yaruki wo atae, soshtie arasoi wo kaiketsu shimasu.

9

-これは誰ですか？
-kore ha dare desuka?

-これは秘書です。彼女は責任があります。
-kore ha hisho desu. kanojo ha sekinin ga arimasu.

-彼女はいつも時間通りに到着しますか？
-kanojo ha itsumo jikandoorini touchaku shimasuka?

-はい、彼女はいつも時間通りに到着します。彼女は時間に正確です。
-hai, kanojo ha itsumo jikandoorini touchaku shimasu. kanojo ha jikanni seikaku desu.

-彼女は残業しないといけませんか？
-kanojo ha zangyou shinaito ikemasenka?

-はい、彼女はよく残業しないといけません。
-hai, kanojo ha yoku zangyou shinaito ikemasen.

10

-あなたは良いCEO(取締役)を持っていますか？
-anata ha ii shi-i-o-(torishimariyaku) wo motteimasuka?

-私たちのCEOは会社を効率的に管理します。
-watashitachi no shi-i-o- ha kaisha wo kouritsuteki ni kanrishimasu.

-彼の任務は何ですか？
-kareno ninmu ha nandesuka?

-彼の任務はよく考え抜いた決断を行うことです。
-kare no ninmu ha yoku kangaenuita ketsudan wo okonaukoto desu.

- motivate others and resolve differences.

9

- Who is this?

- This is a secretary. She is responsible.

- Does she always come to the office on time?

- Yes, she always arrives on time. She is punctual.

- Does she have to work overtime?

- Yes, she often has to work overtime.

10

- Do you have a good CEO (chief executive officer)?

- Our CEO manages the company effectively.

- What are his duties?

- His duties are to make thoughtful decisions.

- Does he help the

- 彼は会社の発展を助けますか？
-kare ha kaisha no hatten wo tasukemasuka?
-かもしれません、けれども彼一人だけではありません。
-kamoshiremasen, keredomo kare hitoridake deha arimasen.

11
-あなたの会社は新しい企画を持っていますか？
-anata no kaisha ha atarashii kikaku wo motteimasuka?
-はい、私たちは新しい製品の製造に携わらなければなりません。
-hai, watashitachi ha atarashii seihin no seizou ni tazusawaranakereba narimasen.
-あなたは沢山の量の製品を持っていますか？
-anata ha takusan no ryou no seihin wo motteimasuka?
-はい、私たちは沢山製品を持っています。私たちは違う商品を持っています。
-hai, watashitachi ha takusan seihin wo motteimasu. watashitachi ha chigau shouhin wo mottemiasu.

12
-協力の条件はあなたにとって適していますか？
-kyouryoku no jouken ha anatanitotte tekishiteimasuka?
-ありがとう、これらの条件はとても有益です。
-arigatou, korerano jouken ha totemo yuueki desu.
-私は金曜日にあなたに電話していいですか？
-watashi ha kinyoubi ni anata ni denwashite ii desuka?
-はい、私の決定は用意できているはずです。
-hai, watashi no kettei ha youi dekiteiru hazu desu.

company's development?
- Perhaps, but he is not the only one.

11
- Does your company have new projects?
- Yes, we have to be engaged in the production of new products.
- Do you have a large amount of products?
- Yes, we have many products. We have different goods.

12
- Are the terms of collaboration suitable for you?
- Thank you, these terms are quite profitable.
- Can I call you on Friday?
- Yes, my decision should be ready.

4

Audio

氷(こおり)を砕(くだ)く
Break the ice

お父(とう)さんと娘(むすめ)は公園(こうえん)から帰宅(きたく)しました。娘(むすめ)は公園(こうえん)に戻(もど)って遊(あそ)びたいらしく。駄々(だだ)をこね始(はじ)めたのです。
"どうしたの？"とお母(かあ)さんは娘(むすめ)に聞(き)くと。"ぱぱがね…子供(こども)たちをいじめているんだ！"と娘(むすめ)は叫(さけ)んだのです。
"子供(こども)たち？"とお母(かあ)さんは言いいました。
"私(わたし)よ！"

A dad and his little daughter return home from the playground. The daughter wants to go back to the playground and continue playing. She begins to cry.
"What happened?" the mom asks.
"This daddy ... our daddy is torturing children!" the little girl shouts.
"What children?" the mom asks.
"Me!" the daughter responds.

otōsan to musume wa kōen kara kitakushimashita. musume wa kōen ni modotte asobitai rashiku. dada o konehajimeta no desu. dō shita no? to okāsan wa musume ni

kiku to. papa ga ne kodomotachi o ijimeteiru n da! to musume wa sakenda no desu. kodomotachi? to okāsan wa iiimashita. watashi yo!

あなたは私の注文を処理するためにどれくらい時間が必要ですか？

How much time do you need to process my order?

単語
Words

1. 1、一 [ichi] - one
2. 2、二 [ni] - two
3. 〜することができる、〜できる [〜surukoto ga dekiru, 〜dekiru] - be able, can
4. 〜に [〜ni] - to
5. 〜も [〜mo] - also
6. いつ [itsu] - when
7. どこ [doko] - where
8. はっきりと、明らかに [hakkirito, akirakani] - clearly
9. シート/表、一覧、リスト [shi-to / hyou, ichiran, risuto] - sheet / list
10. ホテル [hoteru] - hotel
11. 印刷する(動詞)、プリント [insatsu suru (doushi), purinto suru] - print (Verb)
12. 駅 [eki] - station
13. 会う(動詞) [au (doushui)] - meet (Verb)
14. 会議、ミーティング [kaigi, mitingu] - meeting
15. 議論する(動詞)、話し合う [giron suru(doushi), hanashiau] - discuss (Verb)
16. 急いで [isoide] - quickly

17. 公共の場、公共の [koukyou no ba, koukyou no] - public
18. 工場、施設 [koujou, shisetsu] - factory, plant
19. 行く(動詞) [iku (doushi)] - go *(Verb)*
20. 参照する(動詞)、仕事をする [sanshou suru(doushi), shigoto wo suru] - refer *(Verb)* / to turn to
21. 仕事を始める(動詞) [shigoto wo hajimeru (doushi) / modoru] - turn *(Verb)* to / to return
22. 止まる(動詞)、留まる [tomaru (doushi), todomaru] - stop *(Verb)* / to stay
23. 時間、締め切り日 [jikan, shimekiribi] - time, due date
24. 自由 [jiyuu] - free
25. 質問、問い合わせ [shitsumon, toiawase] - inquiry
26. 手短に、要するに [temijikani, yousuruni] - briefly, in short
27. 受け取る [uketoru (doushi)] - receive *(Verb)*
28. 集める(動詞) [atsumeru (doushi)] - collect *(Verb)*
29. 処理する、一掃 [shori suru, issou] - processing, clearance
30. 所有する [shoyuu suru] - own
31. 書く(動詞) [kaku (doushi)] - write *(Verb)*

32. 情報 [jyouhou] - information
33. 水曜日 [suiyoubi] - Wednesday
34. 相応している、適している [souou shiteiru, tekishiteiru] - appropriate
35. 送る、送信する(動詞) [okuru, soushinsuru (doushi)] - send *(Verb)*
36. 待つ(動詞) [matsu (doushi)] - wait *(Verb)*
37. 知る(動詞) [shiru (doushi)] - know *(Verb)*
38. 通して、徹底して、後に(一定時間) [toushite, tetteishite, goni (itteijikan) - through, in (a certain time)
39. 電話する [denwa suru] - call, ring
40. 配達、供給 [haitatsu, kyoukyuu] - delivery, supply
41. 必要、必須 [hitsuyou, hissu] - need, necessary
42. 明日 [asu] - tomorrow
43. 木曜日 [mokuyoubi] - Thursday
44. 夜 [yoru] - evening
45. 予約する(動詞) [yoyaku suru (doushi)] - book *(Verb)*
46. 来る(動詞) [kuru (doushi)] - come *(Verb)*, to arrive
47. 話す(動詞) [hanasu (doushi)] - talk *(Verb)*

B

1

きょう　すいようび
-今日は水曜日ですか？
-kyou ha suiyoubi desuka?
　　　　きょう　すいようび
-はい。今日は水曜日です。
-hai. kyou ha suiyoubi desu.

1

- Is today Wednesday?

- Yes. Today is Wednesday.

-あなたは12時に自由ですか？
-anata ha juniji ni jiyuu desuka?
-はい、私は12時に自由です。
-hai, watashi ha juniji ni jiyuu desu.

2

-私たちは重要な問題について話し合う必要があります。
-watashitachi ha juyouna mondai nitsuite hanashiau hitsuyou ga arimasu.
-1時間後に話し合いをしても良いですか？
-ichijikangoni hanashiai wo shitemo ii desuka?
-わかりました、1時間後にする事ができます。
-wakarimashita, ichijikangoni surukoto ga dekimasu.
-今私は会議に行かなければなりません。
-ima watashi ha kaigini ikanakereba narimasen.
-あなたも行く必要がありますか？
-anata mo ikuhitsuyou ga arimasuka?
-はい、私もそこにいるべきです。
-hai, watashimo sokoni irubeki desu.

3

-あなたはいつ私たちの顧客に電話できますか？
-anata ha itsu watashitachi no kokyakuni denwa dekimasuka?
-私は彼に1時間後に電話できます。
-watashi ha kareni ichijikangoni denwa dekimasu.
-わかりました、彼はあなたの電話を待っています。
-wakarimashita, kare ha anata no denwa wo motteimasu.

4

-私はいつあなたに情報について電話できますか？

- Are you free at twelve o'clock?
- Yes, I'm free at twelve o'clock.

2

- We need to discuss an important issue.
- Can we discuss it in an hour?
- OK, we can do it in an hour.
- Now I have to go to a meeting.
- Do you also need to go?
- Yes, I should also be there.

3

- When can you call our customer?
- I can call him in an hour.
- OK, he's waiting for your call.

4

- When can I contact you for information?

-watashi ha itsu anatani jouhou ni tsuite denwa dekimasuka?
-あなたは明日情報について電話できます。
-anata ha ashita jouhou ni tsuite denwa dekimasu.
-私は配達時間を知る必要がありますか？
-watashi ha haitatsujikan wo shiruhitsuyou ga arimasuka?
-はい、あなたは配達時間を知る必要があります。
-hai, anata ha haitatsujikan wo shiruhitsuyou ga arimasu.

5

-あなたはいつ会議に行く必要がありますか？
-anata ha itsu kaigini ikuhitsuyou ga arimasuka?
-私は木曜日に会議に行く必要があります。
-watashi ha mokuyoubi ni kaigini ikuhitsuyou ga arimasu.
-あなたは私のげすとと駅で会う事は出来ますか？
-anata ha watashi no gesuto to ekide aukoto ha dekimasuka?
-もちろん、私は彼に駅で会う事ができます。
-mochiron, watashi ha kareni eki de aukoto ga dekimasu.

6

-秘書は今何をしなければなりませんか？
-hisho ha ima nani wo shinakereba narimasenka?
-彼女は私たちの顧客にめーるを送らなければなりません。
-kanojo ha watashitachi no kokyaku ni me-ru wo okuranakereba narimasen.
-彼女は急いでそれを行うことはできますか？
-kanojo ha isoide sore wo okonaukotoha dekimasuka?
-はい、彼女はめーるを急いで送る事ができます。
-hai, kanojo ha me-ru wo isoide okurukoto ga dekimasu.

- You can call tomorrow for information.
- Do I need to know the delivery time?
- Yes, you need to know the delivery time.

5

- When do you need to go to a meeting?
- I have to go to a meeting on Thursday.
- Can you meet our guest at the station?
- Of course, I can meet him at the station.

6

- What does the secretary have to do now?
- She has to send an e-mail to our customer.
- Can she do it quickly?
- Yes, she can send the e-mail quickly

7

- 私たちのぱーとなーはどこに泊まる事になっていますか？
-watashitachi no pa-tona- ha doko ni tomarukoto ni natteimasuka?
- 彼はほてるに泊まることになっています。
-kare ha hoteru ni tomarukotoni natteimasu.
- 私たちは彼に部屋を予約することはできますか？
-watashitachi ha kare ni heya wo yoyaku surukoto ha dekimasuka?
-はい、私たちは彼に部屋を予約することができます。
-hai, watashitachi ha kare ni heya wo yoyaku surukoto ga dekimasu.
- 彼はいつ到着することになっていますか？
-kare ha itsu touchaku surukotoni natteimasuka?
- 彼は２日後に到着することになっています。
-kare ha futsukagoni touchaku surukoto ni natteimasu.

8

- 私は注文することはできますか？
-watashi ha chuumon surukoto ha dekimasuka?
-はい、あなたは今注文することができます。
-hai, anata ha ima chuumon surukoto ga dekimasu.
-あなたは私の注文を処理するのにどれくらいの時間が必要ですか？
-anata ha watashi no chuumon wo shorisurunoni dorekuraino jikan ga hitsuyou desuka?
- 私はあなたの注文を処理するのに１時間必要です。
-watashi ha anata no chuumon wo shorisurunoni ichijikan hitsuyou desu.

7

- Where is our partner supposed to stay?
- He is supposed to stay in a hotel.
- Can we book him a room?
- Yes, we can book him a room.
- When is he supposed to arrive?
- He is supposed to arrive in two days.

8

- Can I get my order?
- Yes, you can get your order now.
- How much time do you need to process my order?
- I need an hour to process your order.

9

- せーるすまねーじゃーは何をしなければなりませんか？
- se-rusu mane-ja- ha nani wo shinakereba narimasenka?
- せーるすまねーじゃーはかたろぐを調査しなければなりません。
- se-rusu mane-ja- ha katarogu wo chousa shinakereba narimasen.
- 彼はいつそれをしなければなりませんか？
- kare ha itsu sore wo shinakereba narimasenka?
- 彼は昼食前にそれをしなければなりません。
- kare ha chuushokumaeni sore wo shinakereba narimasen.

10

- 誰が適切な情報を集めるべきですか？
- dare ga tekisetsuna jouhou wo atsumerubeki desuka?
- PRまねーじゃーが情報を集めるべきです。
- pi-a-ru mane-ja- ga jouhou wo atsumerubeki desu.
- 彼女はそれを上手くできますか？
- kanojo ha sore wo umaku dekimasuka?
- はい、彼女はそれを上手くできます。
- hai, kanojo ha sore wo umaku dekimasu.

11

- じぇねらるまねーじゃーはいつ会議に行かなければなりませんか？
- jeneraru mane-ja- ha itsu kaigini ikanakereba narimasenka?
- 彼は夜に会議に行かなければなりません。
- kare ha yoruni kaigi ni ikanakereba narimasen.
- 会議はどこで開かれることになっていますか？
- kaigi ha doko de hirakareru kotoni natteimasuka?
- 会議は事務所で開かれることになっています。
- kaigi ha jimusho de hirakarerukotoni natteimasu.

9

- What does the sales manager have to do?
- The sales manager has to examine the catalogs.
- When does he have to do it?
- He has to do it before lunch.

10

- Who should collect the relevant information?
- The PR-manager should collect the information.
- Can she do it well?
- Yes, she can do it well.

11

- When does the general manager have to go to the meeting?
- He has to go to the meeting in the evening.
- Where should the meeting be?
- The meeting should be in the office.

12

- 彼女は公共の場で話すことはできますか？
-kanojo ha koukyounoba de hanasukoto ha dekimasuka?

- いいえ、彼女は公共の場でで話す方法を知りません。
-iie, kanojo ha koukyounoba de hanasu houhou wo shirimasen.

- 彼女は何をするべきですか？
-kanojo ha nani wo surubeki desuka?

- 彼女ははっきりとそして手短に書きとめるべきです。
-kanojo ha hakkirito soshite temijikani kakitomerubeki desu.

- Is she able to speak in public?
- No, she does not know how to speak in public.
- What should she do?
- She should write it down clearly and briefly.

13

- 私たちの注文が遅れています。
-watashitachi no chumon ga okureteimasu.

- 秘書は今日何をするべきですか？
-hisho ha kyou nani wo surubeki desuka?

- 彼女は問い合わせを書くべきです。
-kanojo ha toiawase wo kakubeki desu.

- 彼女は誰に問い合わせを書くべきですか？
-kanojo ha dare ni toiaawase wo kakubeki desuka?

- 問い合わせは工場に向けて書くべきです。
-toiawase ha koujou ni mukete kakubeki desu.

- Our order is delayed.
- What should the Secretary do today?
- She should write an inquiry.
- To whom should she write the inquiry?
- The inquiry should be written to the factory.

14

- あなたは今日事務所で残業することができますか？
-anata ha kyou jimusho de zangyou surukoto ga dekimasuka?

- はい、私は今日残業することができます。

- Can you stay overtime in the office today?
- Yes, I can stay

-hai, watashi ha kyou zangyou surukoto ga dekimasu.

-あなたは 新しい値段表を印刷することができますか？

-anata ha atarashii nedanhyou wo insatsu surukoto ga dekimasuka?

-はい、私は新しい値段表を印刷することができます。

-hai, watashi ha atarashii nedanhyou wo innsatsu surukoto ga dekimasu.

overtime today.

- Can you print a new price list?

- Yes, I can print a new price list.

5

Audio

氷を砕く
Break the ice

"あなたのくらすには何人女の子がいるの？"とお母さんは娘に聞きました。
"七人いるよ"と娘は答えます。
"男の子は？"とお母さんが聞くと。
"いっぱいいるけど、いつも走り回ってるから数えるのは無理だよ"と答えました。

"How many girls are there in your class?" a mom asks her little daughter.
"There are seven girls in the class," the girl answers.
"What about the boys?" the mom asks.
"There is a lot of the boys. But they always run back and forth. It is impossible to count them," the girl answers.

anata no kurasu ni wa nan nin onnanoko ga iru no? to okāsan wa musume ni kikimashita. nana nin iru yo to musume wa kotaemasu. otokonoko wa? to okāsan ga kiku to.ippai iru kedo, itsumo hashirimawatteru kara kazoeru no wa muri da yo to kotaemashita.

何かお手伝いできませんか？
Can I help you with something?

単語
Words

1. 20、二十 [nijuu] - twenty
2. 〜を超えて、〜の上 [〜wo koete, 〜no ue] - over, above
3. 〜について [〜nitsuite] - about
4. そして、それから [soshite, sorekara] - then
5. どうして [douhsite] - why
6. オープンに [o-punnni] - openly
7. サンプル [sanpuru] - sample
8. ビジネス、企業 [bijinesu, kigyou] - business, enterprise
9. プレゼンテーション [purezente-shon] - presentation
10. 雨 [ame] - rain
11. 学ぶ(動詞)、知るようになる [manabu (doushi), shiruyouni naru] - learn *(Verb)*, to get to know
12. 計画する(動詞) [keikakusuru (doushi)] - plan *(Verb)*
13. 後 [ato] - after
14. 広告、宣伝 [koukoku, senden] - advertising
15. 行われる、通り過ぎる [okonawareru, toorisugiru] - take place, to pass
16. 参加する(動詞) [sankasuru (doushi)] - participate *(Verb)*, to take part
17. 資料 [shiryou] - material
18. 持っている、所有する(動詞) [motteiru, shoyuusuru (doushi)] - have *(Verb)*
19. 持ってくる(動詞) [mottekuru (doushi)] - bring *(Verb)*

20. 集める(動詞)、収集する [atsumeru (doushi), shuushuu suru] - gather *(Verb)*
21. 助ける(動詞) [tasukeru (doushi)] - help *(Verb)*
22. 上げる(動詞) [ageru (doushi)] - raise *(Verb)*
23. 説得力を持って [settokuryoku wo motte] - persuasively
24. 提供する(動詞)、申し出る [teikyō suru (dōshi), mōshideru] - offer *(Verb)*
25. 展覧会 [tenrankai] - exhibition
26. 年 [nen] - year
27. 買う(動詞) [kau (doushi)] - buy *(Verb)*
28. 表現する(動詞) [hyougensuru (doushi)] - express *(Verb)*
29. 品質、質 [hinshitsu, shitsu] - quality
30. 分 [fun] - minute
31. 有益な [yuuekina] - profitable
32. 用意する(動詞) [youisuru (doushi)] - prepare *(Verb)*
33. 要求、需要 [youkyuu, juyou] - demand

B

1

きょう　もくようび
-今日は木曜日ですか？
-kyou ha mokuyoubi desuka?
　　　きょう　もくようび
-はい、今日は木曜日です。
-hai, kyou ha mokuyoubi desu.
　きょう　てんき
-今日の天気はいかがですか？
-kyou no tenki ha ikaga desuka?
　ゆうしょく　のち　あめ　ふ
-夕食の後に雨が降るはずです。
-yuushoku no ato ni ame ga furuhazu desu.

2

なに　てつだ
-何かお手伝いできませんか？
-nanika otetsudai dekimasenka?
　　　　わたし　　　　あたら　せいひん
-はい、私はあなたの新しい製品について
　まな　ひつよう
　学ぶ必要があります。
-hai, watashi ha anata no atarashii seihinni tsuite mababuhitsuyou ga arimasu.

- Is today Thursday?

- Yes, today is Thursday.

- How is the weather today?

- It should rain after dinner.

2

- Can I help you with something?

- Yes, I need to learn about your new products.

- Then I have to bring

-そしたら 私はあなたに新しいかたろぐを持ってこなければなりません。
-soshitara watashi ha anata ni atarashii katarogu wo motte konakereba narimasen.
-これらの商品について私に教えてくれませんか？
-korera no shouhinni tsuite watashi ni oshiete kuremasenka?
-はい、私はあなたにこれらの商品について教えることができます。
-hai, watashi ha anatani korera no shouhinni tsuite oshierukotoga dekimasu.

3

-あなたは何を行う予定ですか？
-anata ha nani wo okonau yotei desuka?
-私は新しい企画に取り掛からなければなりません。
-watashi ha atarashi kikakuni torikakaranakereba narimasen.
-いつこれを行う予定ですか？
-itsu kore wo okonau yotei desuka?
-私はあれを本日行う予定です。
-watashi ha are wo honjitsu okonau yotei desu.

4

-えんじにあはいつ来（こ）なければなりませんか？
-enjinia ha itsu konakereba narimasenka?
-彼らは明日来なければなりません。
-karera ha ashita konakereba narimasen.
-あなたは彼らにほてるを予約しますか？
-anata ha karera ni hoteru wo yoyakushimasuka?
-はい、私たちは彼らに部屋を予約します。
-hai, watashitachi ha karera ni heya wo yoyakushimasu.

you our new catalogs.
- Can you tell me about these goods?
- Yes, I can tell you about these goods.

3

- What are you planning to do?
- I have to work on a new project.
- When do you plan to do this?
- I plan on doing that today.

4

- When do the engineers have to come?
- They have to come tomorrow.
- Are you going to book a hotel room for them?
- Yes, we are going to book a room for them.

5

-これらのえんじにあは 私たちのぱーとなーの会社で働いています。
-korerano enjinia ha watashtiachi no pa-tona- no kaisha de hataraiteimasu.

-どうして彼らは来るべきですか？
-doushite karera ha kurubeki desuka?

-私たちは新しい製品について話し合う必要があります。
-watashitachi ha atarashi seihin nitsuite hanashiau hitsuyou ga arimasu.

-彼らはおーぷんにあいであを表現してもいいですか？
-karera ha o-pun ni aidea wo hyougen dekimasuka?

-はい、彼らはおーぷんにあいであを表現してもいいですよ。
-hai, karera ha o-pun ni aidea wo hyougendekimasu.

6

-展示会はいつ行われますか？
-tenjikai ha itsu okonaware masuka?

-展示会は火曜日と水曜日に行われます。
-tenjikai ha kayoubi to suiyoubi ni okonawaremasu.

-もしかして、私たちの会社も参加するべきですか？
-moshikashite, watashitachi no kaisha mo sanka surubeki desuka?

-はい、私たちは展示会で私たちの製品を発表しなければなりません。
-hai, watashitachi ha tenjikaide watashitachi no seihin wo happyou shinakereba narimasen.

5

- These engineers work in our partner company.

- Why should they come?

- We need to discuss our new project.

- May they openly express their ideas?

- Yes, they may openly express their ideas.

6

- When does the exhibition take place?

- The exhibition takes place on Tuesday and Wednesday.

- Perhaps, our company should also participate?

- Yes, we have to present our products at the exhibition.

- Can you prepare materials for the

-あなたは展示会のための資料を用意することができますか？
-anata ha tenjikai no tameno shiryou wo youisurukoto ga dekimasuka?
-はい、私は会議の後に展示会の資料を用意します。
-hai, watashi ha kaigi no ato ni tenjikai no shiryou wo youishimasu.

7
-誰が展示会に行きますか？
-dare ga tenjikai ni ikimasuka?
-せーるすまねーじゃーが展示会に行きます。
-se-rusu mane-ja- ga tenjikai ni ikimasu.
-まねーじゃーは展示会で何をするべきですか？
-mane-ja- ha tenjikai de nani wo surubeki desuka?
-まねーじゃーは効果的にそして説得力を持って話す必要があります。
-mane-ja- ha koukatekini soshite settokuryoku wo motte hanasu hitsuyou ga arimasu.

8
-私たちの新しい製品のぷれぜんてーしょんはどこで開催されますか？
-watashitachi no atarashii seihin no purezente-shon ha dokode kaisai saremasuka?
-そのぷれぜんてーしょんはびじねすせんたーで開催されます。
-sono purezente-shon ha bijinesusenta-de kaisaisaremasu.
-あなたはいつぷれぜんてーしょんに行きますか？
-anata ha itsu purezente-shon ni ikimasuka?
-私は月曜日にぷれぜんてーしょんに行きます。
-watashi ha getsuyoubi ni purezente-shon ni ikimasu.

exhibition?
- Yes, I'm going to prepare materials for the exhibition after the meeting.

7
- Who is going to go to the exhibition?
- The sales managers are going to go to the exhibition.
- What should the managers do at the exhibition?
- The managers have to speak effectively and persuasively.

8
- Where does the presentation of our new products take place?
- The presentation takes place in the business center.
- When are you going to go to the presentation?
- I'm going to go to the presentation on Monday.

9

- 私たちは有益な条件を共同作業のために申し出る必要があります。
-watashitachi ha yuuekina jouken wo kyoudousagyou no tameni moushideru hitsuyouga arimasu.

- 私たちはこれをどうしたらできますか？
-watashitachi ha kore wo doushitara dekimasuka?

- 私たちは値段を上げるべきではありません。
-watashitachi ha nedan wo agerubekideha arimasen.

- それは私たちにとって有益ですか？
-sore ha watashitachi ni totte yuueki desuka?

- 今年、それは私たちにとって有益です。
-kotoshi, sore ha watashitachi ni totte yuueki desu.

10

- 私たちはあなたの製品のさんぷるをいくつか買いたいです。
-watashitachi ha anata no seihin no sanpuru wo ikutsuka kaitai desu.

- そしたら私たちはあなたの注文を取る必要があります。あなたは待つことができますか？
-soshitara watashitachi ha anata no chuumon wo toru hitsuyou ga arimasu. anata ha matsukoto ga dekimasuka?

- それは沢山時間がかかりますか？
-sore ha takusan jikan ga kakarimasuka?

- いいえ、まねーじゃーがあなたの注文を20分で取ることができます。
-iie, mane-ja- ga anata no chuumon wo nijippun de torukotoga dekimasu.

11

- 私たちの商品の需要をより大きくする

9

- We have to offer profitable conditions for collaboration.

- How can we do this?

- We must not raise prices.

- Is it profitable for us?

- This year, it is profitable for us.

10

- We want to buy a few samples of your products.

- Then we need to place your order. Can you wait?

- Does it take a lot of time?

- No, the manager can place your order in twenty minutes.

11

- How can we motivate a high demand for our

ためにどう動機付すれば良いですか？
-watashitachi no shouhin no juyou wo yori ookusurutame niha dou doukiduke sureba ii desuka?

－私たちは良い宣伝をする必要があります。
-watashitachi ha ii senden wo suru hitsuyou ga arimasu.

－それで充分ですか？
-sorede jubundesuka?

－もちろん違います、私たちの商品は高い品質でなければなりません。
-mochiron chigaimasu, watashitachi no shouhin ha takai hinshitsude nakereba narimasen.

12

－せーるすまねーじゃーは何をするべきですか？
-se-rusu mane-ja- ha nani wo suru beki desuka?

－彼は顧客に必要な情報を提供するべきです。
-kare ha kokyaku ni hitsuyouna jouhou wo teikyousuru beki desu.

－彼は必要な資料を持っていますか？
-kare ha hitsuyouna shorui wo motteimasuka?

－はい、彼は必要な書類とかたろぐを持っています。
-hai, kare ha hitsuyouna shorui to katarogu wo motteimasu.

goods?

- We must do good advertising.

- Is it enough?

- Of course not, our products must be of high quality.

12

- What should a sales manager do?

- He should provide a customer with the necessary information.

- Does he have the necessary materials?

- Yes, he has the necessary materials and catalogs.

6

Audio

氷を砕く
Break the ice

お父さんはたまに、幼い娘のためにしんでれらを読んであげます。
"私の事を愛してくれる人なんか現れないのだわ"とお父さんは読み上げました。娘はお父さんから本を取り上げてこう言いました。
"現れるわよ！"と娘は言い、本をひっくり返しながら"王子様があなたのことを愛してくれるわ！"と言ったのでした。

A dad sometimes reads the story of Cinderella to his little daughter. Today he is reading it again.
"I will never have somebody who loves me, Cinderella said and cried sadly," the dad reads aloud. The daughter quickly takes the book from his hands.
"You will! You will!" she says and flips through the book, "the prince will love you!"

otōsan wa tamani, osanai musume no tameni Shinderera o yondeagemasu. watashi no koto o aishitekureru hito nanka arawarenai no da wa to otōsan wa yomiagemashita. musume wa otōsan kara hon o toriagete kō iimashita. arawareru wa yo! to musume wa ii, hon o hikkurikaeshi nagara ōji sama ga anata no koto o aishitekureru wa! to itta no deshita.

あなたは注文フォームを処理する方法を知っていますか？
Do you know how to process order forms?

単語
Words

1. 3、三 [san] - three
2. 5、五 [go] - five
3. 〜の前 [〜no mae] - before
4. で/いつ [de/itsu] - at / when
5. アプリケーション [apurike-shon] - application
6. エラー [era-] - error
7. カンファレンス、会議 [kanferensu, kaigi] - conference
8. スピーチ、プレゼンテーション [supi-chi, purezente-shon] - speech, presentation
9. チケット [chiketto] - ticket
10. ドイツ [doitsu] - Germany

11. バイヤー、買い手 [baiya-, kaite] - buyer
12. ファイルにまとめる(動詞) [fairu ni matomeru] - file *(Verb)*
13. フォーム、用紙 [fo-mu, youshi] - form
14. フライト [furaito] - flight
15. プログラム [puroguramu] - program
16. 一定の、絶えず続く [itteino, taezu tuzuku] - constant
17. 開催する [kaisai suru] - take place
18. 起こる(動詞)、発生する [okoru (doushi), hassei suru] - happen *(Verb)*, to occur
19. 恐らく [osoraku] - probably
20. 教える(動詞) [oshieru (doushi)] - teach *(Verb)*
21. 交渉 [koushou] - negotiations
22. 考える(動詞)、考慮する、〜だと思う [kangaeru (doushi), kouryosuru, 〜dato omou] - consider *(Verb)*, think *(Verb)*
23. 航空会社、エアライン [koukuu gaisha, earain] - airline
24. 指名する(動詞) [shimeisuru (doushi)] - appoint *(Verb)*
25. 支払い [shiharai] - payment
26. 次 [tsugi] - next
27. 謝る(動詞)、謝罪する [ayamaru (dōshi)、shazai suru] - apologize *(Verb)*
28. 終わる(動詞)/〜に入る/(契約書に)サインする [owaru(doushi)/ 〜ni hairu/ (keiyakushi ni) sain suru] - conclude *(Verb)* / to enter / to sign (a contract)
29. 週 [shuu] - week
30. 処理する(動詞) [shorisuru (doushi)] - process *(Verb)*
31. 尋ねる、聞く(動詞) [tazuneru, kiku (doushi)] - ask *(Verb)*
32. 代表、メンバー [daihyou, menba-] - delegate, member, representative
33. 地図、マップ [chizu, mappu] - map
34. 直す(動詞) [naosu(doushi)] - correct *(Verb)*
35. 到着する(動詞) [touchakusuru (doushi)] - arrive *(Verb)*
36. 導く(動詞) [michibiku (doushi)] - lead *(Verb)*
37. 飛ぶ(動詞) [tobu (doushi)] - fly *(Verb)*
38. 飛行機 [hikouki] - plane, airplane
39. 払う(動詞) [harau (doushi)] - pay *(Verb)*
40. 報告する(動詞) [houkoku suru (doushi)] - report *(Verb)*
41. 方法 [houhou] - method
42. 夜 [yoru] - night
43. 役に立つ [yakunitatsu] - useful
44. 予約する(動詞) [yoyaku suru (doushi)] - book *(Verb)*
45. 話す(動詞)、発表する [hanasu (doushi), happyou suru] - speak *(Verb)*, to present

B

1

- 良い日ですね！
-iihi desune!
- こんにちは！
-konnichiha!
- 元気ですか？
-genkidesuka?
- 全てが良好です、ありがとうございます。
-subete ga ryoukou desu. arigatougozaimasu.

2

- あなたは注文ふぉーむを処理する方法を知っていますか？
-anata ha chuumon fo-mu wo shorisuru houhou wo shitteimasuka?
- いいえ、私は注文ふぉーむを処理する方法を知りません。
-iie, watashi ha chuumon fo-mu wo shorisuru houhou wo shirimasen.
- あなたは知らなければなりません。
-anata ha shiranakereba narimasen.
- 私に教えてくれますか？
-watashi ni oshietekuremasuka?
- はい、あなたに注文の処理を教えることができます。
-hai, anata ni chuumon no shori wo oshierukoto ga dekimasu.

3

- 何が起こりましたか？
-nani ga okorimashitaka?
- 注文の見積もりでえらーが発生しました。
-chuumon no mitsumoride era- ga hasseishimashita.

1

- Good day!
- Hello!
- How are you doing?
- Everything is fine, thank you.

2

- Do you know how to process order forms?
- No, I do not know how to process order forms.
- You have to know.
- Can you teach me?
- Yes, I can teach you to process orders.

3

- What happened?
- An error occurred in the calculations of order processing.

- 手伝いましょうか？
-tetsudaimashouka?

-はい、このえらーを直す手伝いをしてくれませんか？
-hai, kono era- wo naosu tetsudai wo shitekuremasenka?

-買い手はすでにこの事を知っていますか？
-kaite ha sudeni konokoto wo shitte imasuka?

-いいえ、私は直ちに彼に報告し、そして謝るべきです。
-iie, watashi ha tadachini kare ni houkokushi, soshite ayamarubeki desu.

4

-1週間後にどいつでかんふぁれんすが開催されます。
-isshukango ni doitsu de kanfarensu ga kaisaisaremasu.

-私たちの会社はかんふぁれんすに参加しますか？
-watashitachi no kaisha ha kanfarensu ni sanka shimasuka?

-はい、私たちの会社は参加するべきです。CEOが参加に申し込むように言いました。
-hai, watashitachi no kaisha ha sanka surubeki desu. CEO ga sankani moushikomuyouni iimashita.

-あなたはそれを今日できますか？
-anata ha sore wo kyou dekimasuka?

-はい、私はそれを今日できます。
-hai, watashi ha sore wo kyoudekimasu.

5

-あなたのCEOは1人で行きたいですか？
-anata no CEO ha hitori de ikitai desuka?

-いいえ、彼はえんじにあとPRまねーじゃーを連れて行く必要があります。

- Can I help you?

- Yes, you can help me fix this error.

- Did the buyer already know about this?

- No, I should immediately report to him and apologize.

4

- A conference in Germany takes place in a week.

- Does our company participate in the conference?

- Yes, our company should participate. The CEO asks to apply for participation.

- Can you do it today?

- Yes, I can do it today.

5

- Does our CEO want to go alone?

-iie, kare ha enjinia to PR mane-ja- wo tsureteiku hitsuyou ga arimasu.

- 彼らは彼を助けることができますか？
-karera ha kare wo tasukerukoto ga dekimasuka?

-はい、私はそう思います。彼らはぷれぜんてーしょんに役立つことができます。
-hai, watashi ha sou omoimasu. karera ha purezente-shon ni yakudatsukoto ga dekimasu.

6

- 秘書に航空会社のちけっとを予約するように尋ねてくれませんか？
-hisho ni koukuugaisha no chiketto wo yoyaku suruyouni tazunete kuremasenka?

-はい、私は秘書にちけっとを予約するように尋ねることができます。
-hai, watashi ha hisho ni chiketto wo yoyaku suruyouni tazunerukoto ga dekimasu.

- 彼女は何枚のちけっとを予約する必要がありますか？
-kanojo ha nanmai no chiketto wo yoyakusuru hitsuyou ga arimasuka?

- 彼女は3枚のちけっとを予約する必要があります。
-kanojo ha sanmai no chiketto wo yoyaku suruhitsuyou ga arimasu.

7

-CEOはいつそこにいたいと考えますか？
-CEO ha itsu sokoni itaito kangaemasuka?

- 私は彼はそこに5日後にいたいと考えていると思います。
-watashi ha kare ha sokoni itsukago ni itaito kangaeteiru to omoimasu.

- No, he has to take an engineer and a PR-manager with him.

- Can they help him?

- Yes, I think so. They can be useful for the presentation.

6

- Can you ask the secretary to book airline tickets?

- Yes, I can ask the secretary to book the tickets.

- How many tickets does she have to book?

- She has to book three tickets.

7

- When does the CEO want to be there?

- I think he wants to be there in five days.

- Why does he want to

- どうして彼は早く出発したいのですか？
-doushite kare ha hayaku shuppatsu shitaino desuka?
- 彼は新しい情報を学ばないといけないからです。
-kare ha atarashii jouhou wo manabanaito ikenai karadesu.
- 何の情報がCEOにとって興味深いものかもしれませんか？
-nanno jouhou ga CEO nitotte kyoumibukai mono kamoshiremasenka?
- 彼はもだん製造について学びたいと考えています。
-kare ha modanseihin ni tsuite manabitai to kangaeteimasu.

8
- 私たちの代表はかんふぁれんすで何をする予定ですか？
-watashitachi no daihyou ha kanfarensu de nani wo suru yotei desuka?
- 彼らは新しいぱーとなーとの契約書にさいんする予定です。
-karera ha atarashi pa-tona- tono keiyakusho ni sainsuru yotei desu.
- 誰が交渉する予定ですか？
-dare ga koushou suru yotei desuka?
- 私たちの会社の代表が交渉を導きます。
-watashitachi no kaisha no daihyou ga koushou wo michibikimasu.

9
- 彼はいつ飛びますか？
-kare ha itsu tobimasuka?
- 彼は夜に飛ぶ予定です。飛行機は夜に

- leave earlier?
- He needs to learn more new information.
- What information might be of interest to the CEO?
- He wants to learn more about modern manufacturing.

8
- What are our representatives planning to do at the conference?
- They are planning to sign contracts with new partners.
- Who's going to negotiate?
- Our company representative is going to lead the negotiations.

9
- When is he going to fly?
- He's going to fly in

とうちゃく
到着します。
-kare ha yoru ni tobu yotei desu. hikouki ha yoru ni touchaku shimasu.

かれ　　　　　と
- 彼はどこに泊まりたいですか？
-kare ha dokoni tomaritai desuka?

かれ　　　　　と
- 彼はほてるに泊まりたいです。
-kare ha hoteruni tomaritai desu.

10

かれ　なに　　　よてい
- 彼は何をする予定ですか？
-kare ha nani wo suru yoteidesuka?

かれ　じゅうよう　かいぎ　　　　　　よてい
- 彼は重要な会議をせっとする予定です。
-kare ha juuyouna kaigi wo settosuru yotei desu.

かいぎ　じむしょ　かいさい
- この会議は事務所で開催するべきですか？
-kono kaigi ha jimusho de kaisaisuru bekidesuka?

かいぎ　じむしょ　かいさい
- はい、この会議は事務所で開催するべきです。
-hai, kono kaigi ha jimusho de kaisaisuru bekidesu.

11

あたら　　せいぞうほうほう　　　　　　　　　こうりょ
- 新しい製造方法はかんふぁれんすで考慮されるべきです。
-atarashii seizouhouhou ha kanfarensu de kouryosareru beki desu.

だれ　　　　　　　　　　　はな
- 誰がかんふぁれんすで話しますか？
-dare ga kanfarensu de hanashimasuka?

はな　ひと　　　　　　　せいこう　　かいしゃ
- 話す人はえんじにあと成功した会社の
だいひょう
代表です。
-hanasuhito ha enjinia to seikoushita kaisha no daihyou desu.

わたし　　　だいひょうしゃ　なに
- 私たちの代表者は何をするべきですか？
-watashitachi no daihyousha ha nani wo surubeki desuka?

わたし　　　だいひょうしゃ　こうりつてき　あたら
- 私たちの代表者は効率的に新しい
ひつよう
あいであをぷれぜんする必要があります。

---

the evening. The plane arrives at night.

- Where does he want to stay?

- He wants to stay at a hotel.

10

- What is he going to do?

- He's going to set an important meeting.

- Should this meeting take place in the office?

- Yes, this meeting should take place in the office.

11

- New methods of the manufacturing must be considered at the conference.

- Who speaks at the conference?

- The speakers are engineers and successful companies' representatives.

- What should our delegates do?

- Our delegates must effectively present

-watashitachi no daihyousha ha kouritsutekini atarashii aidea wo purezen suruhitsuyou ga arimasu.

12

-あなたは航空会社の電話番号を持っていますか？
-anata ha koukuugaisha no denwabangou wo motteimasuka?
-はい、私は航空会社の電話番号を持っています。私たちは彼らの常連の顧客です。あなたはちけっとを予約したいですか？
-hai, watashi ha koukuugaisha no denwabangou wo motteimasu. watashitachi ha karera no jouren no kokyaku desu. anata ha chiketto wo yoyakushitai desuka?
-はい、私は次のふらいとのちけっとを予約したいです。私はくれじっとかーどでちけっとを払うことができますか？
-hai, watashi ha tsugi no furaito no chiketto wo yoyaku shitaidesu. watashi ha kurejittoka-do de chiketto wo haraukoto ga dekimasuka?

-はい、あなたはくれじっとかーどでちけっとを払うことができます。
-hai, anata ha kurejittoka-do de chiketto wo haraukoto ga dekimasu.

new ideas.

12

- Do you have an airline phone number?

- Yes, I have the airline phone number. We are their regular customer. Do you want to book tickets?

- Yes, I want to book tickets for the next flight. Can I pay for the tickets with a credit card?

- Yes, you can pay for the tickets with a credit card.

7

Audio

氷を砕く
Break the ice

誕生日会には沢山の子供たちが参加をしており、みんなでてーぶるを囲んでけーきを見ています。けーきの上にはちょこでできた動物が飾られています。
"誰かしまうま欲しい?"とお母さんは子供たちに聞きます。
"しまうまさんください"と女の子は言いました。
"お魚さんください"ともう一人の女の子が言いました。

There are many little children at a birthday party. They all sit at the table. A big cake is on the table. There are chocolate animals on the cake.
"Who wants the zebra?" the mom asks the children.
"Give me the zebra please," a girl says.
"Give me the fish please," another girl says.

"きりんさんください" と 男の子が言いました。
"すぷーんください" と 別の男の子が言いました。

"Give me the giraffe please," a boy says.
"Give me a spoon please," another boy says.

tanjōbikai ni wa takusan no kodomotachi ga sanka o shiteori, minna de te-buru o kakonde ke-ki o miteimasu. ke-ki no ueni wa choko de dekita dōbutsu ga kazarareteimasu. dare ka shimauma hoshii? to okāsan wa kodomotachi ni kikimasu. shimauma san kudasai to onnanoko wa iimashita. o sakana san kudasai to mō ichi nin no onnanoko ga iimashita. kirin san kudasai to otokonoko ga iimashita. supu-n kudasai to betsu no otokonoko ga iimashita.

解決する手伝いをしてくれませんか？
Can you help me to figure it out?

単語
Words

1. (料金が)無料 [(ryoukin ga) muryou] - free (of charge)
2. 2番 [niban] - second
3. 30分 [sanjuppun] - half an hour
4. 3番 [sanban] - third
5. かかる(動詞) [kakaru (doushi)] - cost *(Verb)*
6. アンチウィルスソフト [anchi uirusu sofutowea] - antivirus software
7. インターネット [inta-netto] - Internet
8. コピー機 [kopi-ki] - copy machine, Xerox, copier
9. コンピューター [konpu-ta-] - computer

10. サービス [sa-bisu] - service
11. システム [sisutemu] - system
12. ソフトウェア、プログラム [sofutouea, puroguramu] - software, program
13. ディスク [disuku] - disk
14. ネットワーク [nettowa-ku] - network
15. ノード [no-do] - node
16. 会議室 [kaigishitsu] - conference room
17. 会計士 [kaikeishi] - accountant
18. 解決する、理解する [kaiketsusuru, rikaisuru] - figure out
19. 壊す [kowasu] - break
20. 階 [kai] - floor
21. 確認する(動詞)、調査する [kakuninsuru (doushi), chousasuru] - check *(Verb)*, to examine
22. 近い [chikai] - near, close
23. 銀行 [ginkou] - bank
24. 見せる(動詞) [miseru (doushi)] - show *(Verb)*
25. 口座、アカウント [kouza, akaunto] - account
26. 最初、始め、1番 [saisho, hajime, ichiban] - first
27. 残す(動詞) [nokosu (doushi)] - leave *(Verb)*
28. 使う(動詞) [tsukau (doushi)] - use *(Verb)*
29. 事務所 [jimusho] - office
30. 事務所の [jimusho] - of the office
31. 準備する、用意する [junbisuru, youisuru] - ready
32. 署名する(動詞)、サインする [shomeisuru (doushi), sainsuru] - sign *(Verb)*
33. 相談する (動詞) [soudansuru (doushi)] - consult *(Verb)*
34. 代理店 [dairiten] - agency
35. 大きくない、小さい [ookikunai, chiisai] - not big, small
36. 通訳 [tsuuyaku] - interpreter
37. 天気 [tenki] - whether
38. 読む(動詞) [yomu(doushi)] - read *(Verb)*
39. 法律家、弁護士 [houritsuka, bengoshi] - lawyer, attorney
40. 有線の、接続した、繋がった [yuusen no, setuzokushita, tsunagatta] - wired, connected

B

1

-おはようございます！何 時ですか？
-ohayougozaimasu! nanji desuka?
- 朝 の 10時です。
-asa no juuji desu.
- 今日は水曜日ですか？
-kyou ha suiyoubi desuka?

1

- Good morning! What time is it?

- It's ten o'clock in the morning.

- Is today Wednesday?

-いいえ、今日は木曜日です。
-iie, kyou ha mokuyoubi desu.

2

-この階にこぴー機はありますか？
-konokaini kopi-ki ha arimasuka?

-いいえ。この階には、こぴー機はありません。
-iie. konokai niha, kopi-ki ha arimasen.

-私はここにこれらのどきゅめんとを残していってもいいですか？
-watashi ha kokoni korera no dokyumento wo nokoshite ittemo ii desuka?

-はい、あなたはここにどきゅめんとを残していってもいいです。
-hai, anata ha kokoni dokyumento wo nokoshite ittemo ii desu.

3

-この建物に会議室はありますか？
-konotatemononi kaigishitsu ha arimasuka?

-はい、この建物に会議室はあります。それは地上階に位置します。
-hai, konotatemononi kaigishitsu ha arimasu. sore ha chijoukaini ichishimasu.

-この会議室は大きいですか？
-konokaigishitsu ha ookii desuka?

-いいえ。この会議室は小さいです。
-iie. konokaigishitsu ha chiisai desu.

4

-てーぶるの上には新しいかたろぐはありますか？
-te-buru noue niha atarashii katarogu ha arimasuka?

-いいえ。てーぶるの上に新しいかたろぐはありません。
-iie. te-buru noueni atarashii katarogu ha arimasen.

- No, today is Thursday.

2

- Is there a copier on this floor?

- No. On this floor, there is no copier.

- Can I leave these documents here?

- Yes, you can leave your documents here.

3

- Is there a conference room in this building?

- Yes, this building has a conference room. It is located on the ground floor.

- Is this conference room large?

- No. This conference room is small.

4

- Is there a new catalog on the table?

- No. There is no new catalog on the table.

- ねだんひょう
値段表はどこで手に入れることができますか？
-nedanhyou ha dokode teni irerukoto ga dekimasuka?

- まねーじゃーが値段表を持っています。
-mane-ja- ga nedanhyou wo motteimasu.

5

- 新しい事務所を見せてくれませんか？
-atarashii jimusho wo misete kuremasenka?

- いいえ、私は新しい事務所をあなたに見せることができません。まだ準備ができていません。
-iie, watashi ha atarashii jimusho wo anatani miserukotoga dekimasen. mada junbi ga dekiteimasen.

- 来週には見れますか？
-raishuu niha miremasuka?

- はい、あなたは来週見ることができます。
-hai, anata ha raishuu mirukoto ga dekimasu.

6

- あなたには通訳はいますか？
-anata niha tsuuyaku ha imasuka?

- いいえ。私たちの会社は通訳を持っていません。私たちは代理店のさーびすを使っています。
-iie. watashitachi no kaisha ha tsuuyaku wo motteimasen. watashitachi ha dairiten no sa-bisu wo tsukatteimasu.

- ここに会計士はいますか？
-kokoni kaikeishi ha imasuka?

- いいえ、会計係はここにはいません。彼女は隣の部屋にいます。
-iie, kaikeigakari ha kokoniha imasen. kanojo ha tonari no heyani imasu.

- Where can I get a price list?
- The manager has the price list.

5

- Can you show me the new office?
- No, I cannot show you the new office. It is not ready yet.
- Can I see it next week?
- Yes, you can see it next week.

6

- Do you have an interpreter?
- No. Our company has no interpreter. We use the services of an agency.
- Is there an accountant here?
- No, the accountant is not here. She's in the next room.

7

-あんちうぃるすそふとは事務所のこんぴゅーたーにいんすとーるされていますか？
-anchi uirusu sofuto ha jimusho no konpyu-ta- ni insuto-ru sareteimasuka?

-はい。もちろんです、あんちうぃるすそふとは事務所のこんぴゅーたーにいんすとーるされています。
-hai. mochiron desu. anchi uirusu sofuto ha jimusho no konpyu-ta- ni insuto-ru sareteimasu.

-2階にはしすてむのーどはありますか？
-nikai niha shisutemu no-do ha arimasuka?

-いいえ。2階にはしすてむのーどはありません。それは3階に位置します。
-iie. nikai niha shisutemu no-do ha arimasen. soreha sankaini ichishimasu.

8

-あなたは新しいそふとうぇあを持っていますか？
-anata ha atarashii sofutouea wo motteimasuka?

-はい、私たちは新しいそふとうぇあを持っています。
-hai, watashitachi ha atarashii sofutouea wo motteimasu.

-それを理解する手伝いをしてくれませんか？
-sore wo rikaisuru tetsudai wo shitekuremasenka?

-はい。私は手伝うことができます。
-hai. watashi ha tetsudaukoto ga dekimasu.

9

-建物にはいんたーねっとはありますか？私はびじねすにゅーすを読みたいです。
-tatemono niha inta-netto ha arimasuka? watashi ha bijinesunyu-su wo yomitai desu.

-はい。建物にはいんたーねっとはあります。
-hai. tatemono niha inta-netto ha arimasu.

7

- Is antivirus software installed on the office computers?

- Yes. Of course, antivirus software is installed on our computers.

- Does the second floor have the system node?

- No. The second floor does not have the system node. It is located on the third floor.

8

- Do you have the new software?

- Yes, we have the new software.

- Can you help me to figure it out?

- Yes. I can help you.

9

- Is there Internet in the building? I want to read the business news.

- Yes. There is Internet in this

わたし　　　　　　　　　　　　むりょう　つか
- 私 はいんたーねっとを 無 料 で 使 えますか？
-watashi ha inta-netto wo muryou de tsukaemasuka?
　　　わたし　　　　　　　　　　　せつぞく
-はい。 私 はねっとわーくに 接 続 したこんぴゅー
　　　　　　　　　　み
たーを見せることができます。
-hai. watashi ha nettowa-kuni setsuzokushita konpyu-ta-wo miserukoto ga dekimasu.

10

　　　　じむしょ　　べんごし　　　　　　　わたし　かれ
-この事 務 所 には弁護 士 はいますか？ 私 は彼 に
　そうだん　　　ひつよう
 相 談 する 必 要 があります。
-konojimusho niha bengohi ha imasuka? watashi ha kare ni soudansuru hitsuyou ga arimasu.
　　　　　べんごし　げんざいじむしょ
-いいえ。弁護士は 現 在 事務所にいません。
-iie. bengoshi ha genzai jimushoni imasen.
　　わたし　　　　かれ　あ
- 私 はいつ 彼 と会 うことができますか？
-watashi ha itsu kare to aukoto ga dekimasuka?
　かれ　　　じかんご　　　じむしょ
- 彼 は１時 間 後には事務 所 にいるはずです。
-kare ha ichijikango niha jimushoni iruhazu desu.

11

　じむしょ　ちか　　ぎんこう　　　　　　　　わたし
-事務所の 近 くに 銀 行 はありますか？ 私 は
　じぶん　こうざ　かくにん　　　ひつよう
 自分の口 座 を 確 認 する 必 要 があります。
-jimusho no chikakuni ginkou ha arimasuka? watashi ha jibun no kouza wo kakuninsuru hitsuyou ga arimasu.
　　　　じむしょ　ちか　　ぎんこう
-はい。事務 所 の 近 くに 銀 行 があります。
-hai. jimusho no chikakuni ginkou ga arimasu.
　ぎんこう　ひるやす
- 銀 行 に昼 休 みはありますか？
-ginkou ni hiruyasumi ha arimasuka?
　　　　ぎんこう　ひるやす
-はい。 銀 行 に昼 休 みはあります。
-hai. ginkou ni hiruyasumi ha arimasu.

12

　　　　　　どうい　　　ふぉーむ　も　　　　　わたし
-あなたは同 意 ふぉーむを持っていますか？ 私 はそ

building.
- Can I use the Internet for free?
- Yes. I can show you a computer connected to the network.

10

- Is there a lawyer in the office? I need to consult him.
- No. The lawyer is not currently in the office.
- When can I see him?
- He should be in the office in an hour.

11

- Is there a bank near the office? I have to check my account.
- Yes. There is the bank near the office.
- Does the bank have a lunch break?
- Yes. The bank has a lunch break.

12

- Do you have the agreement form? I

れを読みたいです。
-anata ha douifo-mu wo motteimasuka? watashi ha sore wo yomitai desu.

-はい、もちろんです。私たちは同意ふぉーむを持っています。CEOがそれに署名する必要があります。
-hai, mochiron desu. watashitachi ha douifo-mu wo motteimasu. CEO ga soreni shomeisuru hitsuyou ga arimasu.

- 私は今彼に会うことができますか？
-watashi ha ima kareni aukotoga dekimasuka?

-いいえ、あなたは彼に30分後に会うことができます。
-iie. anata ha kareni sanjuppungoni aukoto ga dekimasu.

13

-これは私たちの新しい企画が入ったこんぴゅーたーでぃすくですか？
-kore ha watashitachi no atarashii kikaku ga haitta konpyu-ta- disuku desuka?

-いいえ。これはおふぃすぷろぐらむが入ったこんぴゅーでぃすくです。
-iie. koreha ofisu puroguramu ga haitta konpyu-ta-disuku desu.

-りんだは企画が入ったこんぴゅーたーでぃすくを持っていますか？
-rinda ha kikaku ga haitta konpyu-ta-disuku wo motteimasuka?

-いいえ。えんじにあがこのこんぴゅーたーでぃすくを持っています。
-iie. enjinia ga kono konpyu-ta-disuku wo motteimasu.

want to read it.

- Yes, of course. We have an agreement form. The CEO has to sign it.

- Can I see him now?

- No, you can see him in half an hour.

13

- Is this the computer disk with our new project?

- No. This is a computer disk with the office program.

- Does Linda have the computer disk with the project?

- No. The engineer has this computer disk.

8

Audio

氷を砕く
Break the ice

"どうだかね、ってどういう意味？"と少年はお母さんに聞きました。
"疑わしいってことは真実か真実じゃないか確かじゃない時よ。でもたまに真実の時もあるの。"
後に二人がスープを食べている時、少年は座って窓を眺めていました。
"早く食べちゃいなさい"とお母さんは言いました。
息子はお母さんを見ています。息子は何やら考

"What does 'I doubt it' mean?" a little boy asks his mom.
"It means rather no than yes. But it can mean yes in other situations," the mom explains to her son. Later the son and the mom have some soup. The boy sits and looks at the window.
"Finish your soup, please," the mom says to him. The son looks at his mom. The mom sees that he is thinking hard.

え込んでいる様子です。
"どうだかね"と息子は最後に言いました。

"I doubt it," he says at last.

dō da ka ne, tte dōiu imi? to shōnen wa okāsan ni kikimashita. utagawashii tte koto wa shinjitsu ka shinjitsu janai ka tashika janai toki yo. demo tamani shinjitsu no toki mo aru no.go ni ni nin ga su-pu o tabeteiru toki, shōnen wa suwatte mado o nagameteimashita. hayaku tabe chai nasai to okāsan wa iimashita. musuko wa okāsan o miteimasu. musuko wa naniyara kangaekondeiru yōsu desu. dō da ka ne to musuko wa saigo ni iimashita.

これらの責任は誰のですか？
Whose are these responsibilities?

単語
Words

1. コピー/サンプル[kopi-/sanpuru] - copy/sample
2. タスク、仕事[tasuku,shigoto] - task
3. ディレクトリー[direkutori-] - directory
4. ファイル/フォルダ[fairu/foruda-] - file/folder
5. レポート、報告[repo-to,houkoku] - report
6. 横になる[yokoninaru] - laydown
7. 会社の、組織の[kaishano,soshikino] - corporate

8. 開発する(動詞)[kaihatsusuru(doushi)] - develop*(Verb)*
9. 管理者[kanrisha] - administrator
10. 財務[zaimu] - financial
11. 車[kuruma] - car
12. 手紙[tegami] - letter
13. 商業[shougyou] - trade
14. 戦略[senryaku] - strategy
15. 相談する(動詞)[soudansuru(doushi)] - consult*(Verb)*
16. 棚[tana] - shelve
17. 誰の[dareno] - whose
18. 部門、部[bumon,bu] - department,division
19. 問題[mondai] - problem

B

1

-これらのどきゅめんとは 誰 のですか？
-korera no dokyumento ha dareno desuka?

-これらはみかえるのどきゅめんとです。彼 はよくそれらをてーぶるの 上 に 残 します。
-korera ha mikaeru no dokyumento desu. kare ha yoku sorera wo te-buru no ueni nokoshimasu.

-ぽーるのどきゅめんとはどこですか？
-po-ru no dokyumento ha doko desuka?

-ぽーるのどきゅめんとはふぉるだの 中 にあります。
-po-ru no dokyumento ha foruda no nakani arimasu.

2

-このかたろぐは 誰 のですか？
-kono katarogu ha dare no desuka?

-もしかしたらこのカタログはサンドラのかもしれません。
-moshikashitara kono katarogu ha sandora no kamo shiremasen.

- 私 のかたろぐのこぴーはどこですか？
-watashi no katarogu no kopi- ha doko desuka?

-あなたのかたろぐのこぴーは秘書の 所 にあります。
-anata no katarogu no kopi- ha hisho no tokoroni arimasu.

1

- Whose are these documents?

- These are Michael's documents. He often leaves them on the table.

- Where are Paul's documents?

- Paul's documents are in the folder.

2

- Whose is this catalog?

- Perhaps this catalog is Sandra's.

- Where's my copy of the catalog?

- Your copy of the catalog is at the secretary's.

3

-あなたは会議のぷろぐらむを持っていますか？
-anata ha kaigi no puroguramu wo motteimasuka?
-はい、私は会議のぷろぐらむを持っています。
-hai, watashi ha kaigi no puroguramu wo motteimasu.
-それは誰のですか？
-soreha dare no desuka?
-このぷろぐらむはみかえるのです。
-kono puroguramu ha mikaeru no desu.

4

-これらの責任は誰のですか？
-korera no sekinin ha dare no desuka?
-これらは弁護士の責任です。
-korera ha bengoshi no sekinin desu.
-せーるすまねーじゃーの責任は何ですか？
-se-rusu mane-ja- no sekinin ha nandesuka?
-彼はくらいあんとにあどばいすをする必要があります。
-kare ha kuraianto ni adobaisu wo suruhitsuyou ga arimasu.

5

-このでぃすくは誰のですか？
-kono disuku ha dare no desuka?
-これはりんだのでぃすくです。
-kore ha rinda no disuku desu.
-みかえるのでぃすくはどこですか？
-mikaeru no disuku ha doko desuka?
-みかえるのでぃすくは棚の上にあります。
-mikaeru no disuku ha tana no ueni arimasu.

6

-この契約書は誰のですか？
-kono keiyakusho ha dare no desuka?

3

- Do you have a conference program?

- Yes, I have a conference program.

- Whose is it?

- This program is Michael's.

4

- Whose are these responsibilities?

- These are the lawyer's responsibilities.

- What are the responsibilities of the sales manager?

- He has to advise clients.

5

- Whose is this disk?

- This is Linda's disk.

- Where is Michael's disk?

- Michael's disk is on the shelf.

6

- Whose is this contract?

- This is Paul's contract.

　　　　　　　　けいやくしょ
-これはぽーるの 契 約 書 です。
-kore ha po-ru no keiyakusho desu.
　　　　　　　けいやくしょ
-さんどらの 契 約 書 はどこですか？
-sandora no keiyakusho ha doko desuka?
　　　　　　けいやくしょ　　　　ところ
-さんどらの 契 約 書 はCEOの 所 にあります。
-sandora no keiyakusho ha CEO no tokoroni arimasu.

7
　　　　　　　だれ
-このあいであは 誰 ですか？
-kono aidea ha dare no desuka?
-これはりーどえんじにあのあいであです。
-kore ha ri-do enjinia no aidea desu.
　だれ　　かれ　　そうだん
- 誰 が彼と相 談 しますか？
-dare ga kare to soudan shimasuka?
　かれ　　べんごし　そうだん
- 彼は弁護士と相 談 します。
-kare ha bengoshi to soudanshimasu.

8
　　　　　みつ　　　　だれ
-これらの見積もりは 誰 のですか？
-korera no mitsumori ha dare no desuka?
　　　　　　　　みつ
-これらはぽーるの見積もりです。
-korera ha po-ru no mitsumori desu.
　だれ　　　みつ　　　　もんだい　も
- 誰 がその見積もりに 問 題 を持っていますか？
-dare ga sono mitsumorini mondai wo motteimasuka?
　　　　　　　　みつ　　　　もんだい　も
-りんだがその見積もりに 問 題 を持っています。
-rinda ga sono mitsumorini mondai wo motteimasu.

9
　　　だれ
-これは 誰 のでぃれくとりですか？
-kore ha dare no direkutori desuka?
　　　　わたし
-これは 私 のでぃれくとりです。
-kore ha watashi no direkutori desu.
-みかえるのでぃれくとりはどこですか？

- Where is Sandra's contract?

- Sandra's contract is at the CEO's.

7

- Whose is this idea?

- This is the lead engineer's idea.

- Who consults him?

- He consults with a lawyer.

8

- Whose are these calculations?

- These are Paul's calculations.

- Who has problems with the calculations?

- Linda has problems with the calculations.

9

- Whose directory is this?

- This is my directory.

- Where is Michael's

-mikaeru no direkutori ha doko desuka?
- 彼のでぃれくとりは 車 の 中 にあります。
-kare no direkutori ha kuruma no nakani arimasu.

10
-これらは 誰 の 問題 ですか？
-korera ha dare no mondai desuka?
-これはまねーじゃーの 問題 です。彼自身がそれらを解決しなければなりません。
-kore ha mane-ja- no mondai desu. karejishin ga sorera wo kaiketsu shinakereba narimasen.
-あなたは 彼 と 相談 できますか？
-anata wo kare to soudan dekimasu.
-はい、 私 は 彼 と 相談 できます。
-hai, watashi ha kare to soudan dekimasu.

11
-このぷろじぇくとは 誰 のですか？
-kono purojekuto ha dare no desuka?
-これはPRまねーじゃーのぷろじぇくとです。
-kore ha PR mane-ja- no purojekuto desu.
-ぽーるのぷろじぇくとはどこですか？
-po-ru no purojekuto ha doko desuka?
- 彼 のぷろじぇくとはまだ 準備 できていません。
-kareno purojekuto ha mada junbi dekiteimasen.

12
-この財務のれぽーとは 誰 のですか？
-kono zaimuno repo-to ha dare no desuka?
-これは 会計士 のれぽーとです。
-kore ha kaikeishi no repo-to desu.
- 誰 がそのれぽーとを 用意 しましたか？
-dare ga sono repo-to wo youi shimashitaka?
-さんどらが 用意 しました。

- directory?
- His directory is in the car.

10
- Whose problems are this?
- This is the manager's problems. He himself must solve them.
- Can you consult him?
- Yes, I can consult him.

11
- Whose is this project?
- This is the PR- manager's project.
- Where is Paul's project?
- His project is not ready.

12
- Whose is this financial report?
- This is the accountant's report.
- Who prepared the report?

-sandora ga youi shimashita.

13

- 会社のろごぺーぱーに書かれたあなたの手紙はどこですか？
-kaisha no rogope-pa- ni kakareta anata no tegami ha doko desuka?
- 私の手紙は秘書の所にあります。
-watashi no tegami ha hisho no tokoroni arimasu.
- りんだの手紙はどこですか？
-rinda no tegami ha doko desuka?
- 彼女の手紙はまねーじゃーの所にあります。
-kanojo no tegami ha mane-ja-no tokoroni arimasu

14

- これは誰の電話番号ですか？
-kore ha dare no denwabangou desuka?
- これは私たちのくらいあんとの電話番号です。
-kore ha watashitachi no kuraianto no denwabangou desu.
- しすてむ管理者の電話番号はどこですか？
-shisutemu kanrisha no denwabangou ha doko desuka?
- 秘書が彼の電話番号を知っています。
-hisho ga kare no denwabangou wo shitteimasu.

15

- これは誰の取引戦略ですか？
-kore ha dare no torihikisenryaku desuka?
- これはみかえるの戦略です。彼は成功する政略を発展させます。
-kore ha mikaeru no senryaku desu. kare ha seikousuru senryaku wo hattensasemasu.
- さんどらの戦略は効率的ではありませんか？
-sandora no senryaku ha kouritsuteki deha arimasenka?

- Sandra prepared it.

13

- Where is your letter on the company logo paper?

- My letter is at the secretary's.

- Where's Linda's letter?

- Her letter is at the manager's.

14

- Whose is this phone number?

- This is our client's phone number.

- Where's the phone number of the system administrator?

- The secretary knows his phone number.

15

- Whose is this trading strategy?

- This is Michael's strategy. He develops successful strategies.

- Are Sandra's strategies

-はい、彼女の戦略はそこまで効率的ではありません。
-hai, kanojo no senryaku ha sokomade kouritsutekideha arimasen.

- Yes, her strategies are not as effective.

16

-このすたっふは誰のですか？
-kono sutaffu ha dare no desuka?

-これは他の部門のすたっふです。
-kore ha hokano bumon no sutaffu desu.

-彼らはどこですか？
-karera ha dokodesuka?

-彼らは今会議にいます。
-karera ha ima kaigini imasu.

- Whose is this staff?

- This is the staff from another department.

- Where are they?

- They are now at the meeting.

9

Audio

氷を砕く
Break the ice

お父さんと 幼い息子は散歩から 戻りました。
お母さんは息子が 両 手をあげたままでテレビを見ているのを見つけました。
"何で手を挙げているの？"とお母さんは聞きました。
"お父さんがそうしてと言ったから"と 彼は言いました。
お父さんが部屋に 入ってきました。
"セーターを脱がせてあげたんだけど"とお父さんは

A dad and his little son come home from a walk. The mom comes into the room and sees that the son is standing, watching TV with his hands up.
"Why are your hands up?" she asks him.
"It is because of daddy," he answers.
The dad comes into the room.
"I took the sweater off him," he explains, "Dear

せつめい　　　　て　お　　　　　そふぁ　すわ
説明しました。"手を下ろしてソファーに座って
てれび　み　　　　　　　　　むすこ　い
テレビを見なさい"とお父さんは息子に言った。

put your hands down and take a seat on the sofa, please."

otōsan to osanai musuko wa sanpo kara modorimashita. okāsan wa musuko ga ryōte o ageta mama de terebi o miteiru no o mitsukemashita. nani de te o ageteiru no? to okāsan wa kikimashita. otōsan ga sō shite to itta kara to kare wa iimashita. otōsan ga heya ni haittekimashita. se-ta- o nugaseteageta n da kedo to otōsan wa setsumeishimashita. te o oroshite sofuxa- ni suwatte terebi o mi nasai to otōsan wa musuko ni itta.

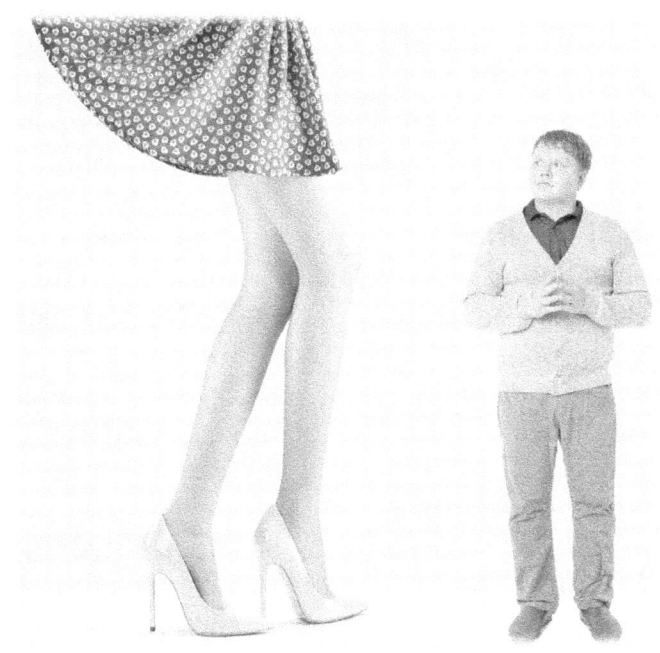

私のためにファックスを受理してくれませんか？
Can you accept a fax for me?

単語
Words

1. 〜から [〜kara] - from
2. あげる(動詞) [ageru (doushi)] - give (Verb)
3. このような/こんな [konoyouna/ konna] - such / so
4. しばらくの間、短い間 [shibaraku no aida, mijikaiaida] - for a while, for a short time
5. すでに、もう/また/同じ [sudeni, mou/ mata/ onaji] - already / again / same

6. それぞれ、皆 [sorezore, mina] - each, everybody
7. つまり、そして [tsumari, soshite] - so, then
8. キーボード [ki-bo-do] - keyboard
9. システム [shisutemu] - system
10. セクション/ブロック [sekushon/burokku] - section / block
11. パッケージ [pakke-ji] - package
12. ファックス [fakkusu] - fax
13. フォーマット、フォーム [fo-matto, fo-mu] - format, form
14. プラスチック [purasuchikku] - plastic
15. プリンター [purinta-] - printer
16. マウス [mauseu] - mouse
17. メッセージ [messe-ji] - message
18. モニター [monita-] - monitor
19. 一致する(動詞) [icchisuru (doushi)] - match *(Verb)*, to correspond
20. 過ぎた/最後の [suugita/saigono] - past / last
21. 会計 [kaikei] - accounting
22. 開ける [akeru (doushi)] - open *(Verb)*
23. 管理、制御、監督 [kanri, seigyo,kantoku] - control, supervision
24. 許可する(動詞) [kyokasueu (doushi)]] - allow *(Verb)*
25. 金属の [kinzokuno] - metallic
26. 決意する(動詞)、定義する [ketsuisuru (doushi), teigisuru] - determine *(Verb)*, to define
27. 月 [tsuki] - month
28. 建設、建物、構造[kensetsu, tatemono, kouzou] - construction, structure
29. 源、リソース [minamoto, reso-su] - resource
30. 言う(動詞) [iu (doushi)] - tell *(Verb)*
31. 高い [takai] - high
32. 紙 [kami] - paper
33. 資産、財産 [shisan, zaisan] - funds, means
34. 失敗、衝突 [shippai, shoutotsu] - failure, crash
35. 終わり [owari] - end
36. 終わる(動詞) [owaru (doushi)] - finish *(Verb)*
37. 暑い [atsui] - hot
38. 助ける [tasukeru] - help
39. 小さい [chiisai] - small
40. 招待する(動詞) [shoutaisuru (doushi)] - invite *(Verb)*
41. 色 [iro] - color
42. 窓 [mado] - window
43. 送る、送信する(動詞) [okuru, soushinsuru (doushi)] - send *(Verb)*
44. 待合室 [machiaishitsu] - waiting room
45. 暖かい [atatakai] - warm
46. 調査する(動詞)、見る [chousasuru (doushi), miru] - examine *(Verb)*, to view
47. 調整する(動詞)、修正する [chousei suru (doushi), shuuseisuru] - adjust *(Verb)*, to tune
48. 提案する(動詞) [teiansuru (doushi)] - suggest *(Verb)*, to offer
49. 電話 [denwa] - phone
50. 部屋 [heya] - room
51. 保管する(動詞) [hokansuru (doushi)] - store *(Verb)*
52. 保存する(動詞)/保つ/保管する [hozonsuru (doushi)/ tamotsu/ hokansuru] - save *(Verb)* / to keep / to store
53. 予算 [yosan] - budget
54. 要求 [youkyuu] - requirement

B

1

-こんにちは！本日は良い天気ですね。
-konnichiha! Honjitsu ha iitenki desune.
-はい。天気は暖かいです。今日は金曜日ですか？
-hai. tenki ha atatakai desu. kyou ha kinyoubi desuka?
-はい。今日はもう金曜日です。
-hai. kyou ha mou kinyoubi desu.

- Good day! The weather today is good.
- Yes. The weather is warm. Is today Friday?
- Yes. Today is Friday already.

2

-どうしてふぁっくすましーんは動いていないのですか？
-doushite fakkusumashi-n ha ugoite inaino desuka?
-もしかしたらそれにふぁっくす用紙が入っていないのかもしれません。
-moshikashitara soreni fakkusuyoushi ga haitte inaino kamoshiremasen.
-事務所にはふぁっくす用紙がありますか？
-jimusho niha fakkusuyoushi ga arimasuka?
-はい。事務所にふぁっくす用紙があります。秘書のところにあります。
-hai. Jimushoni fakkusuyoushi ga arimasu. hishono tokoroni arimasu.

- Why isn't the fax machine working?
- Perhaps there is no fax paper in it.
- Does the office have fax paper?
- Yes. The office has fax paper. It is at the secretary's.

3

-あなたはいつふぁっくすを送るつもりですか？
-anata ha itsu fakkusu wo okuru tsumori desuka?
-私たちは2時間後にあなたにふぁっくすを送ることができます。
-watashitachi ha nijikangoni anatani fakkusu wo okurukoto ga dekimasu.
-良かった。私はあなたからの電話を楽しみにしています。

- When are you going to send a fax?
- We can send you a fax in two hours.
- Good. I look forward

-yokatta. watashi ha anatakara no denwa wo tanoshimini shiteimasu.
-わかりました。私達の秘書があなたに知らせます。
-wakarimashita. watashitachi no hisho ga anatani shirasemasu.

4

-私のこんぴゅーたーまうすが動きません。
-watashi no konpyu-ta-mausu ga ugokimasen.
-あなたは秘書にそれを言わなければなりません。
-anata ha hishoni sore wo iwanakereba narimasen.
-彼女はいつ新しいこんぴゅーたーまうすを頼むことができますか？
-kanojo ha itsu atarashii konpyu-ta-mausu wo tanomukoto ga dekimasuka?
-彼女は毎週月曜日に注文します。
-kanojo ha maishuu getsuyoubini chuumonshimasu.

5

-これは誰のこんぴゅーたーまうすですか？
-kore ha dare no konpyu-ta-mausu desuka?
-これはみかえるのこんぴゅーたーまうすです。
-kore ha mikaeru no konpyu-ta-mausu desu.
-私は彼のこんぴゅーたーまうすをしばらく持って行ってもいいですか？
-watashi ha kare no konpyu-ta-mausu wo shibaraku motteittemo ii desuka?
-大丈夫です。あなたは彼のこんぴゅーたーまうすを持っていくことができます。
-daijoubu desu. anata ha kare no konpyu-ta-mausu wo motteikukoto ga dekimasu.

6

-部屋の窓を開けてくれませんか？部屋が暑いです。
-heya no mado wo aketekuremasenka? heya ga atsui desu.

---

to your phone call.
- OK. Our secretary will inform you.

4

- My computer mouse does not work.
- You must tell the secretary.
- When can she order a new computer mouse?
- She places orders every Monday.

5

- Whose is this computer mouse?
- This is Michael's computer mouse.
- Can I take his computer mouse for a while?
- OK. You can take his computer mouse.

6

- Can you open the window in the room?

-いいえ、できません。部屋の窓は高い所にあります。待合室の窓を開けることはできます。
-iie, dekimasen. heya no mado ha takaitokoroni arimasu. machiaishitsu no mado ha akerukotoga dekimasu.

-これらの窓はぷらすちっくの窓ですか？
-korera no mado ha purasuchikku no mado desuka?

-はい。これらはぷらすちっくの窓です。
-hai. korera ha purasuchikku no mado desu.

7

-私たちの製品はぷらすちっくのぱっけーじに保管されていますか？
-watashitachi no seihin ha purasuchikku no pakke-ji ni hokan sareteimasuka?

-はい。私達の製品はぷらすちっくのぱっけーじに保管されています。
-hai. watashitachi no seihin ha purasuchikku no pakke-ji ni hokansareteimasu.

-せーるすまねーじゃーは紙のぱっけーじを注文するよう私達に提案しています。
-se-rusumane-ja- ha kami no pakke-ji wo chuumon suruyou watashitachini teianshiteimasu.

-これは誰のあいであですか？
-kore ha dare no aidea desuka?

-これはぽーるのあいであです。
-kore ha po-ru no aidea desu.

8

-教えてください、ふぁっくすはすでに動いていますか？それにはふぁっくす用紙が入っていますか？
-oshietekudasai, fakkusu ha sudeni ugoiteimasuka? Sore niha fakkusuyoushi ga haitteimasuka?

The room is hot.

- No, I cannot. The window in the room is high up. We can open the window in the waiting room.

- Are these plastic windows?

- Yes. These are plastic windows.

7

- Are our products stored in plastic packages?

- Yes. Our products are stored in plastic packages.

- The sales manager suggests that we order paper packaging.

- Whose idea is this?

- This is Paul's idea.

8

- Tell me please, is the fax already working?

-はい。ふぁっくすはすでに動いています。
-hai. fakkusu ha sudeni ugoiteimasu.
-あなたは私のためにふぁっくすを受理してくれませんか？
-anata ha watashi no tameni fakkusu wo juri shitekuremasenka?
-はい、私はあなたのためにふぁっくすを受理することができます。
-hai, watashi ha anata no tameni fakkusu wo jurisurukoto ga dekimasu.

9

-私たちはぷりんたー用紙を持っていますか？
-watashitachi ha purintayoushi wo motteimasuka?
-はい。私たちはぷりんたー用紙を持っています。
-hai. watashitachi ha purintayoushi wo motteimasu.
-しかしこれは色のついた紙です。はまりません。
-shikashi kore ha ironotsuita kami desu. hamarimasen.

10

-彼女は財務れぽーとのための新しいふぉーまっとを開発しています。
-kanojo ha zaimurepo-to no tameno atarashii fo-matto wo kaihatsu shiteimasu.
-彼女はいつそれを終わらせる予定ですか？
-kanojo ha itsu sorewo owaraseru yotei desuka?
-彼女は財務れぽーとを週の終わりに終わらせる予定です。
-kanojo ha zaimurepo-to wo shuu no owarini owaraseru yotei desu.
-つまり、週の終わりには財務れぽーとは用意されているはずです。
-tsumari, shuu no owarini ha zaimurepo-to ha youi sareteiruhazu desu.

Does it have fax paper?
- Yes, fax is already working.
- Can you accept a fax for me?
- Yes, I can accept a fax for you.

9

- Do we have printer paper?
- Yes, we have printer paper.
- But this is color paper. It does not fit.

10

- She is developing a new format for a financial report.
- When is she planning to finish it?
- She is planning to finish the financial report at the end of the week.
- So, at the end of the week the financial report should be ready.

11

-りんだはこんぴゅーたーぷろぐらむを使ってれぽーとを作成していますか？
-rinda ha konpyu-ta- puroguramu wo tsukatte repo-to wo sakusei shiteimasuka?

-はい、彼女はこんぴゅーたーぷろぐらむを使ってそれを作成しています。
-hai, kanojo ha konpyu-ta- puroguramu wo tsukatte sore wo sakusei shiteimasu.

-このぷろぐらむは要求を満たしていますか？
-kono puroguramu ha youkyuu wo mitashite imasuka?

-はい。それは要求を満たしています。
-hai. sore ha youkyuu wo mitashite imasu.

-これは新しい会計のそふとうぇあですか？
-kore ha atarashii kaikei no sofutouea desuka?

-はい。これは新しい会計ぷろぐらむです。
-hai. kore ha atarashii kaikei puroguramu desu.

12

-これは会社の予算を制御下で管理することを可能としますか？
-kore ha kaisha no yosan wo seigyokade kanrisurukoto wo kanouto shimasuka?

-はい。これは十分な資金を節約することを可能とします。
-hai. kore ha juubunna shisan wo setsuyakusurukoto wo kanouto shimasu.

-私たちの会社は新しいぷろじぇくとのための財源を持っていますか？
-watashitachi no kaisha ha atarashii purojekuto no tame no zaigen wo motteimasuka?

11

- Is Linda making a report using a computer program?

- Yes, she is making it using the computer program.

- Does this program meet the requirements?

- Yes. It meets the requirements.

- Is this new accounting software?

- Yes, this is a new accounting program.

12

- Does this allow keeping the company's budget under the control?

- Yes. This allows to save enough funds.

- Does our company have financial resources for a new project?

- 先月の費用が新しい企画で利用可能な財源を決定します。
-sengetsu no hiyou ga atarashii kikaku de riyoukanouna zaigen wo ketteishimasu.

13

-あなたのこんぴゅーたーしすてむは正しく動いていますか？
-anata no konpyu-ta-shisutemu ha tadashiku ugoiteimasuka?

-いいえ、私のこんぴゅーたーしすてむは落ちています。
-iie, watashi no konpyu-ta-shisutemu ha ochiteimasu.

-専門家がしすてむぶろっく機能を調節する必要があるかもしれませんか？
-senmonka ga shisutemu burokku kinou wo chouseisuru hitsuyou ga arukamo shiremasenka?

-はい。私たちはしすてむ管理者を呼ぶ必要があります。
-hai. watashitachi ha shisutemukanrisha wo yobu hitsuyou ga arimasu.

14

-さんどらのこんぴゅーたーもにたーは適していません。それは小さいです。
-sandora no konpyu-ta-monita- ha tekishite imasen. sore ha chiisai desu.

-どうしてあなたは大きなもにたーが必要ですか？
-doushite anata ha ookina monita- ga hitsuyou desuka?

-私たちは注意深く金属構造を調査する必要があります。
-watashitachi ha chuuibukaku kinzokukouzou wo chousa suruhitsuyou ga arimasu.

-大きなこんぴゅーたーもにたーはどこですか？

- Last month's expenses determine the financial resources available for a new project.

13

- Is your computer system working well?

- No. My computer system is failing.

- Maybe a specialist has to adjust the system block functioning?

- Yes. We must call in the system administrator.

14

- Sandra's computer monitor is not a good fit. It's small.

- Why do you need a large computer monitor?

- We have to carefully examine the design of the metal structure.

- Where is there a large computer monitor?

-ookina konpyu-ta-monita- ha doko desuka?
- 秘書がそのようなもにたーを持っています。
-hisho ga sonoyouna monita- wo motteimasu.

- The secretary has such a computer monitor.

15

- これは誰のこんぴゅーたーきーぼーどですか？
-kore ha dare no konpyu-ta-ki-bo-dodesuka?
- これはぽーるのきーぼーどです。
-kore ha po-ru no ki-bo-do desu.
- 彼のこんぴゅーたーきーぼーどはとても使い心地が良いです。
-kare no konpyu-ta-ki-bo-do ha totemo tsukai gokochiga ii desu.
- 私たちは同じ種類のきーぼーどをあなたのために注文することができます。
-watashitachi ha onaji shurui no ki-bo-do wo anatanotameni chumonsurukoto ga dekimasu.

- Whose computer keyboard is this?

- This is Paul's keyboard.

- His computer keyboard is very comfortable.

- We can order you the same kind of computer keyboard.

10

Audio

氷を砕く
Break the ice

電話が鳴っています。お母さんが電話に出ました。息子がかけているようです。

"ママ、窓の外を見て！"と息子は言いました。

"汚れたズボンを履いて水たまりで遊んでいる人、見える？それ、僕だよ！二回も転んだん

The phone rings. The mom answers the phone. Her son is calling.

"Mom! Look out of the window!" her son says, "Can you see somebody in dirty pants running on puddles? It is me! I fell two times already!"

だ！" と息子は言いました。

denwa ga natteimasu. okāsan ga denwa ni demashita. musuko ga kaketeiru yō desu. mama, mado no soto o mite! to musuko wa iimashita. yogoreta zubon o haite mizutamari de asondeiru hito, mieru? sore, boku da yo! ni kai mo koronda n da! to musuko wa iimashita.

何時に会議は始まりますか？
At what time will the conference start?

単語
Words

1. IT スペシャリスト、IT 専門家 [IT supesharisuto, IT senmonka] - IT-specialist, IT-professional
2. あれ [are] - that
3. よりも [yorimo] - instead
4. アメリカ女性 [amerikajosei] - American woman
5. イギリス女性 [igirisujosei] - British woman
6. イタリアの、イタリア人 [itariano, itariajin] - Italian
7. ウェブデザイン [uebudezain] - Web designer
8. ギリシャの、ギリシャ人 [girishano, girishajin] - Greek

9. スペインの [supeinno] - Spain
10. スペイン女性 [supeinjosei] - Spanish woman
11. ドイツ語、ドイツの、ドイツ人 [doitsugo, doitsuno, doitsujin] - German
12. ビジネスセンター [bijinesusenta-] - business-center
13. フランスの、フランス人 [furansuno, furansujin] - French, Frenchman
14. フランス語、フランスの、フランス人 [furansugo, furansuno, furansujin] - French
15. フランス女性 [furansujosei] - French woman
16. ロシア語、ロシアの、ロシア人 [roshiago, roshiano, roshiajin] - Russian
17. 英語、イギリスの、イギリス人 [eigo, igirisuno, igirisujinno] - British, English
18. 会う(動詞)/紹介する [au (doushi)/ shoukaisuru] - meet *(Verb)* / to introduce
19. 開始する(動詞)、始める [kaishisuru (doushi), hajimeru] - start *(Verb)*, to begin
20. 記事、論文 [kiji, ronbun] - article
21. 記者 [kisha] - journalist
22. 議論する(動詞)、話し合う [gironsuru (doushi), hanashiau] - discuss *(Verb)*
23. 許す(動詞)、言い訳をする [yurusu (doushi), iiwake wo suru] - excuse *(Verb)*
24. 強い [tsuyoi] - strong
25. 強いられる [shiirareru] - be forced
26. 経済学者 [keizaigakusha] - economist
27. 計画 [keikaku] - scheme
28. 建てる(動詞) [tateru(doushi)] - build *(Verb)*
29. 見る(動詞) [miru (doushi)] - view *(Verb)*, to watch, to look
30. 言語 [gengo] - language
31. 効率的、能率的 [kouritsuteki, nouritsuteki] - effective, efficient
32. 購入 [kounyuu] - purchase
33. 国 [kuni] - country
34. 国際的な [kokusaitekina] - international
35. 雑誌 [zasshi] - magazine
36. 参加 [sanka] - participation
37. 指揮する(動詞)、導く [shikisuru(doushi), michibiku] - conduct *(Verb)*, to lead
38. 事業家 [jigyouka] - Entrepreneur
39. 時間 [jikan] - time
40. 若い [wakai] - young
41. 女性 [josei] - woman
42. 職業、業務 [shokugyou, gyoumu] - profession, occupation
43. 尋ねる(動詞) [tazuneru (doushi)] - ask *(Verb)*
44. 製品 [seihin] - product
45. 全て [subete] - all
46. 中国語、中国の、中国人 [chuugokugo, chuugokuno, chuugokujin] - Chinese
47. 中国女性 [chuugokujosei] - Chinese woman
48. 導く(動詞)、指揮を執る [michibiku (doushi), shiki wo toru] - lead *(Verb)*, to control
49. 飛ぶ(動詞) [tobu (doushi)] - fly *(Verb)*
50. 北京 [pekin] - Beijing
51. 融資する(動詞) [yuushisuru (doushi)] - finance *(Verb)*

B

1

-おはようございます！
-ohayougozaimasu!

-おはようございます！遅れて申し訳ありません。
-ohayougozaimasu! okurete moushiwake arimasen.

-今の天気は何ですか？
-ima no tenki ha nandesuka?

-今は激しい雨です。
-ima ha hageshii ame desu.

2

-明日、会議が私たちの建物で開催されます。
-ashita, kaigi ga watashitachi no tatemono de kaisai saremasu.

-今日は何曜日ですか？
-kyou ha nanyoubi desuka?

-今日は水曜日です。
-kyou ha suiyoubi desu.

-明日びじねすせんたーは1日中占領されます。
-ashita bijinesusenta- ha ichinichijuu senryou saremasu.

-会議は何時に始まりますか？
-kaigi ha nanjini hajimarimasuka?

-会議は12時に始まります。
-kaigi ha juuniji ni hajimarimasu.

3

-様々な国の会社の代表たちが会議に参加します。
-samazama na kuni no kaisha no daihyoutachi ga kaigini sankashimasu.

1

- Good morning!

- Good morning! Sorry that I am late.

- What is the weather now?

- Now there is a heavy rain.

2

- A conference will take place in our building tomorrow.

- What day is today?

- Today is Wednesday.

- Tomorrow the business center will be occupied all day.

- At what time will the conference start?

- The conference will start at twelve o'clock.

3

- Representatives of companies from different countries will participate in the

-つまりこれは国際的な会議ですか？
-tsumari kore ha kokusaitekina kaigi desuka?

-はい。これは国際的な会議です。
-hai. kore ha kokusaitekina kaigi desu.

-私たちの会社はこれに参加しますか？
-watashitachi no kaisha ha koreni sanka shimasuka?

-はい、私たちの会社の専門家たちが会議に参加します。
-hai, watashitachi no kaisha no senmonkatachi ga kaigini sanka shimasu.

4

-私たちの製品の情報を様々な言語で用意できますか？
-watashitachi no seihin no jouhou wo samazama na gengo de youi dekimasuka?

-はい、私たちの製品の情報を用意することができます。
-hai, watashitachi no seihin no jouhou wo youisurukoto ga dekimasu.

-あなたは資料を英語、どいつ語そしてふらんす語で用意することができますか？
-anata ha shiryou wo eigo, doitsugo soshite furansugo de youisurukoto ga dekimasuka?

-はい。私は資料を英語とどいつ語で用意できます。けれども私はふらんす語を知りません。
-hai. watashi ha shiryou wo eigo to doitsugo de youi dekimasu. keredomo watashi ha furansugo wo shirimasen.

-そしたら、あなたは資料をすぺいん語で用意すべきです。
-soshitara, anata ha shiryou wo supeingo de youisubeki desu.

- So this is an international conference?

- Yes. This is an international conference.

- Does our company participate in it?

- Yes, our company specialists participate in the conference.

4

- Can you prepare information about our products in different languages?

- Yes, I can prepare information about our products.

- Can you prepare materials in English, German, and French?

- Yes. I can prepare materials in English and German. But I do not know French.

- Then, instead you should prepare materials in Spanish.

5

- この女性は誰ですか？
-konojosei ha dare desuka?
- 彼女はあめりか人です。
-kanojo ha amerikajin desu.
- 彼女の職業は何ですか？
-kanojo no shokugyou ha nandesuka?
- 彼女は経済学者です。彼女は銀行で働いています。この銀行は新しい企画を融資しています。
-kanojo ha keizaigakusha desu. kanojo ha ginkoku de hataraiteimasu. konoginkou ha atarashii kikaku wo yuushi shiteimasu.
- 彼女はどいつ語を話しますか？
-kanojo ha doitsugo wo hanashimasuka?
- いいえ。彼女は英語のみを話します。
-iie. kanojo ha eigo nomi wo hanashimasu.

6

- このえんじにあはどいつから来ました。彼はどいつ人です。
-kono enjinia ha doitsu kara kimashita. kare ha doitsujin desu.
- 彼は英語を話しますか？
-kare ha eigo wo hanashimasuka?
- はい、彼は英語を知っています。
-hai, kare ha eigo wo shitteimasu.
- 彼は何を建てますか？
-kare ha nan wo tatemasuka?
- 彼は建物を建てます。
-kare ha tatemono wo tatemasu.
- これらの建物の計画を見てもいいですか？

5

- Who is this woman?

- She's an American.

- What is her profession?

- She is an economist. She works in a bank. This bank is financing new projects.

- Does she speak German?

- No. She only speaks English.

6

- This engineer is from Germany. He is German.

- Does he speak English?

- Yes, he knows English.

- What does he build?

- He builds buildings.

- Can I see schemes of these buildings?

- Yes. These schemes

-korera no tatemono no keikaku wo mitemo iidesuka?
-はい。これらの計画はこんぴゅーたーぷろぐらむで見ることができます。
-hai. korera no keikaku ha konpyu-ta-puroguramu de mirukotoga dekimasu.

7

-それらのいぎりす人の職業は何ですか?
-sorera no igirisujin no shokugyou ha nandesuka?
-彼らはまねーじゃーです。彼らは大きなな会社で働きます。会議の後、私たちは彼らと交渉を行う予定です。
-karera ha mane-ja-desu. karera ha ookina kaisha de hatarakimasu. kaigi no ato, watashitachi ha karera to koushou wo okonau yotei desu.
-私たちはいぎりす人と何を議論する予定ですか?
-watashitachi ha igirisujin to nani wo gironsuru yotei desuka?
-私たちの会社は彼らの製品を購入するために契約書に署名する予定です。
-watashitachi no kaisha ha karera no seihin wo kounyuu surutameni keiyakushoni shomeisuru yotei desu.

8

-この女性は誰ですか?
-konojosei ha dare desuka?
-彼女はすぺいん人です。彼女は通訳です。
-kanojo ha supeinjin desu. kanojo ha tsuuyaku desu.
-彼女はどいつ語を話しますか?
-kanojo ha doitsugo wo hanashimasuka?
-はい、彼女は英語とどいつ語を知っています。
-hai, kanojo ha eigo to doitsugo wo shitteimasu.

can be viewed in a computer program.

7

- What are the occupations of those British?

- They are managers. They work in a large company. After the conference, we will have negotiations with them.

- What are we going to discuss with the British?

- Our company is going to sign a contract for the purchase of their products.

8

- Who is this woman?

- She is Spanish. She is an interpreter.

- Does she speak German?

- Yes, she knows English and German.

9

- このふらんす人は誰ですか？
-kono furansujin ha dare desuka?
- 彼はITすぺしゃりすとです。
-kare ha IT supesharisuto desu.
- 彼は何をしますか？
-kare ha nani wo shimasuka?
- 彼は新しいしすてむ製品とそふとうぇあを開発します。
-kare ha atarashii shisutemu seihin to sofutouea wo kaihatsu shimasu.
- 私は彼は優れた専門家だと思います。
-watashi ha kare ha sugureta senmonka dato omoimasu.
- はい、彼は優れた専門家です。
-hai, kare ha sugureta senmonka desu.

10

- あなたはすぺいん語の製品かたろぐを持っていますか？
-anata ha supeingo no seihinkatarogu wo motteimasuka?
- いいえ。私たちは英語の製品かたろぐを持っています。
-iie. watashitachi ha eigo no siehinkatarogu wo motteimasu.
- 私たちのすぺいん人のぱーとなーがそれを見たいと考えています。
-watashitachi no supeinjin no pa-tona- ga sore wo mitai to kangaete imasu.
- 私は通訳者を招待することができます。
-watashi ha tsuuyakusha wo shoutaisurukoto ga dekimasu.
- 良かったです。私たちは彼の助けが必要だと

9

- Who is this Frenchman?

- He is an IT- specialist.

- What does he do?

- He develops new system products and software.

- I think he's a good specialist.

- Yes, he's a good specialist.

10

- Do you have a product catalog in Spanish?

- No. We have a product catalog in English.

- Our Spanish partners want to see it.

- I can invite an interpreter.

- Good. I think we need his help.

思います。
-yokattadesu. watashitachi ha kare no tasuk ga hitsuyoudato omoimasu.

11

- 私たちの会社はどいつ人たちとの契約に署名したいです。
-watashitachi no kaisha ha doitsujintachi tono keiyaku ni shomei shitai desu.

- 契約書のこぴーをいくつ用意する必要がありますか？
-keiyakusho no kopi- wo ikutsu youisuru hitsuyou ga arimasuka?

- どいつ語と英語で２つこぴーを用意してくれますか？
-doitsugo to eigo de futatsu kopi- wo youi shitekuremasuka?

- はい、私は契約書のこぴーをどいつ語と英語で用意することができます。
-hai, watashi ha keiyakusho no kopi- wo doitsugo to eigo de youisurukoto ga dekimasu.

- ぽーるは交渉に参加しますか？
-po-ru ha koushou ni sankashimasuka?

- はい、彼は効率的に交渉し、そしてどいつ語を知っています。
-hai, kare ha kouritsuteki ni koushoushi, soshite doitsugo wo shitteimasu.

12

- このぎりしゃ人の職業は何ですか？
-kono girishajin no shokugyou ha nandesuka?

- 彼はPRまねーじゃーです。私たちは彼とすぺいんの展示会で会いました。
-kare ha PR mane-ja- desu. watashitachi ha karera to supein no tenjikai de aimashita.

11

- Our company wants to sign a contract with the Germans.

- How many copies of the contract do we need to prepare?

- Can you prepare two copies - in German and in English?

- Yes, I can prepare contract copies in German and in English.

- Does Paul participate in the negotiations?

- Yes, he effectively negotiates and knows German.

12

- What is this Greek's profession?

- He's a PR-manager. We met him at the exhibition in Spain.

- What company does

かれ　　　　　かいしゃ　だいひょう
-彼 はどの会 社 の代 表 ですか？
-kare ha dono kaisha no daihyou desuka?
かれ　　　　　　　　かいしゃ　だいひょう
-彼 はぎりしゃの会 社 の代 表 です。
-kare ha girisha no kaisha no daihyou desu.

13

かいしゃ　　かいぎ　さんか
-いたりあの会 社 は会議に参加しますか？
-itaria no kaisha ha kaigini sankashimasuka?
　　　　だんせい　　　　　　じん　　かれ　べんごし
-はい。あの男 性 はいたりあ人 です。彼 は弁護士です。
-hai. ano dansei ha itariajin desu. kare ha bengoshi desu.
かれ　えいご　し
-彼 は英語を知っていますか？
-kare ha eigo wo shitteimasuka?
　　　　かれ　　　　　ご　　　　　　　　　　　ご　はな
-いいえ。彼 はすぺいん語ともしかするとどいつ語を話します。
-iie, kare ha supeingo to moshikasuruto doitsugo wo hanashimasu.

14

　　　　ひとびと　だれ
-これらの人 々 は誰ですか？
-korera no hitobito ha daredesuka?
　　　　　わたしたち　ちゅうごく　　　　　　　　　かれ
-これらは私 達 の中 国 のぱーとなーです。彼
　ぺきん　と
らは北 京 から飛んできました。
-korera ha watashitachi no chuugoku no pa-tona-desu. karera ha pekin kara tonde kimashita.
　　　かれ　　えいご　はな
-彼 らは英語を話しますか？
-karera ha eigo wo hanashimasuka?
　　　　かれ　　えいご　　　ご　　　　はな
-はい、彼 らは英語とろしあ語をよく話します。
-hai, karera ha eigo to roshiago wo yoku hanashimasu.

15

　　　　　　じじょせい　しょくぎょう　なに
-このふらんす人女 性 の職 業 は何ですか？
-kono furansujin josei no shokugyou ha nandesuka?
　　　　　　じじょせい
-このふらんす人女 性 はうぇぶでざいなーです。

---

he represent?
- He represents a Greek company.

13

- Do Italian companies participate in the conference?
- Yes. That man is Italian. He's a lawyer.
- Does he know English?
- No. He speaks Spanish and possibly German.

14

- Who are these people?
- These are our Chinese partners. They flew from Beijing.
- Do they speak English?
- Yes, they speak English and Russian well.

15

- What is this French woman's occupation?

-kono furansujinjosei ha uebudezaina- desu.
- 彼女はどいつ語を話しますか？
-kanojo ha doitsugo wo hanashimasuka?
-いいえ、彼女はどいつ語を話しません、彼女はふらんす語のみを知っています。
-iie, kanojo ha doitsugo wo hanashimasen. kanojo ha furansugonomi wo shitteimasu.

16

-このいぎりす人女性はとても若く見えます。彼女の職業は何ですか？
-kono igirisujinjosei ha totemo wakaku miemasu. koanojo no shokugyou ha nandesuka?
- 彼女は記者です。彼女は英語とどいつ語の雑誌のために記事を書きます。
-kanojo ha kishadesu. Kanojo ha eigo to doitsugo no zasshinotameni kiji wo kakimasu.
- 私は彼女にろしあ語でいくつか質問することはできますか？
-watashi ha kanojoni roshiago de ikutsuka shitsumon surukoto ha dekimasuka?
-はい。彼女はろしあ語を話します。
-hai, kanojo ha roshiago wo hanashimasu.

17

-この中国女性の職業は何ですか？
-kono chugokujosei no shokugyou ha nandesuka?
- 彼女はまねーじゃーです。
-kanojo ha mane-ja-desu.
- 彼女に会うのはこれが初めてではありません。
-kanojoni auno ha kore ga hajimete deha arimasen.
-はい。彼女はどいつの会議に参加しました。
-hai. kanojo ha doitsu no kaigi ni sankashimashita.

- This French woman is a web designer.

- Does she speak German?

- No, she does not speak German; she knows only French.

16

- This British woman looks very young. What is her profession?

- She's a journalist. She writes articles for English and German magazines.

- Can I ask her some questions in Russian?

- Yes. She speaks Russian.

17

- What is this Chinese woman's occupation?

- She is a manager.

- This isn't the first time I'm meeting her.

- Yes. She participated in the conference in Germany.

18

- この女性は誰ですか？
-kono josei ha dare desuka?
- 彼女はろしあ人です。彼女は事業家です。
-kanojo ha roshiajin desu. kanojo ha jigyouka desu.
- 彼女は何をしますか？
-kanojo ha nani wo shimasuka?
- 彼女はろしあの会社を導きます。
-kanojo ha roshia no kaisha wo michibikimasu.

18

- Who is this woman?

- She is Russian. She is an entrepreneur.

- What does she do?

- She leads a Russian company.

11

Audio

氷を砕く
Break the ice

幼いロバートはおじいちゃんにシンデレラを読んでもらうのが好きでした。おじいちゃんはすでに本のセリフを一言一句知っています。ロバートはおじいちゃんにもう一回読んで欲しいとお願いしましたが、おじいちゃんは車にメガネを忘れていたので本を読む事はできません。幸運にも彼は物語をよく知っているので、字は読めなくても読むフリをし始めました。
シンデレラの叔母が魔法をかける時のことです。
"古い車を、新品の車に変えておくれ" と

Little Robert likes it when his granddad reads him the book about Cinderella. His granddad already knows every word, on every page by heart. Robert asks him to read Cinderella again, however his granddad's glasses are in his car. Luckily, he knows the story very well. So, the granddad takes the book and pretends to "read". He comes to the moment when Cinderella's aunt does the magic.
"The aunt turned an old

おじいちゃんは言いました。

ロバートは怪しげにおじいちゃんを見つめ、こう言ったのです。

"待って、おじいちゃん。メガネ持ってきてあげる"

Ford into a gold cart," the granddad "reads". Little Robert looks at him attentively.
"Wait granddad," the boy says, "I will bring you your glasses."

osanai Roba-To wa ojiichan ni Shinderera o yondemorau no ga suki deshita. ojiichan wa sudeni hon no serifu o hitokoto ichi ku shitteimasu. Roba-To wa ojiichan ni mō ichi kai yonde hoshii to onegaishimashita ga, ojiichan wa kuruma ni megane o wasureteita node hon o yomu koto wa dekimasen. kōun ni mo kare wa monogatari o yoku shitteiru node, ji wa yomenakute mo yomu furi o shihajimemashita. Shinderera no oba ga mahō o kakeru toki no koto desu. furui kuruma o, shinpin no kuruma ni kaete okure to ojiichan wa iimashita. Roba-To wa ayashige ni ojiichan o mitsume, kō itta no desu. matte, ojiichan. megane mottekiteageru

ミカエルの方がより責任があると思いますか？

Do you think Michael is more responsible?

単語
Words

1. (専門)領域、プロフィール
   [(senmon)ryouiki, purofi-ru] - area (of specialization), profile

2. 〜〜のために/〜となるように/〜するために [〜no tameni/〜tonaruyouni/〜surutameni] - to / so that / in order

3. かかる [kakaru] - cost
4. さらにもっと [saranimotto] - much more
5. たいてい、ほとんど [taitei, hotondo] - almost
6. はっきり、明確、理解できる [hakkiri, meikaku, rikaidekiru] - clear, understandable
7. または [mataha] - or
8. より、更に [yori, sarani] - more
9. よりシンプルな、より簡単な [yori shinpuruna, yori kantanna] - simpler, easier
10. より高価な [yori koukana] - more expensive
11. より少ない [yorisukunai] - less
12. より速い、より早い [yorihayai, yorihayai] - faster
13. より良い [yoriyoi] - better
14. アクティブ、活発 [akutibu, kappatsu] - active
15. コマーシャル広告 [koma-sharu koukoku] - commercial advertising
16. 安い [yasui] - cheap
17. 貨物 [kamotsu] - cargo
18. 割り当てる(動詞) [wariateru (doushi)] - assign *(Verb)*
19. 競争者 [kyousousha] - competitor
20. 経験した、経験のある [keikenshita, keiken no aru] - experienced
21. 古い [furui] - old
22. 更に複雑な / 難しい [sarani fukuzatsuna, muzukashii] - more complex / difficult
23. 購入する(動詞) [kounyuusuru (doushi)] - purchase *(Verb)*
24. 最も [mottomo] - most
25. 最新の [saishinno] - the newest
26. 最良の、最高、最も [sairyouno, saikou, mottomo] - best
27. 削減する(動詞)、切る [sakugensuru (doushi), kiru] - reduce *(Verb)*, to cut
28. 自信をもって [jishin wo motte] - confidently
29. 従順な [juujunna] - obedient
30. 出席する [shussekisuru] - be present
31. 正確な、精密な [saikakuna, seimitsuna] - exact, precise
32. 製図 [seizu] - drawing
33. 説得力のある [settokuryoku no aru] - convincing
34. 前の、前回の [maeno, zenkaino] - previous
35. 増加する(動詞)、増える [zoukasuru (doushi), fueru] - increase *(Verb)*
36. 速い、早い [hayai, hayai] - fast
37. 中国 [chuugoku] - China
38. 注文する(動詞)、予約する [chuumonsuru, yoyakusuru] - order *(Verb)*, to book
39. 低い [hikui] - low
40. 読む [yomu] - read
41. 配達 [haitatsu] - delivery
42. 複数 [fukusuu] - multiple
43. 方法 [houhou] - way
44. 量 [ryou] - volume

B

1

-みかえるとぽーるでは、誰がより高いくおりてぃーのぷれぜんてーしょんを用意できますか？
- mikaeru to po-ru deeha, dare ga yoritakai kuoriti- no purezente-shon wo youi dekimasuka?

-あなたはそれをみかえるに割り当てることができます。
-anata ha sorewo mikaeru ni wariaterukoto ga dekimasu.

-あなたはみかえるの方がより責任感があると思いますか？
-anata ha mikaeru no hou ga yori sekininkan ga aruto omoimasuka?

-はい、私はみかえるの方がより責任感があり、そして従順です。
-hai, watashi ha mikaeru no hou ga yori sekininkan ga ari, soshite juujun desu.

2

- 私たちの今月の製品の製造には前回よりも値段はかかりますか？
-watashitachi no kongetsu no seihin no seizou niha zenkai yorimo nedan ha kakarimasuka?

-はい、私たちの今月の費用の方が高いです。
-hai, watashitachi no kongetsu no hiyou no hou ga takai desu.

-それらを削減できますか？
-sorera wo sakugen dekimasuka?

-はい。私たちはそれらを削減することができます。
-hai. watashitachi ha sorera wo sakugen surukoto ga dekimasu.

1

- Who can prepare a higher quality presentation - Michael or Paul?

- You can assign it to Michael.

- Do you think Michael is more responsible?

- Yes, I think Michael is more responsible and obedient.

2

- Are our production costs this month more than the last one?

- Yes, our expenses this month are larger.

- Can we reduce them?

- Yes. We can make them smaller.

3

- りんだは広告記事を用意しましたか？
-rinda ha koukoku kiji wo youi shimashitaka?
- はい。りんだは面白い広告記事を用意しました。
-hai. rinda ha omoshiroi koukoku kiji wo youi shimashita.
- あなたはぽーるの記事を読むべきです。それはより面白くて明確です。
-anata ha po-ru no kiji wo yomubeki desu. sore ha yori omoshirokute meikaku desu.

4

- ぷれぜんてーしょんでは何が議論されるべきですか？
-purezente-shon deha nani ga giron sarerubeki desuka?
- 機材がぷれぜんてーしょんで考慮されるべきです。
-kizai ga purezente-shon de kouryosareru bekidesu.
- これは新しい機材ですか？
-kore ha atarashii kizai desuka?
- はい、これはどいつの会社からの最新の機材です。
-hai, kore ha doitsu no kaishakara no saishin no kizai desu.

5

- どうしたら製品の製造をより効率的にできますか？
-doushitara seihin no seizou wo yori kouritsutekini dekimasuka?
- 製造をより効率的にするためには機材をさらに新しくするべきです。
-seizou wo yori kouritsutekini surutame niha kizai wo sarani atarashiku surubeki desu.
- 私たちは最新でより高い品質の機材を

3

- Did Linda prepare an advertising article?
- Yes. Linda prepared an interesting advertising article.
- You should read Paul's article. It is more interesting and clearer.

4

- What should be discussed at the presentation?
- Equipment should be considered at the presentation.
- Is this new equipment?
- Yes. This is the newest equipment from a German company.

5

- How can the production be made more efficient?
- The equipment should be newer to make the production more efficient.

注文したいと考えます。
-watashitachi ha saishin de yori takai hinshitsu no kizai wo chuumonshitaito kangaemasu.

6

-このえんじにあは誰ですか？
-kono enjinia ha daredesuka?

-このえんじにあはどいつからの専門家です。
-kono enjinia ha doitsu karano senmonka desu.

-彼は経験のある専門家ですか？
-kare ha keiken no aru senmonka desuka?

-はい、彼はこの会社の中でこの領域で最も経験のある専門家です。
-hai, kare ha konokaisha no naka de konoryouiki de mottomo keiken no aru senmonka desu.

7

-このえんじにあは何をする予定ですか？
-kono enjinia ha nani wo suru yotei desuka?

-彼は金属構造のための企画をする予定です。
-kare ha kinzokukouzou no tameno kikaku wo suru yotei desu.

-彼は頑丈な構造を作れますか？
-kare ha ganjouna kouzou wo tsukuremasuka?

-はい。これらの構造はとても頑丈です。
-hai. korera no kouzou ha totemo ganjou desu.

8

-この女性は誰ですか？
-kono josei ha daredesuka?

-彼女は私たちの会社で最も経験のある中国の通訳です。
-kanojo ha watashitachi no kaisha de mottomo keiken no aru chugoku no tsuuyaku desu.

- We want to order the newest and higher quality equipment.

6

- Who is this engineer?
- This engineer is a specialist from Germany.
- Is he an experienced professional?
- Yes. He is the most experienced specialist in his area in this company.

7

- What is this engineer going to do?
- He's going to do a project for metal structures.
- Can he make sturdy structures?
- Yes. These structures are very sturdy.

8

- Who is this woman?
- She is the most experienced Chinese interpreter in our

- 彼女は正確な翻訳を行いますか？
-kanojo ha seikakuna honyaku wo okonaimasuka?
-はい、彼女は最良のそして最も正確な翻訳を行います。
-hai, kanojo ha sairyouno soshite mottomo seikakuna honyaku wo okonaimasu.

- Does she make accurate translations?
- Yes, she makes the best and the most accurate translations.

9

- 誰が交渉に出席していそうですか？
-dare ga koushouni shusseki shiteisou desuka?
-さんどらが交渉に出席しているかもしれません。
-sandora ga koushou ni shusseki shiteiru kamoshiremasen.
- 彼女は公共の場でより自信をもって話しますか？
-kanojo ha koukyounoba de yori jishin wo motte hanashimasuka?
-はい。さんどらは公共の場でより自信を持って話します。
-hai. sandora ha koukyounoba de yori jishin wo motte hanashimasu.

- Who may be present at the negotiations?
- Sandra may be present at the negotiations.
- Does she speak more confidently in public?
- Yes. Sandra speaks more confidently in public.

10

-せーるすまねーじゃーの今月の働きはどうですか？
-se-rusu mane-ja- no kongetsu no hataraki ha dou desuka?
- 彼らは今月より良く働いています。
-karera ha kongetsu yori yoku hataraite imasu.
- それは彼らは更に効率的に働いているという意味ですか？
-soreha karera ha sarani kouritsutekini hataraiteiru toiu imi desuka?
-はい、彼らはより効率的です。

- How do the sales managers work this month?
- They work better this month.
- Does it mean they work more effectively?
- Yes, they are more

-hai, karera ha yori kouritsuteki desu.

- 彼らは 何 をしていますか？
-karera ha nani wo shiteimasuka?

- 彼らは 更に売り上げをあげます。
-karera ha sarani uriage wo agemasu.

11

-これらは 良品質の製品ですか？
-korera ha ryouhinshitsu no seihin desuka?

-はい。これらの製品は私たちの競争相手の物よりもよい良い品質です。
-hai. korarano seihin ha watashitachi no kyousouaite no mono yorimo ii hinshitsu desu.

-これらの製品は高価ですか？
-korerano seihin ha kouka desuka?

-はい。高品質製品はほとんど必ずより高価です。
-hai. kouhinshitsu seihin ha hotondo kanarazu yori kouka desu.

12

- 売上の量をあげるためにはどうすればいいですか？
-uriage no ryou wo agerutame niha dousureba iidesuka?

-売り上げの量をあげるためには広告に説得力を持たせるべきです。
-uriage no ryou wo agerutame niha koukokuni settokuryoku wo motaserubeki desu.

-どうして私たちはよりあくてぃぶにならないといけませんか？
-doushite watashitachi ha yori akutibuni naranaito ikemasenka?

effective.

- What are they doing?

- They make more sales.

11

- Are these high-quality products?

- Yes. These products are of better quality than those of our competitors.

- Are these products expensive?

- Yes. Quality products are almost always more expensive.

12

- How to increase the sales volume?

- Advertising must be convincing in order to increase the sales volume,.

- Why do we need to be more active?

- 私たちは成功するためによりあくてぃぶに働かないといけません。
-watashitachi ha seikousuru tameni yori akutibuni hatarakanaito ikemasen.

13

- どいつの会社はどうやってなっていますか？
-doitsu no kaisha ha dounatte imasuka?
- 彼らは他よりもより良く働きます。
-karera ha hokayorimo yori yoku hatarakimasu.
- 中国のぱーとなーはより早く働きますか？
-chuugoku no pa-tona- ha yori hayaku hatarakimasuka?
- はい。彼らはより早く働けます。
-hai. karera ha yori hayaku hatarakemasu.

14

- 今月私たちは北京にある中国の会社から商品を購入しなければなりません。
-kongetsu watashitachi ha pekinniaru chuugoku no kaisha kara shouhin wo kounyuu shinakereba narimasen.
- 彼らはより安い製品を持っていますか？
-karera ha yori yasui seihin wo motteimasuka?
- はい、彼らの値段はより低いです。
-hai, karera no nedan ha yori hikui desu.
- 彼らと働くことは私たちにとってより有益ですか？
-karerato hatarakukoto ha watashitachini totte yori yuueki desuka?
- はい、彼らと働くことはさらにもっと有益です。
-hai. karerato hatarakukoto ha sarani motto yuueki desu.

- We need to work more actively in order to be successful.

13

- How do German companies work?
- They work better than many others.
- Do the Chinese partners work faster?
- Yes. They can work faster.

14

- This month we have to purchase goods from the Chinese company based in Beijing.
- Do they have cheaper products?
- Yes, their prices are lower.
- Is working with them more profitable for us?
- Yes, working with them is much more profitable.

15

- 中国から商品を届ける最も早い方法は何ですか？
-chugoku kara shouhin wo todokeru mottomo hayai houhou ha nandesuka?
- 最も早い方法は貨物飛行機に乗せることです。
-mottomo hayai houhou ha kamotsuhikouki ni noseru kotodesu.
-そのような配達の費用は高いですか？
-sonoyouna haitatsu no hiyou ha takai desuka?
-いいえ。この配達の費用はあまり高くありません。
-iie. kono haitatsu no hiyou ha amari takaku arimasen.

16

-あなたの事務所はどのような様子ですか？
-anata no jimusho ha donoyouna yousu desuka?
- 私たちの新しい事務所は古いのよりも良いです。
-watashitachi no atarashii jimusho ha furui no yorimo iidesu.
-あなたは便利な事務所を持っていますか？
-anata ha benrina jimusho wo motteimasuka?
-はい。この事務所はとても便利です。
-hai. kono jimusho ha totemo benri desu.

17

-あなたの最良のせーるすまねーじゃーは誰ですか？
-anata no sairyou no se-rusu mane-ja- ha daredesuka?
- 私たちの最良のせーるすまねーじゃーはみかえるです。
-watashitachi no sairyou no se-rusu mane-ja- ha mikaeru desu.

15

- What is the fastest way to deliver the goods from China?
- The fastest delivery method is on a cargo plane.
- Is the cost of such a delivery high?
- No. The cost of this delivery is not very high.

16

- What does your office look like?
- Our new office is nicer than the old one.
- Do you have a convenient office?
- Yes. This office is very convenient.

17

- Who is your best sales manager?
- Our best sales manager is Michael.

- 彼は責任感がありますか？
-kare ha sekininkan ga arimasuka?
-はい。しかしぽーるの方がより交渉に自信があります。
-hai. shikashi po-ru no houga yori koushouni jishin ga arimasu.

18
- 新しいかたろぐはどう見えるべきですか？
-atarashii katarogu ha dou mieru bekidesuka?
- 新しいかたろぐはより便利でより美しいべきです。
-atarashii katarogu ha yori benride yori utsukushii bekidesu.
-それらはより良い品質であるべきですか？
-sorera ha yori ii hinshitsu de arubeki desuka?
-はい、もちろん、それらはより良い品質であるべきです。
-hai, mochiron, soreraha yori ii hinshitsu de arubeki desu.

19
- 私たちのえんじにあは金属の構造の製図を作りました。
-watashitachi no enjinia ha kinzoku no kouzou no seizu wo tsukurimashita.
-これらの製図はよりしんぷるですか、またはよりふくざつ複雑ですか？
-korera no seizu ha yori shinpuru desuka, mataha yori fukuzatsu desuka?
-これらの製図は前回のよりもさらにもっとふくざつ複雑です。
-korera no seizu ha zenkai no yorimo sarani motto fukuzatsu desu.

- Is he responsible?
- Yes. But Paul is more confident in negotiations.

18
- What should the new catalogs look like?
- New catalogs should be more convenient and more beautiful.
- Should they be of better quality?
- Yes, of course, they should be of better quality.

19
- Our engineer made drawings of metal structures.
- Are these drawings simpler or more complex?
- These drawings are much more complex than the previous ones.

20

-これらは良いそふとうぇあですか？
-korera ha ii sofutouea desuka?

-はい、このそふとうぇあはより早く動きます。
-hai, kono sofutouea ha yori hayaku ugokimasu.

-それは私たちの仕事に役立つかもしれません。
-soreha watashitachi no shigoto ni yakudatsu kamoshiremasen.

-はい。これは私たちの仕事をより効率的にします。
-hai. kore ha watashitachi no shigoto wo yori kouritsutekini shimasu.

- Is this good software?

- Yes, this software works a lot faster.

- It may help with our work.

- Yes. This makes our work more effective.

12

Audio

氷を砕く
Break the ice

季節は冬です。外は雪がふっていて地面は滑りやすくなっています。お父さんは仕事から帰ってくると
「ひどい天気だ！すぐに滑ってしまう。二回も転んでしまったよ。」とお母さんに言いました。お父さんのズボンは濡れてシミがいくつか出来ていました。ここでちょうど息子さんが学校から帰ってきました。
「外はすごく寒いよ！」息子さんは嬉しそうに言いました。「すごく滑りやすいんだ。二回も転んじ

It is winter. It is snowy and slippery outside. The dad comes home from work.
"The weather is terrible! It is very slippery. I fell two times," he says to the mom. His pants have several wet spots. The dad is unhappy. At this moment the little son comes home from school.
"It is so cool outside!" the son cries happily. "It is very slippery. I fell two

やったんだよ！」息子さんはとても嬉しい様子でした。

times!" The son is very happy.

kisetsu wa fuyu desu. soto wa yuki ga futteite jimen wa suberi yasuku natteimasu. otōsan wa shigoto kara kaettekuru to" hidoi tenki da! sugu ni subetteshimau. ni kai mo korondeshimatta yo." to okāsan ni iimashita. otōsan no zubon wa nurete shimi ga ikutsu ka dekiteimashita. koko de chōdo musuko san ga gakkō kara kaettekimashita." soto wa sugoku samui yo!" musuko san wa ureshisō ni iimashita." sugoku suberi yasui n da. ni kai mo koron jatta n da yo!" musuko san wa totemo ureshii yōsu deshita.

私はあなたをどう紹介するべきですか？
How should I introduce you?

単語
Words

1. (商品の)バッチ、一部 [(shouhin no) bacchi, ichibu] - batch (of goods)
2. 〜になった(動詞) [〜ni natta (doushi)] - became *(Verb)*
3. 〜になる(動詞)、来る [〜ni naru (doushi), kuru] - become *(Verb)*, will be
4. すぐ [sugu] - soon

5. する(動詞) [suru (doushi)] - do (Verb)
6. ずいぶん前、昔 / 長く [zuibun mae, mukashi/ nagaku] - long ago / for long
7. で/の上 [de / no ue] - by / on
8. はまる(動詞)、合う / アレンジする [hamaru (doushi), au/ arenjisuru] - suit (Verb) / to arrange
9. もし [moshi] - if
10. より安い [yori yasui] - cheaper
11. より高い / の上 [yori takai/ no ue] - higher / above
12. より自信を持って [yori jishin wo motte] - more confidently
13. より説得力のある [yori settokuryoku no aru] - more convincing
14. より低い / 低い、下 [yori hikui/ hikui, shita] - lower / below
15. より有益な [yori yuuekina] - more profitable
16. を必要とする [hitsuyouto suru] - be in need
17. アップデート、リニュー [appude-to, rinyuu] - update, renew
18. アンチウィルスソフトウェア [anchi uirusu sofutouea] - antivirus software
19. シールド [shi-rudo] - shield
20. セットアップ、インストール、設置する [setto appu, insuto-ru, secchisuru] - set up, to install
21. ソフトウェア [sofutouea] - software
22. マーケット [ma-ketto] - market
23. ライセンスのある、認証された [raisensu no aru, nintei sareta] - licensed, certified
24. 悪く、不十分に [waruku, fujuubunni] - badly, poorly
25. 安全に / 頼りになるように、壊れることなく [anznni, tayorininaru youni, kowarerukoto naku] - safely / reliably
26. 卸売り [oroshiuri] - wholesale
27. 割引 [waribiki] - discount
28. 興味深い、面白い [kyoumibukai, omoshiroi] - interesting
29. 緊急に [kinkyuuni] - urgently
30. 後で / 後 [atode/ ato] - later / after
31. 高くない [takakunai] - inexpensive
32. 今 [ima] - now
33. 使う(動詞) [tsukau (doushi)] - use (Verb)
34. 取引する(動詞) [torihiki suru (doushi)] - trade (Verb)
35. 守る(動詞) [mamoru (doushi)] - defend (Verb)
36. 少々、少し、ちょっと [shoushou, sukoshi, chotto] - slightly, a bit, a little bit
37. 紹介する(動詞) [shoukaisuru (doushi) - introduce (Verb)
38. 上手に [jyouzuni] - tactfully
39. 設置 [secchi] - installation
40. 値段、レート [nedan, re-to] - price, rate
41. 遅い [osoi] - slow
42. 著しく、ずいぶん、とても [ichijirushiku, zuibun, totemo] - significantly, considerably, much
43. 挑戦する(動詞)、試す [chousen suru(doushi), kokoromiru] - try (Verb)
44. 導く(動詞) [michibku (doushi)] - lead (Verb), to conduct
45. 売る(動詞) [uru (doushi)] - sell (Verb)
46. 必ずしも、やむをえず、避けられない[kanarazushimo, yamuoezu,

sakerarenai] - necessarily, unavoidably
47. 評価する、尊重する(動詞)、感謝する [hyoukasuru, souchou suru (doushi), kansha suru] - value *(Verb)*, to appreciate
48. 評判 [hyouban] - reputation
49. 本当に、とても [hontouni, totemo] - really
50. 予防メンテナンス [yobou mentenansu] - preventative maintenance
51. 要求する、求める(動詞) [youkyuu suru, motomeru (doushi)] - require *(Verb)*
52. 利益の無い [rieki no nai] - unprofitable
53. 率、パーセンテージ [ritsu, pa-sente-ji] - percent

B

1

-こんにちは。会えて嬉しいです。
-konnichiha. aete ureshii desu.
-おはようございます！あなたのじぇねらるまねーじゃーと会うことはできますか？
-ohayougozaimasu! anata no jeneraru mane-ja- to aukotoha dekimasuka?
-あなたは少し待つ必要があります。彼はもうすぐここに来ます。
-anata ha sukoshi matsu hitsuyou ga arimasu. kare ha mousugu koko ni kimasu.
-私はあなたをどう紹介するべきですか？
-watashi ha anata wo dou shoukai surubeki desuka?
-私はしーるど会社の代表です。私は認証されたそふとうぇあのいんすとーるの件でここにいます。
-watashi ha shi-rudo geisha no daihyou desu. watashi ha ninteisareta sofutouea no insuto-ru no ken de kokoni imasu.

2

-私たちはずいぶん前にこんぴゅーたーのそふとうぇ

1

- Hello. Glad to see you.

- Good morning! Can I see your general manager?

- You need to wait a bit. He will be here soon.

- How should I introduce you?

- I am a representative of The Shield company. I'm here regarding the installation of licensed software.

2

- Have we updated the software on our

あをあっぷでーとしましたか？
-watashitachi ha zuibun mae ni konpyu-ta- no sofutouea wo appude-to shimashitaka?
-はい、私たちは私たちの事務所のこんぴゅーたーのそふとうぇあをずいぶん前にあっぷでーとしました。
-hai, watashitachi ha watashitachi no jimusho no konpyu-ta- no sofutouea wo zuibun mae ni appude-to shimashita.
-そふとうぇあ会社の代表が今私たちの事務所にいます。
-sofutoueakaisha no daihyou ga ima watashitachi no jimusho ni imasu.
-彼は急いであんちうぃるすそふとうぇあをいんすとーるすることができますか？
-kare ha isoide anchi uirusu sofutouea wo insuto-ru wo surukoto ga dekimasuka?
-はい。彼はあんちうぃるすそふとうぇあを急いでいんすとーるすることができます。
-hai. kare ha anchi uirusu sofutouea wo isoide insuto-ru surukoto ga dekimasu.

3

-私たちはこの会社のさーびすを長い間使ってきました。
-watashitachi ha kono kaisha no sa-bisu wo nagaiaida tsukattekimashita.
-それは有益ですか？
-sore ha yuueki desuka?
-はい、それは私たちの会社にとって有益です。
-hai. sore ha watashitachi no kaisha ni totte yuueki desu.
-私たちはこれらのさーびすの割引はありますか？
-watashitachi niha korera no sa-bisu no waribiki ha arimasuka?

computers long ago?
- Yes, we have updated the software on our office computers long ago.
- The software company representative is now in our office.
- Can he quickly install antivirus software?
- Yes. He can install antivirus software quickly.

3

- We have been using this company's services for a long time.
- It is profitable?
- Yes, it is profitable for our company.
- Do we have a discount on these services?
- Yes, we have a large discount for this

-はい、私たちにはこの会社のさーびすの大きな割引があります。
-hai, watashitachi niha kono kaisha no sa-bisu no ookina waribiki ga arimasu.

4

-これは新しい会社ですか？
-kore ha atarashii kaisha desuka?

-いいえ、彼らは長い間まーけっとにいます。
-iie, karera ha nagaiaida ma-ketto ni imasu.

-彼らは彼らの評判を尊重しますか？
-karera ha karera no hyouban wo sonchou shimasuka?

-はい、彼らは早く良い仕事をします。
-hai, karera ha hayaku iishigoto wo shimasu.

5

-あなたの値段は変わりました。それは私たちにとって高すぎます。
-anata no nedan ha kawarimashita. sore ha watashitachi ni totte takasugimasu.

-値段はより高くなりました。けれども私たちは少し割引を増やすことができます。
-nedan ha yori takakunarimashita. keredomo watashitachi ha sukoshi waribiki wo fuyasukoto ga dekimasu.

-それは私たちにとって有益になりますか？
-sore ha watashitachi ni totte yuueki ni narimasuka?

-はい、今はあなたにとってはより安いです。
-hai, ima ha anatanitotte ha yori yasui desu.

6

-あなたはいつ新しいそふとうぇあをいんすとーるしたいですか？
-anata ha itsu atarashii sofutouea wo insuto-ru shitai desuka?

company's services.

4

- Is this a new company?

- No, they have been on the market for a long time.

- Do they value their reputation?

- Yes, they work quickly and with high quality.

5

- Your prices have changed. It is too expensive for us.

- The prices became higher. But we can slightly increase the discount.

- Will it be profitable for us?

- Yes, now it is much cheaper for you.

6

- When do you want to

-それは緊急に行われなければいけません。今日です。
-sore ha kinkyu ni okonawarenakereba ikemasen. kyou desu.
-あなたは全てのこんぴゅーたーが壊れることなく、そして早く動いてほしいですか？
-anata ha subete no konpyu-ta- ga kowarerukoto naku, soshite hayaku ugoite hoshii desuka?
-はい、私たちは全てのこんぴゅーたーが壊れることなく、そして早く動いてほしいです。
-hai, watashitachi ha subeteno konpyu-ta- ga kowarerukoto naku, soshite hayaku ugoite hoshii desu.

7

-あんちうぃるすそふとうぇあは効率的にこんぴゅーたーを守りますか？
-anchi uirusu sofutouea ha kouritsuteki ni konpyu-ta- wo mamorimasuka?
-はい、それは効率的にこんぴゅーたーを守ります。
-hai, sore ha kouritsuteki ni konpyu-ta- wo mamorimasu.
-私たちはどきゅめんとをより安全に保管できますか？
-watashitachi ha dokyumento wo yori anzenni hokan dekimasuka?
-はい、あなたはどきゅめんとを安全に保管できます。
-hai, anata ha dokyumento wo anzenni hokan dekimasu.

8

-あなたは緊急に全てのこんぴゅーたーに新しいそふとうぇあをいんすとーるしたいですか？
-anata ha kinkyu ni subeteno konpyu-ta- ni atarashii sofutouea wo insuto-ru shitai desuka?

install the new software?
- It must be done urgently. Today.
- Do you want all of your computers to work more reliably?
- Yes, we want all our computers to work reliably and quickly.

7

- Does antivirus software effectively protect computers?
- Yes, it effectively protects computers.
- Can we store our documents more reliably?
- Yes, you can store your documents reliably.

8

- Do you want to urgently install new software on all

-はい、それはより急いで行わなければなりません。
-hai, sore ha yori isoide okonawanakereba narimasen.
-けれどもあなたの3台のこんぴゅーたーは予防めんてなんすが必要です。
-keredomo anata no sandai no konpyu-ta- ha yobou mentenansu ga hitsuyou desu.
-それは本当に必要ですか？
-sore ha hontou ni hitsuyou desuka?
-はい。それらは不十分でとても遅い動きをします。
-hai. sorera ha fujuubun de totemo osoi ugoki wo shimasu.

9

-私たちの製造の量は今月より高くなりました。
-watashitachi no seizou no ryou ha kongetsu yori takaku narimashita.
-これをどう私たちのあどばんてーじに使うことができますか？
-kore wo dou watashitachi no adobante-ji ni tsukaukoto ga dekimasuka?
-私たちは売り上げを著しく増やす必要があります。
-watashitachi ha uriage wo ichijirushiku fuyasu hitsuyou ga arimasu.

10

-誰が電話交渉をより説得力のあるように行うことができますか？
-dare ga denwakoushou wo yori settokuryoku no aruyouni okonaukoto ga dekimasuka?
-りんだがより説得力のある交渉をすることができます。
-rinda ga yori settokuryoku no aru koushou wo surukoto ga

computers?
- Yes, it must be done more quickly.
- But three of your computers are in need of preventative maintenance.
- Is it really necessarily?
- Yes. They perform poorly and very slowly.

9

- The volume of our production became higher this month.
- How can we use this to our advantage?
- We need to increase sales significantly.

10

- Who can conduct phone negotiations more convincingly?
- Linda can negotiate more convincingly.

dekimasu.
-さんどらの方がより自信があるかもしれませんか？
-sandora no houga yori jishin ga arukamo shiremasenka?
-いいえ、りんだははっきりとそして上手に話すことができます。
-iie, rinda ha hakkirito soshite jouzu ni hanasukoto ga dekimasu.

11
-私たちは製品をより低い値段で売らなければなりません。
-watashitachi ha seihin wo yori hikui nedan de uranakereba narimasen.
-それは本当に有益ですか？
-sore ha hontou ni yuueki desuka?
-はい、より買い手がいれば有益になります。
-hai, yori kaite ga ireba yuueki ni narimasu.
-誰と取引をするのがより有益ですか？
-dare to torihiki wo suruno ga yori yuueki desuka?
-卸売りの買い手と取引するのがより有益です。
-oroshiuri no kaite to torihiki suruno ga yori yuueki desu.

12
-私たちは製品の大きな一部を卸売り会社に提供したいです。
-watashitachi ha seihin no ookina ichibu wo oroshiuri kaisha ni teikyou shitai desu.
-私たちは彼らにより大きな割引をあげますか？
-watashitachi ha karerani yori ookina waribiki wo agemasuka?
-はい、20%割引をあげることができます。
-hai, nijippa-sento waribiki wo agerukoto ga dekimasu.

- Maybe Sandra is more confident?
- No, Linda can speak clearly and tactfully.

11
- We have to sell products at lower prices.
- Is it really profitable?
- Yes, it will be profitable if there are more buyers.
- With whom would it be more profitable for us to trade?
- It is more profitable for us to trade with wholesale buyers.

12
- We want to offer a large batch of products to wholesale companies.
- Will we give them a bigger discount?
- Yes, a twenty percent discount can be made.

かれ　　　　きょうみ　も
-それは 彼らに 興 味 を持たせますか？
-sore ha karera ni kyoumi wo motasemasuka?
　　　もう　で　かれ　　きょうみ　も
-はい、この 申 し出は 彼らに 興 味 を持たせます。
-hai, kono moushide ha karera ni kyoumi wo motasemasu.

13

　　　　　かいしゃ　おろしう　しょうひん　やす　か
-それぞれの 会 社 は 卸 売り 商 品 を安く買お
　　こころ
うと 試 みます。
-sorezore no kaisha ha oroshiuri shouhin wo yasuku kaouto kokoromimasu.
　　　　かれ　　　　　おこな
-どうして 彼らはそれを 行 いますか？
-doushite karera ha sore wo okonaimasuka?
　　　　かれ　　　　　　しょうひん　　たか　う
-そして 彼らはこれらの 商 品 をより 高 く売りま
す。
-soshite karera ha korerano shouhin wo yori takaku urimasu.
　かれ　　　　　　しょうひん　はや　う
- 彼らはこれらの 商 品 を早く売れますか？
-karera ha korera no shouhin wo hayaku uremasuka?
　　　　　　さら　じかん　ひつよう
-いいえ、それは 更に時間を 必 要 とします。
-iie, sore ha sara ni jikan wo hitsuyouto shimasu.

14

　かれ　　わたし　　　しょうひん　　　　か
- 彼らは 私 たちの 商 品 をもっと買いたいです。
-karera ha watashitachi no shouhin wo motto kaitai desu.
　　わたし　　　じょうけん　かれ　あ
- 私 たちの 条 件 は彼らに合いますか？
-watashitachi no jouken ha karerani aimasuka?
　　　　かれ　　　　ひく　ねだん
-いいえ、彼らはより 低い値段がほしいです。
-iie, karera ha yori hikui nedan ga hoshii desu.
　　　かれ　　おお　　　　　　　やす　か
-では 彼らは 大 きなばっちを、より 安く買うことはで
きますか？
-deha karera ha ookina bacchi wo, yori yasuku kaukoto ha dekimasuka?
　　　　かれ　おお　　　　　　　やす　か
-はい、彼らは 大 きなばっちを、より 安く買うことが
できます。

- Will it interest them?

- Yes, this offer will interest them.

13

- Each company tries to buy wholesale goods cheaply.

- Why do they do it?

- Then they sell these goods more expensively.

- Can they sell these goods quickly?

- No, it requires more time.

14

- They want to buy more of our goods.

- Do our terms suit the buyer?

- No, they want a lower price.

- So can they buy a large batch, but more cheaply?

- Yes, they can buy a large batch, but more

-hai, karera ha ookina bacchi wo, yori yasuku kaukoto ga dekimasu.

15

-2つの卸売り顧客と働くことは私たちにとって有益ですか？
- futatsu no oroshiuri kokyaku to hatarakukoto ha watashitachi nitotte yuueki desuka?

-いいえ、それは私たちにとって有益ではありません。より沢山の買い手がいるべきです。
-iie, sore ha watashitachi nitotte yuuekideha arimasen. yori takusan no kaite ga irubeki desu.

-もし更に買い手がいれば私たちの取引はより有益になりますか？
-moshi sarani kaite ga ireba watashitachi no torihiki ha yori yuuekini narimasuka?

-はい、私たちの取引はより有益になります。
-hai, watashitachi no torihiki ha yori yuueki ni narimasu.

cheaply.

15

- Is it profitable for us to work with two wholesale customers?

- No, it is not profitable for us. There should be more buyers.

- Does our trade become more profitable if there are more buyers?

- Yes, our trade becomes more profitable.

Elementary Course

13

氷を砕く
Break the ice

　幼いレオンは公園で彼のお父さんと一緒にいます。レオンは彼の友達らと遊んでいます。

"パパ、ズボンの上にパンツ履いていい?"とレオンはお父さんに聞きました。

"なぜだい?"とお父さんは聞きました。

"だって、スーパーマンになれるから!"とレオンは言いました。

"わかった、じゃあ家でやろうね"とお父さんは言いました。

Little Leon is on the playground with his dad. He is playing with his friends.
"Daddy, may I put underpants over the pants?" he asks his dad.
"Why?" the dad asks the son.
"I will be Superman!"
"Okay. But let's do it at home," the dad says.
"I will be a

そう言うとレオンは嬉しそうに"僕はスーパーマンになれるんだ!"と友達に言いました。

superman!" Leon cries happily to his friends.

osanai Reon wa kōen de kare no otōsan to issho ni imasu. Reon wa kare no tomodachira to asondeimasu. papa, zubon no ueni pantsu haite ii? to Reon wa otōsan ni kikimashita. naze dai? to otōsan wa kikimashita. datte, su-pa-man ni nareru kara! to Reon wa iimashita. wakatta, jā ie de yarou ne to otōsan wa iimashita. sō iu to Reon wa ureshisō ni boku wa su-pa-man ni nareru n da to tomodachi ni iimashita.

アンチウィルスソフトウェア
Antivirus software

単語
Words

1. (〜に)興味を持つ / 興味を持たせる [kyoumi wo motsu/ kyoumi wo motaseru] - get (be) interested / to interest
2. 15、十五 [juugo] - fifteen
3. 〜で来る [〜de kuru] - come by
4. 〜以外、〜を除いて [〜igai, 〜wo nozoite] - except, besides, but
5. あれ [are] - that
6. なぜなら [nazenara] - because
7. ウィルスの [uirusuno] - viral
8. サービス [sa-bisu] - service
9. セットアップ、設置する、置く [setto appu, secchisuru, oku] - set up, to put, to place
10. デザイン、開発 [dezain, kaihatsu] - design, development
11. ドル [doru] - dollar

12. ハッカー [hakka-] - hacker
13. パッケージ、包み、バッチ [pakke-ji, tsutsumi, bacchi] - package, parcel, batch
14. ポジティブ [pojitibu] - positive
15. リーダーシップ [ri-da-shippu] - leadership
16. リニューアル [rinyu-aru] - renewal
17. 悪意のある [akui no aru] - malicious
18. 一度に、すぐに、てきぱきして [ichidoni, suguni, tekipakishite] - at once, right away, promptly
19. 応答する(動詞) [outousuru (doushi) - respond (Verb)
20. 何もない [nanimo nai] - nothing
21. 希望する(動詞)、願う、期待する [kibou suru (doushi), negau, kitaisuru] - hope (Verb) / to expect
22. 期間、時間、フェーズ [kikan, jikan, fr-zu] - period, time, phase
23. 気づく(動詞) [kizuku (doushi)] - notice (Verb)
24. 結果 [kekka] - result
25. 好き [suki (doushi)] - like (Verb)
26. 行動、アクション [koudou, akushon] - action
27. 購入、買う [kounyuu, kau] - purchase, buy
28. 参照、調査する、評判 [sanshou, chousasuru, hyouban] - reference, review
29. 取引、広告、宣伝 [torihiki, koukou, senden] - trading, commercial
30. 守備、保護 [shubi, hogo] - defense, protection
31. 出る(動詞)、去る [deru (doushi), saru] - exit (Verb), to leave
32. 詳細な [shousaina] - detailed
33. 説明する [setsumei suru (doushi)] - explain (Verb)
34. 定期刊行の [teikikankouno] - periodical
35. 読む(動詞) [yomu (doushi)] - read (Verb)
36. 日本 [nihon] - Japan
37. 入る(動詞)、〜に入る [hairu (doushi), 〜ni hairu] - enter (Verb), to go in, to get into
38. 聞く(動詞) [kiku (doushi)] - hear (Verb), listen (Verb)
39. 訪問者 [houmonsha] - visitor
40. 明示する(動詞) [meijisuru] - specify (Verb), to itemize
41. 免許、ライセンス [menkyo, raisensu] - license
42. 余分に払う [yobun ni harau] - pay extra

B

"こんにちは。お困りですか？" 秘書は言います。
"konnichiha. okomaridesuka?" hisho ha iimasu.

"おはようございます。あなたのしすてむ管理者に会うことはできますか？" 訪問者は尋ねます。
"ohayougozaimasu. anata no shisutemu kanrisha ni aukotoha dekimasuka?" houmonsha ha tazunemasu.

"Hello. How can I help you?" says the secretary.

"Good morning. Can I see your system administrator?" asks

"あなたはどう紹介されたいですか?" 秘書は尋ねます。
"anata ha dou shoukai saretai desuka?" hisho ha tazunemasu.

"私はしーるど会社の代表です。私は認証されたそふとうぇあをいんすとーるするためにいます。" 訪問者は言います。
"watashi ha shi-rudogaisha no daihyou desu. watashi ha ninshousareta sofutouea wo insuto-ru surutameni imasu." houmonsha ha iimasu.

"あなたは少し待たなければなりません。" "anata ha sukosh imatanakereba narimasen."

秘書は部屋を去ります。しばらくした後、秘書としすてむ管理者が入ります。
hisho ha heya wo sarimasu. shibarakushita ato, hisho to shisutemukanrisha ga hairimasu.

"こんにちは。私は会社のしすてむ管理者です。あなたは私に会いたかったのですか?" 彼は尋ねます。
"konnichiha. watashi ha kaisha no shisutemu kanrisha desu. Anata ha watashi ni aitakattano desuka?" kare ha tazunemasu.

"こんにちは。はじめまして。私はしーるどの代表です。あなたは私の為に時間はありますか?" 訪問客は尋ねます。
"konnichiha. hajimemashite. watashi ha shi-rudo no daihyou desu. anata ha watashi no tameni jikan ha arimasuka?" houmonkyaku ha tazunemasu.

"はい、私はあなたの話を聞く準備ができています。あなたは何か申し出がありますか?" 管理者は言います。

the visitor.

"How do you want to be introduced?" asks the secretary.

"I am a representative of The Shield company. I'm here to install licensed software," says the visitor.

"You have to wait a little."

The secretary leaves the room. After some time, the secretary and the system administrator enter.

"Hello. I am the system administrator of the company. Did you want to see me?" he asks.

"Hello. Nice to meet you. I am a representative of The Shield. Do you have some time for me?" asks the visitor.

"Yes, I am ready to

"hai, watashi ha anata wo hanashi wo kiku junbi ga dekiteimasu. anata ha nanika moushide ga arimasuka?" kanrisha ha iimasu.

"私たちは認証されたそふとうぇあを提供します。あなたはそれに興味がありますか？"彼は言います。

"watashitachi ha ninshousareta sofutouea wo teikyoushimasu. anata ha soreni kyoumi ga arimasuka?" kare ha iimasu.

"はい。私にもっと教えてくれませんか？"しすてむかんりしゃは尋ねます。

"hai. watashi ni motto oshiete kuremasenka?" shisutemu kanrisha ha tazunemasu.

"私はあなたに日本で作られたあんちうぃるすそふとうぇあを提供したいです。それは信頼でき、そして高品質です。この会社は長い間そふとうぇあ開発に携わってきました。彼らは沢山経験を持ちます。彼らは10年以上もまーけっとにいます。"訪問者は言います。

"watashi ha anata ni nihonde tsukurareta anchi uirusu sofutouea wo teikyoushitai desu. sore ha shinraideki, soshite kouhinshitsu desu. kono kaisha ha nagaiaida sofutouea kaihatsu ni tazusawatte kimashita. karera ha takusan keiken wo mochimasu. karera ha juunenijou mo ma-ketto ni imasu." houmonsha ha iimasu.

"はい、私はこの会社について沢山の良い評判を聞いています。"管理者は言います。"このそふとうぇあは何のぷろぐらむで動きますか？"彼は尋ねます。

"hai, watashi ha kono kaisha nit suite takusan no iihyouban wo kiiteimasu." kanrisha ha iimasu. "kono sofutouea ha nanno

listen to you. Do you have something to offer?" says the administrator.

"We offer licensed software. May it be of interest for you?" he says.

"Yes. Can you tell me more?" asks the system administrator.

"I want to offer you antivirus software made in Japan. It is reliable and high quality. This company has long been engaged in software development. They have a lot of experience. They have been on the market for more than ten years," says the visitor.

"Yes, I've heard a lot of good reviews of this company," says the administrator. "With

puroguramu de ugokimasuka?" kare ha tazunemasu.

"それはうぃるす、まるうぇあそしてはっかーから守ります。もし毎月あっぷでーとされていれば、あなたは強固な守備を持つことができます。"訪問者は言います。

"sore ha uirusu, maruea soshite hakka- kara mamorimasu. moshi maitsuki appude-to sareteireba, anata ha kyoukona shubi wo motsukoto ga dekimasu." houmonsha ha iimasu.

"私たちはあっぷでーとに対して定期的にお金を払わなければなりませんか、それともそれは年間さーびすのぱっけーじに含まれていますか？"しすてむ管理者は尋ねます。

"watashitachi ha appude-to ni taishite teikitekini okane wo harawanakereba narimasenka, soretomo soreha nenkan sa-bisu no pakke-ji ni fukumarete imasuka?" shisutemu kanrisha ha tazunemasu.

"一年分のぱっけーじを購入すると、あなたは余計にお金を払う必要はありません。加えて、今月私たちはとても有利な条件を持っています。"訪問者は言います。

"ichinenbun no pakke-ji wo kounyuusuruto, anata ha yokeini okani wo harau hitsuyou ha arimasen. kuwaete, kongetsu watashitachi ha totemo yuurina jouken wo motteimasu." houmonsha ha iimasu.

"それでは私たちはこのあんちうぃるすをより安く買うことができますか？"管理者は尋ねます。

"soredeha watashitachi ha kono anchiuirusu wo yori yasuku kaukoto ga dekimasuka?" kanrisha ha tazunemasu.

"はい。私たちの会社はぷろもーしょんを行っ

what programs does this software work?" he asks.

"It protects against viruses, malware and hackers. If it is updated every month, you can have a solid defense," says the visitor.

"Do we have to pay for the updates periodically, or it is included in the package of annual services?" asks the system administrator.

"When you purchase a package for the whole year, you do not have to pay extra. In addition, this month we have very favorable terms," says the visitor.

"So can we now buy this antivirus cheaper?" asks the administrator.

"Yes. Our company is

137

ています。15 らいせんす買うと、あなたは25% 割引を受けます。私はこれはあなたにとって有利になると思います。"訪問者は言います。

"hai. watashitachi no kaisha ha puromo-shon wo okonatteimasu. juugo raisensu kauto, anata ha nijuugopa-sento waribiki wo ukemasu. watashi ha kore ha anatani totte yuurini naruto omoimasu." houmonsha ha iimasu.

"あなたのあんちうぃるすそふとうぇあはいくらですか？どの期間分を直ちに払わなければなりませんか？"
管理者は尋ねます。

"anata no anchi uirusu sofutouea ha ikura desuka? dono kikanbun wo tadachini harawanakereba narimasenka?" kanrisha ha tazunemasu.

"このそふとうぇあはらいせんすあたり年間20どるかかります。割引によって、値段は更に低くなります。そのためもし今月購入することができれば、あなたにとってより有利になります。"訪問者は答えます。

"kono sofutouea ha raisensu atari nenkan nijuudoru kakarimasu. waribikiniyotte, nedan ha sarani hikuku narimasu. sonotame moshi kongetsu kounyuusurukoto ga dekireba, anatani totte yori yuuri ni narimasu." houmonsha ha kotaemasu.

"どのような会社がこのそふとうぇあを使っていますか？彼らのれびゅーを読むことはできますか？"しすてむ管理者は尋ねます。

"donoyouna kaisha ga kono sofutouea wo tsukatte imasuka? Karerano rebyu- wo yomukoto ha dekimasuka?" shisutemu kanrisha ha tazunemasu.

"はい。これらがそにー、HTC、さむすんなどの大きな

doing a promotion. When buying fifteen licenses, you get a twenty-five percent discount. I think this will be advantageous for you," says the visitor.

"How much is your antivirus software? What period must be paid immediately?" asks the administrator.

"This software costs twenty dollars per year per license. With the discount, the price becomes much lower. Therefore it will be more advantageous for you if you can make a purchase this month," answers the visitor.

"What companies use this software? Can I read their reviews?" asks the system administrator.

会社です。"訪問者は応答します。
"hai. korera ga soni-, HTC, samusun nadono ookina kaisha desu." houmonsha ha outoushimasu.

"他にはどのような会社があなたのくらいあんとですか？"管理者は尋ねます。
"hokaniha donoyouna kaisha ga anata no kuraianto desuka?" kanrisha ha tazunemasu.

"私たちのくらいあんとは3大銀行、そしてたくさんの広告企業です。彼らは3年以上私たちのくらいあんとです。私たちは彼らとうまく協力しています。彼らは私たちのさーびすの品質に良い応答をします。"訪問者は言います。
"watashitachi no kuraianto ha sandaiginkou, soshite takusan no koukokukigyou desu. karera ha sannenijou watashitachi no kuraianto desu. watashitachi ha karerato umaku kyouryoku shiteimasu. karera ha watashitachi no sa-bisu no hinshitsu ni ii outou wo shimasu." houmonsha ha iimasu.

"私は財政問題を経営と話さなければいけません。私はぽじてぃぶな結果を期待します。私はあなたの提案が好きです。"しすてむ管理者は言います。
"watashi ha zaiseimondai wo keiei to hanasanakereba ikemasen. watashi ha pojitibuna kekka wo kitaishimasu. watashi ha anata no teian ga suki desu." shisutemu kanrisha ha iimasu.

"Yes. These are large companies, such as Sony, HTC, Samsung," responds the visitor.

"What other companies are your clients?" asks the administrator.

"Our clients are the three major banks and many commercial firms. They have been our clients for more than three years. We successfully collaborate with them. They respond well to the quality of our services," says the visitor.

"I have to discuss financial issues with the management. I hope for a positive outcome. I like your proposal," says the system administrator.

C

テキストについての質問	Questions about the text

1. 秘書(ひしょ)はなんと言(い)いますか？
2. しーるど会社(かいしゃ)の代表(だいひょう)は誰(だれ)ですか？
3. 何(なに)の問題(もんだい)に関(かん)して訪問者(ほうもんしゃ)は来(き)ましたか？
4. 誰(だれ)が部屋(へや)を出(で)ますか？
5. 誰(だれ)がしばらくした後(のち)来(き)ますか？
6. どのような種類(しゅるい)のそふとうぇあを訪問者(ほうもんしゃ)は提供(ていきょう)しますか？
7. 誰(だれ)があんちうぃるすそふとうぇあの製造業者(せいぞうぎょうしゃ)ですか？
8. そふとうぇあは何(なに)から守(まも)りますか？
9. 今月(こんげつ)の彼(かれ)らの購入(こうにゅう)の条件(じょうけん)は何(なに)ですか？
10. 彼(かれ)らはあんちうぃるすそふとうぇあをより安(やす)く買(か)うことができますか？
11. どのようなあくしょんを会社(かいしゃ)は抱(かか)えますか？
12. あんちうぃるすそふとうぇあはいくらですか？
13. しすてむ管理者(かんりしゃ)はどのような質問(しつもん)を議論(ぎろん)しなければなりませんか？

1. What does the secretary say?
2. Who is the representative of The Shield company?
3. Regarding what issue did the visitor come?
4. Who leaves the room?
5. Who comes after some time?
6. What kind of software does the visitor offer?
7. Who is the manufacturer of antivirus software?
8. From what does the software protect?
9. What are their terms of purchase this month?
10. Can they buy antivirus software cheaper?
11. What kind of action does the company carry?
12. How much is the antivirus software?
13. What question does the system administrator have to discuss?

14

Audio

氷を砕く
Break the ice

"ママ、小さい時はどんなスマートフォンを使ってたの？"と幼い息子がお母さんに聞きました。
"持てなかったわよ"
"タブレット持ってた？"と彼はもう一回聞きました。
"ママが幼い頃は、スマートフォンも、タブレットもなかったのよ。"とお母さんは答えました。息子はとても驚いていました。
"ママが小さいとき、恐竜見たことある？"

"Mommy, what smartphone did you have when you were little?" a little son asks his mom.
"None," his mom answers.
"Did you have a tablet?" he asks again.
"When I was little, there were neither tablets nor smartphones," the mom says to her son. Her son is very surprised.
"Mom, did you see dinosaurs, when you were a little child?" he asks

と息子は聞きました。
"見たことないわよ、ママはそんなに歳をとってないわ"

again.
"No, I did not, dear. I am not that old."

mama, chiisai toki wa donna Suma-To fuxon o tsukatteta no? to osanai musuko ga okāsan ni kikimashita. motenakatta wa yo taburetto motteta? to kare wa mō ichi kai kikimashita. mama ga osanai koro wa, Suma-To fuxon mo, taburetto mo nakatta no yo. to okāsan wa kotaemashita. musuko wa totemo odoroiteimashita. mama ga chiisai toki, kyōryū mita koto aru? to musuko wa kikimashita. mita koto nai wa yo, mama wa sonnani toshi o tottenai wa

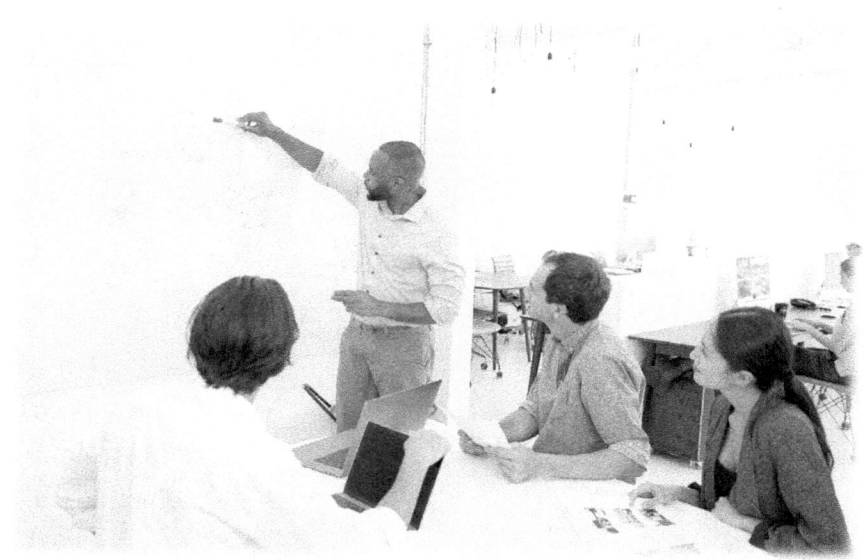

卸売り会社
A wholesale company

単語
Words

1. 1000、千 [sen] - thousand
2. 2番目の [nibanmeno] - secondary
3. 30、三十 [sanjuu] - thirty
4. 7、七 [nana] - seven
5. 〜をより好む(動詞)、〜をより望む [〜 wo yori konomu (doushi), 〜 wo yori nozomu] - prefer *(Verb)*
6. 〜から構成される / 〜と同等の [〜 kara kouseisareru/ 〜to doutouno] - consist of / be equal to
7. いくつか [ikutsuka] - some
8. お金 [okane] - money
9. これ [kore] - this

10. やっと、最後に [yatto, saigoni] - finally
11. より詳細に [yorishousaini] - more detailed
12. より便利に [yori benrini] - more convenient
13. キロメートル [kirome-toru] - kilometer
14. コーヒー [ko-hi-] - coffee
15. ドア [doa] - door
16. ユニット、単位 [yunitto, tani] - unit
17. 違い [chigai] - difference
18. 運ぶ、抱える(動詞) [hakobu, kakeru (doushi)] - carry (Verb)
19. 延長 [enchou] - extension
20. 応答する(動詞) [outousuru (doushi)] - respond (Verb)
21. 価値、重要性 [kachi, juuyousei] - value, significance
22. 加える、追加する(動詞) [kuwaeru, tuikasuru(doushi)] - add (Verb)
23. 議論する(動詞)、話し合う [gironsuru (doushi), hanashiau] - discuss (Verb)
24. 興味 [kyoumi] - interest
25. 繋ぐ、接続 [tsunagu, setsuzoku] - connect
26. 考える(動詞) [kangaeru (doushi)] - think (Verb)
27. 賛成する(動詞) [sanseisuru(doishi)] - agree (Verb)
28. 指名した、任命した、指定した [shimeishita, ninmeishita, shiteishita] - appointed
29. 指名する(動詞)、任命する、指定する [shimeisuru (douishi), ninmeisuru, shiteisuru] - appoint (Verb)
30. 持ってくる(動詞) [mottekuru (doushi)] - bring (Verb)
31. 持つ(動詞) / エスコート [motsu (doushi)/ esuko-to] - hold (Verb) / to escort
32. 時々 [tokidoki] - sometimes
33. 重要な、著しく [juuyouna, ichijirushiku] - significant
34. 商業の、コマーシャル [shougyouno, koma-sharu] - commercial
35. 少ない [sukuna] - less
36. 詳細 / アイテム [shousai/ aitemu] - detail / item
37. 状況 [joukyou] - occasion
38. 尋ねる[tazuneru] (動詞) [doushi] - ask (Verb)
39. 遂行する [suikō suru] (動詞) [doushi]、実行する [jikkō suru] - execute (Verb)
40. 正しい [tadashii] - right
41. 洗練 [senen] - refinement
42. 全て [suubete] - full
43. 倉庫 [souko] - warehouse
44. 大きさ、サイズ [ookisa, saizu] - size
45. 追加した [tsuikashita] - added
46. 提案する、勧める、アドバイスする(動詞) [teiansuru, susumeru, adobaisusuru] - advise (Verb)
47. 点、その時 [ten, sonotoki] - point, moment
48. 電話する(動詞)、名前をつける [denwasuru (doushi), namae wo tsukeru] - call (Verb), to name
49. 当座預金(口座) [touzayokin (kouza)] - checking (account)
50. 内容 [naiyou] - content
51. 能力、可能性、機会 [nouryoku, kanousei, kikai] - ability, possibility, opportunity
52. 配達 [deribari-] - delivery
53. 売る(動詞) [kau (doushi)] - buy (Verb)

54. 表にする(動詞) [hyounisuru] - list (Verb)
55. 閉じる(動詞) [toziru (doushi)] - close (Verb)
56. 鳴らす(動詞)、呼ぶ [narasu, yobu] - ring (Verb), to call
57. 来る(動詞)、到着する [kuru (doushi), touchakusuru] - come (Verb), to arrive
58. 利益、もうけ [rieki, mouke] - profit, benefit
59. 話す(動詞) [hanasu(doushi)] - talk (Verb)

B

会社の応接えりあにて。電話が鳴ります。
kaisha no ousetsueria nite. denwa ga narimasu.
"ゆーろびっと会社です。ご用件はなんですか?"
秘書は答えます。
"yu-robittogaishadesu. goyouken ha nandesuka?" hisho ha kotaemasu.
"こんにちは。私は卸売り会社の代表です。私たちはあなたの申し出を受け取りました。私は誰とこのことについて話すことができますか?"卸売り会社の代表は尋ねます。
"konnichiha. watashi ha oroshiurigaisha no daihyou desu. watashitachi ha anata no moushide wo uketorimashita. watashi ha dare to konokoto nitsuite hanasukoto ga dekimasuka?" oroshiurigaisha no daihyou ha tazunemasu.
"少々お待ちください。あなたを私たちのせーるすまねーじゃーに繋ぎます。"秘書は応答します。
"shoushou omachikudasai. anata wo watashitachi no se-rusu mane-ja- ni tsunagimasu." hisho ha outoushimasu.
"こんにちは。私はあなたが私たちの申し出に応答してくれて嬉しいです。私はあなたに私たちの条件についてより詳細に教え

In the reception area of the company. The phone rings.

"Eurobit Company. How can I help you?" answers the secretary.

"Hello. I represent a wholesale company. We have received your offer. Who can I talk to about this?" asks the wholesale company representative.

"Wait a minute. I am connecting you with our sales manager," responds the secretary.

"Good afternoon. We are glad that you have responded to our offer. I can tell you in more

ることができます。私の事務所でこの話し合いをすることができます。それは都心部に位置します。あなたは今日私たちの事務所に来ることはできますか?"まねーじゃーは尋ねます。
"konnichiha. watashi ha anata ga watashitachi no moushide ni outou shitekurete ureshii desu. watashi ha anata ni watashitachi no jouken nitsuite yori shousai ni oshierukoto ga dekimasu. watashi no jimusho de kono hanashiai wo surukoto ga dekimasu. sore ha toshinbu ni ichishimasu. anata ha kyou watashitachi no jimusho ni kurukoto ha dekimasuka?" mane-ja- ha tazunemasu.
"わかりました。私たちの会議を午後3時にせっとしてくれませんか?"代表は言います。
"wakarimashita, watashitachi no kaigi wo gogosanji ni settoshite kuremasenka?" daihyou ha iimasu.
"もちろん、あなたの希望通りに。私たちはあなたが3時に来ることを期待しています。"みかえるは言います。
"mochiron, anata no kibou doorini. Watashitachi ha anata ga sanji ni kurukoto wo kitaishiteimasu." mikaeru ha iimasu.
卸売り会社の代表は指定された時間に事務所に来ます。彼は秘書に迎えられます。
oroshiurigaisha no daihyou ha shiteisareta jikan ni jimusho ni kimasu. kare ha hisho ni mukaeraremasu.
"こんにちは。私があなたを案内します。"彼女は言います。
"konnichiha. watashi ga anata wo annaishimasu." kanojo ha iimasu.
"ありがとうございいます。"訪問者は言います。
"arigatougozaimasu." houmonsha ha iimasu.

detail about our terms. We can discuss this in our office. It is located downtown. Do you have an ability to come to our office today?" asks the manager.

"OK. Can you set our meeting for three p.m.?" says the representative.

"Of course, as you prefer. We are expecting you at three o'clock," says Michael.

The wholesale company representative comes to the office at the appointed time. He is greeted by the secretary.

"Good afternoon. I'll escort you," she says.

"Thank you," says the visitor.

The sales manager

せーるすまねーじゃーのみかえるが訪問者と会います。
Se-rusu mane-ja- no mikaeru ga houmonsha to aimasu.

"私はみかえるです。お会いできて嬉しいです。全ての重要な点をより詳細に話し合いましょう。"みかえるは申し出ます。
"watashi ha mikaeru desu. oaidekite ureshiidesu. subete no juuyouna ten wo yori shousai ni hanashiaimashou." mikaeru ha moushidemasu.

"私の名前はへんりーです。はい、私はあなたの話を聞き、そしてあなたの申し出を考える準備ができています。"訪問者は賛成します。
"watashi no namae ha henri-desu. hai, watashi ha anata no hanashi wo kiki, soshite anata no moushide wo kangaeru junbi ga dekiteimasu." houmonsha ha sanseishimasu.

"こーひーはどうですか?"みかえるは尋ねます。
"ko-hi- ha dou desuka?" mikaeru ha tazunemasu.

"はい、喜んで。"へんりーは賛成します。
"hai, yorokonde." henri- ha sanseishimasu.

秘書はこーひーを持ってきてそしてどあを閉じます。
hisho ha ko-hi- wo mottekite soshite doa wo tojimasu.

"私たちの会社は製品の製造と卸売り取引に携わっています。この時点では私たちは製品の製造の拡大に繋がる協力のための魅力的な条件を提供する準備ができています。あなたは私たちのかたろぐの内容をよく知っていますか?"みかえ

Michael meets the visitor.

"I'm Michael. Glad to meet you. Let's discuss all the important points in more details," offers Michael.

"My name is Henry. OK, I am ready to listen to you and consider your offer," agrees the visitor.

"Can I offer you some coffee?" asks Michael.

"Yes, with pleasure," agrees Henry.

The secretary brings coffee and closes the door.

"Our company is engaged in manufacturing and wholesale trade of products. At this point we are ready to offer favorable conditions for collaboration in

るは始めます。
"watashitachi no kaisha ha seihin no seizou to oroshiuri torihiki ni tazusawatteimasu. Kono jiten deha watashitachi ha seihin no seizou no kakudai ni tsunagaru kyouryoku no tameno miryokutekina jouken wo teikyousuru junbi ga dekiteimasu. anata ha watashitachi no katarogu no naiyou wo yoku shitteimasuka?" mikaeru ha hajimemasu.

"はい、私は2012年のかたろぐを見ました。"
代表は言います。
"hai, watashi ha nisenjuuninen no katarogu wo mimashita." daihyou ha iimasu.

"あなたは私たちの新しいかたろぐを見るべきです。私はあなたにそれを見せることができます。"みかえるは言います。
"anata ha watashitachi no atarashii katarogu wo mirubeki desu. watashi ha anatani sore wo miserukoto ga dekimasu." mikaeru ha iimasu.

5分後事務所のどあが開き、秘書が中に入ります。彼女は3つの新しいかたろぐを持っています。
gofungo jimusho no doa ga hiraki, hisho ga nakani hairimasu. kanojo ha mittsu no atarashii katarogu wo motteimasu.

"ありがとうございます。"みかえるは秘書に言います。"へんりー、このかたろぐを持って行ってください。それらは私たちの製品の最新の情報を持っています。今それらは更に良くそしてより高い品質です。それらはあなたに興味を持たせると思います。"みかえるは加えます。
"arigatougozaimasu." mikaeru ha hisho ni iimasu. "henri-, kono katarogu wo motteitte kudasai. sorera ha watashitachi

connection with the expansion of production. Are you familiar with the content of our catalog?" Michael begins.

"Yes, I saw the catalog for the year two thousand twelve," says the representative.

"I think you should see our new catalog. I can show you it," says Michael.

Five minutes later the office door opens, and the secretary enters. She carries three new catalogs.

"Thank you," says Michael to the secretary, "Henry, take these catalogs. They have latest information about our products. They are now even better and of higher quality. I think they are

147

no seihin no saishin no jouhou wo motteimasu. ima sorera ha sarani yoku soshite yori takai hinshitsu desu. sorera ha anata ni kyoumi wo motaseruto omoimasu." mikaeru ha kuwaemasu.

"はい、もちろん。私はあなたの製品が高い品質で最新の要求を満たしていると知っています。"卸売り会社の代表は賛成します。

"hai, mochiron. watashi ha anata no seihin ga takai hinshitsude saishin no youkyuu wo mitashiteiru to shitteimasu." oroshiurigaisha no daihyou ha sanseishimasu.

"卸売りぱっけーじの大きさは3000ゆにっとより少なくてはいけません。5000ゆにっとより多く購入すると、私たちの会社は20%の割引を提供します。それはあなたの会社の重要な利益として貢献するかもしれません。もしあなたが7000ゆにっとから買うと、私たちは25%の割引を提供します。ごめんなさい、私は製品の1ゆにっとの全体の値段は15どるだと言いませんでした。加えて、昨年のもでるには、更に大きな割引を提供します。それは同じ状態の下30%です。"せーるすまねーじゃーは説明します。

"oroshiuri pakke-ji no ookisa ha sanzenyunitto yori sukunakuteha ikemasen. gosenyunitto yori ooku kounyuusuruto, watashitachi no kaisha ha nijuppa-sento no waribiki wo teikyou shimasu. sore ha anata no kaisha no juuyouna riekini toshite koukensuru kamoshiremasen. moshi anata ga nanasenyunitto kara kauto, watashitachi ha

of interest to you," adds Michael.

"Yes, of course. I know that your products are of high quality and meet the latest requirements," agrees the representative of the wholesale company.

"The size of the wholesale package must not be less than three thousand units. When you purchase five thousand units or more, our company offers twenty percent discount. It may add up as significant profit for your company. If you buy starting from seven thousand units, we offer a discount of twenty-five percent. Sorry, I did not say that the full cost of one unit of the product is fifteen dollars. In addition, for last year's model, we offer an even greater discount. It is thirty percent under the same conditions," explains

nijuugopa-sento no waribiki wo teikyou shimasu. gomennasai, watashi ha seihin no ichiyunitto no zentai no nedan ha juugodoru dato iimasendeshita. kuwaete, kyonen no moderuniha, sarani ookina waribikiwo teikyoushimasu. sore ha onaji joutai no moto sanjippa-sento desu." se-rusu mane-ja- ha setsumeishimasu.

"それらは最新のもでるよりよりしんぷるですか?" 訪問者は尋ねます。

"sorera ha saishin no moderuyori yori shinpuru desuka?" houmonsha ha tazunemasu.

"大きな違いはありません。ただいくつかまいなーな内容が加えられました。あなたは気づかないかもしれません。" みかえるは応答します。

"ookina chigaiha arimasen. tada ikutsuka maina-na naiyou ga kuwaeraremashita. anata ha kizukanaikamo shiremasen." mikaeru ha outoushimasu.

"あなたは何を提案しますか?" 卸売り会社の代表は尋ねます。

"anata ha nani wo teianshimasuka?" oroshiurigaisha no daihyou ha tazunemasu.

"あなたはよく考え通すべきです。けれども私はより新しい製品を好みます。改善点の内容は時々大きな価値を持ちます。" みかえるは応答します。

"anata ha yoku kangaetoosu bekidesu. keredomo watashi ha yori atarashi seihin wo konomimasu. kaizenten no naiyou ha tokidoki ookina kachi wo mochimasu." mikaeru ha outoushimasu.

"はい、あなたは正しいです。私は供給条件を明確にしたいです。" へんりーは言います。

the sales manager.

"Are they much simpler than the latest models?" asks the visitor.

"It's not a big difference. Just some minor details were added. You may not notice," Michael responds.

"What do you advise?" asks the representative of the wholesale company.

"You should think it through. But I prefer the newer products. The refinement of details sometimes also has great value," Michael responds.

"Yes, you're right. I want to clarify the supply terms," says Henry.

"Our firm supplies at its

"hai, anata ha tadashii desu. watashi ha kyoukyuu jyouken wo meikakuni shitaidesu." henri- ha iimasu.

"私たちの会社は自分たちの費用で供給します。私たちは会社の銀行口座に支払いが入った次の日に製品を配達します。製品は私たちの会社の倉庫にあり、それは都心部から10きろめーとるに位置します。"せーるすまねーじゃーは応答します。
"watashitachi no kaisha ha jibuntachi no hiyou de kyoukyuu shimasu. watashitachi ha kaisha no ginkokukouza ni shiharai ga haitta tsuginohi ni seihin wo haitatsushimasu. seihin ha watashitachi no kaisha no soukoniari, sore ha toshinbukara jukkirome-toru ni ihishimasu." se-rusu mane-ja- ha outoushimasu.

"私たちはあなたの申し出を最終考慮しなければなりません。私たちは費用を2日後に移行するかもしれません。"訪問者は言います。
"watashitachi ha anata no moushide wo saishuukouryo shinakereba narimasen. watashitachi ha hiyou wo futsukago ni ikou surukamo shiremasen" houmonsha ha iimasu.

"私は協力できて嬉しいです。また会いましょう。"みかえるは応答します。
"watashi ha kyouryokudekite ureshii desu. mata aimashou." mikaeru ha outoushimasu.

own expense. We deliver products the next day after the payment comes into the company's bank account. The products are in our company warehouse, located ten kilometers from the downtown," the sales manager responds.

"We have to give your offer a final consideration. We may transfer funds in two days," says the visitor.

"I am glad to collaborate. See you," Michael responds.

C

テキストについての質問

1. 誰が申し出を受け取りましたか？
2. 卸売り会社の代表は何を尋ね

Questions about the text

1. Who received an offer?
2. What does the representative of the

ますか？
　　　じむしょ
3. 事務所はどこですか？
　　だいひょう　なに　あき
4. 代表は何を明らかにしますか？
　　だれ　おろしう　かいしゃ　だいひょう　あ
5. 誰が卸売り会社の代表と会いますか？
　　　　　　なに　もう　で
6. みかえるは何を申し出ますか？
　　ほうもんしゃ　なまえ　なに
7. 訪問者の名前は何ですか？
　　かいしゃ　なに
8. 会社は何をしますか？
　　かれ　　なに　ていきょう　　じゅんび
9. 彼らは何を提供する準備ができていますか？
　　だいひょう　　み　　　　　なんねん
10. 代表が見たかたろぐは何年でしたか？
　　おろしう
11. 卸売りぱっけーじのさいずはどのくらいであるべきですか？
　　　　かいしゃ　わりびき　ていきょう
12. どの会社が割引を提供しますか？
　　せいひん　　　　　ぜんたい　ねだん　なに
13. 製品の1ゆにっと全体の値段は何ですか？
　　せいひん
14. 製品はどこですか？

wholesale company ask?
3. Where is the office?
4. What does the representative clarify?
5. Who meets the representative of the wholesale company?
6. What does Michael offer?
7. What is the name of the visitor?
8. What does the company do?
9. What are they ready to offer?
10. From what year was the catalog that the representative saw?
11. What should the size of a wholesale package be?
12. What company offers a discount?
13. What is the full cost of one unit of the product?
14. Where are the products?

15

Audio

氷を砕く
Break the ice

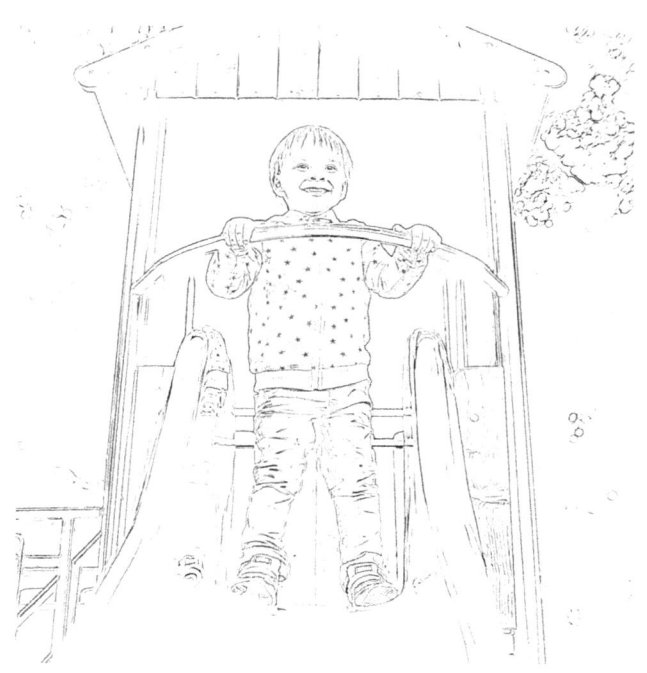

幼いロバートは公園で遊んでいます。
"ロバート、お家に帰ってきなさい！"と彼のお母さんが言いました。
ロバートはお母さんを見上げて"僕は疲れてるの？"とお母さんに聞きました。
"違うわよ、ロバート"
"僕は寒いのかな？"

Little Robert is playing on the playground.
"Robert, come home!" his mother calls. Robert looks up at his mom.
"Am I tired?" he asks his mom.
"No, dear," Robert's mom answers.
"Am I cold?" he asks again.
"No, honey. You are hungry," the mom says.

"違うわ、あなたはお腹が減っているの"
"そっか！今帰るよ！"と嬉しそうに言って足早に帰宅した。

"Okay, mommy! I am coming!" Robert says happily and runs home quickly.

osanai Roba-To wa kōen de asondeimasu. Roba-To, oie ni kaetteki nasai! to kare no okāsan ga iimashita. Roba-To wa okāsan o miagete boku wa tsukareteru no? to okāsan ni kikimashita. chigau wa yo, Roba-To boku wa samui no ka na? chigau wa, anata wa onaka ga hetteiru no so ka! ima kaeru yo! to ureshisō ni itte ashibaya ni kitakushita.

経営陣が決断を下しました
The management has made a decision

単語
Words

1. 8、八 [hachi] - eight
2. 9、九 [kyuu] - nine
3. 〜を除いて [〜wo nozoite] - without
4. その間に / 〜まで [sonoaidani/ 〜made] - meanwhile / until
5. どれ [dore] - which
6. スキャンする(動詞) [sukyan suru (doushi)] - scan *(Verb)*
7. ダウンロードする(動詞) / ロードする [daunro-do- suru/ ro-dosuru] - download *(Verb)* / to load
8. ライン、線 [rain, sen] - line
9. 加えて、更に [kuwaete, sarani] - additionally, further
10. 会う(動詞) [au (doushi)] - meet *(Verb)*
11. 開始から、始めから [kaishikara, hajimekara] - from the start, from the beginning, first
12. 完了する(動詞) [kanryou suru (doushi)] - complete *(Verb)*
13. 危険 [kiken] - danger
14. 銀行業 [ginkougyou] - banking

15. 経過する(動詞) [tsuukasuru] - pass (Verb)
16. 見る(動詞) [miru (doushi)] - watch (Verb), to look
17. 硬い [katai] - hard
18. 再起動する(動詞) [saikidou suru (doushi)] - restart (Verb)
19. 支払い [shiharai] - payment
20. 持つ、持っていく(動詞) [motsu, motteiku (doushi)] - take (Verb)
21. 実行 [zikkou] - execution
22. 取り除く(動詞) [torinozoku (doushi)] - eliminate (Verb)
23. 受け取る(動詞) / 了解する [uketoru (doushi)/ ryoukaisuru] - receive (Verb) / to perceive
24. 受け入れる(動詞) [ukeireru (doushi)] - accept (Verb) / to take
25. 十分でない [juubun de nai] - not enough
26. 障害、不利 [shougai, furi] - drawback, disadvantage
27. 冗談を言う(動詞) [jyoudan wo iu (doushi)] - joke (Verb)
28. 場所 [basho] - place
29. 真面目な、重要な [majimena, juuyouna] - serious
30. 設定、セットアップ [settei, settoappu] - set up
31. 設定する、チューニング [setteisuru, chu-ningusuru] - setting, tuning
32. 掃除 / 清掃 [souji, seisou] - cleaning / clearing
33. 走る(動詞) [hashiru (doushi)] - run (Verb)
34. 通常、普通、普段 [tsuujyou, futsuu, fudan] - regular, normal
35. 発見する、確認する / 明確にする [hakken sur, kakunin suru/ meikakunisuru] - find out / to clarify
36. 発売、開始 [hatsubai, kaishi] - launch, startup
37. 部門 [bunon] - department
38. 聞く(動詞) [kiku (doushi)] - listen (Verb)
39. 変更する(動詞) [henkou suru (doushi)] - change (Verb)
40. 保証する(動詞) [hoshousuru] - guarantee (Verb)
41. 望ましくない [nozomashikunai] - undesirable
42. 本当 [hontou] - really
43. 予定、摂生 [yotei, sessei] - schedule, regimen
44. 理由 [riyuu] - reason
45. 励ます(動詞) [hagemasu (doushi)] - cheer (Verb)

B

"こんにちは。 私はゆーろびっと会社のしすてむ管理者です。 私の名前はういりあむです。2日前に私たちの事務所にいたあなたの従業員に話すことはできますか？"ういりあむ

"Hello. I am the system administrator for Eurobit company. My name is William. Can I speak to your employee, who was in

"konnichiha. watashi ha yu-robittokaisha no shisutemu kanrisha desu. watashi no namae ha uiriamudesu. futsukamae ni watashitachi no jimusho ni ita anata no juugyouin ni hanasukoto ha dekimasuka?" uiriamu ha tazunemasu.

"わかりました。私はその質問を確認します。らいんにいてください。"うぃりあむは言われます。
"wakarimashita. watashi ha sono shitsumon wo kakunin shimasu. rain ni itekudasai." uiriamu ha iwaremasu.

"私は聞いています。私はぴーたーです。私は2日前にあなたの会社を訪問し、そしてあんちうぃるすそふとうぇあをいんすとーるするぱっけーじを提供しました。"そふとうぇあ会社の代表は応答します。
"watashi ha kiiteimasu. watashi ha pi-ta- desu. watashi ha futsukamae ni anata no kaisha wo houmonshi, soshite anchi uirusu sofutouea wo insuto-ru suru pakke-ji wo teikyou shimashita." sofutoueakaisha no daihyou ha outoushimasu.

"ぴーたー、経営陣はあなたの会社からそふとうぇあを買うことにぽじてぃぶな決断を下しました。私たちはあなたの条件で大丈夫です。私たちはらいせんすがこんぴゅーたー22台分必要です。"うぃりあむは言います。
"pi-ta-, keieijin ha anata no kaishakara sofutouea wo kaukoto ni pijitibu na ketsudan wo kudashimashita. watashitachi ha anata no jouken de daijoubu desu. watashitachi ha raisensu ga konpyu-ta- nijuunidaibun hitsuyou desu." uiriamu ha iimasu.

"私はとても嬉しいです。私はあなたが私たちの会社のさーびすに満足すると思います。し

かも、あなたの割引が増幅しまして、今は28%です。"ぴーたーは応答します。

"watashi ha totemo ureshii desu. watashi ha anata ga watashitachi no kaisha no sa-bisu ni manzokusuruto omoimasu. shikamo, anata no waribiki ga zoufukushite, ima ha nijuuhachipa-sento desu." pi-ta- ha outoushimasu.

"教えてください、あなたはいつ私たちが支払いをあなたの銀行口座に移動することを好みますか?"うぃりあむは尋ねます。

"oshietekudasai, anata ha itsu watashitachi ga shiharai wo anata no ginkoukouza ni idoususukoto wo konomimasuka?" uiriamu ha tazunemasu.

"私たちの会社は仕事が終わってから支払いを受け取ることを好みます。これはさーびすの質を更に保証します。"ぴーたーは答えます。

"watashitachi no kaisha ha shigoto ga owattekara shiharai wo uketorukoto wo konomimasu. kore ha sa-bisu no shitsu wo sarani hoshoushimasu." pi-ta- ha kotaemasu.

"あなたはいつ新しいそふとうぇあをいんすとーるし、始動するために私たちの事務所に来ることができますか?"しすてむ管理者は尋ねます。

"anata ha itsu atarashii sofutouea wo insuto-rushi, shidousurutameni watashitachi no jimusho ni kurukoto ga dekimasuka?" shisutemu kanrisha ha tazunemasu.

"私たちはあぽいんとめんとを明日の9時に設定することができます。"ぴーたーは言います。

"watashitachi ha apointomento wo ashita no kuji ni settei surukoto ga dekimasu." pi-ta- ha iimasu.

ぴーたーとうぃりあむはゆーろびっと事務所で会います。

"discount has increased, and it is twenty-eight percent for now," Peter replies.

"Tell me, when do you prefer us to transfer our payment to your bank account?" asks William.

"Our company prefers to receive payments after the work is done. This further guarantees the quality of the services," Peter answers.

"When can you come to our office to install and run the new software?" asks the system administrator.

"We can make an appointment at nine o'clock tomorrow," says Peter.

Peter and William meet at the Eurobit office.

pi-ta- to uiriamu ha yu-robittojimusho de aimasu.

"おはようございます。私たちはいんすとーるを始めることができます。"ぴーたーは言います。
"ohayougozaimasu. watashitachi ha insuto-ru wo hajimerukoto ga dekimasu." pi-ta- ha iimasu.

"しすてむを設定するのにどのくらいの時間必要ですか？"みかえるは尋ねます。
"shisutemu wo setteisurunoni donokurai no jikan hitsuyou desuka?" mikaeru ha tazunemasu.

"3時間以上はかかりません。"ぴーたーは答えます。
"sanjikan ijuou ha kakarimasen." pi-ta- ha kotaemasu.

"良かった。私たちのせっとあっぷは従業員の普段のおぺれーしょんすけじゅーるを少しだけ変えると思います。"みかえるは言います。
"yokatta. watashitachi no settoappu ha juugyouin no fudan no opera-shonsukeju-ru wo sukoshidake kaeruto omoimasu." mikaeru ha iimasu.

"始めに私たちはしすてむゆにっとを始動しなければいけません。そして私たちはほすとこんぴゅーたーにそふとうぇあをろーどします。もししすてむが新しいぷろぐらむをえらーなしで受け取れば、私たちはいんすとーるしたあんちうぃるすそふとうぇあをほすとしすてむを通して全てのこんぴゅーたーに送ることができます。"ぴーたーは提案します。
"hajimeni watashitachi ha shisutemuyunitto wo shidou shinakerebaikemasen. soshite watashitachi ha hosutokonpyu-ta- ni sofutouea wo ro-do shimasu. moshi shisutemu ga atarashii puroguramu wo era-nashi de uketoreba, watashitachi ha insuto-rushita anchi uirusu sofutouea wo

"Good morning. We can start the installation," says Peter.

"How much time do you need to configure the system?" asks Michael.

"It takes no more than three hours," Peter answers.

"Good. I think our setup will briefly change the normal operation schedule of the employees," says Michael.

"First we have to run the system unit. Then we load the software on the host computer. If the system receives a new program without errors, we can send the installed antivirus software to every computer through the host system," Peter

hosutoshisutemu wo tooshite subete no konpyu-ta- ni okurukoto ga dekimasu." pi-ta- ha teianshimasu.

"これは良いあいであです。"うぃりあむは言います。
"kore ha ii aidea desu." uiriamu ha iimasu.

しすてむ管理者とそふとうぇあ会社の代表はそふとうぇあのいんすとーるを開始します。
shisutemukanrisha to sofutoueagaisha no daihyou ha sofutouea no insuto-ru wo kaishishimasu.

"私ははーどどらいぶをすきゃんしてしすてむを再起動する必要があると思います。"しすてむ管理者は言います。
"watashi ha ha-dodoraibu wo sukyanshite shisutemu wo saikidousuru hitsuyou ga aruto omoimasu." Shisutemu kanrisha ha iimasu.

"見て、あんちうぃるすぷろぐらむが5台目のこんぴゅーたーにまるうぇあの存在を検知しました。これは望ましくありませんがその間重要なりすくはありません。"ぴーたーは説明します。
"mite, anchi uirusu puroguramu ga godaime no konpyu-ta- ni maruuea no sonzai wo kenchishimashita. kore ha nozomashiku arimasen ga sonoaida juuyouna risuku ha arimasen." pi-ta- ha setsumeishimasu.

せーるす部門からの電話。
se-rusu bumon karano denwa.

"うぃりあむ、さんどらです。私たちのこんぴゅーたーが不十分な動きをしています。理由を発見してくれませんか?"さんどらは尋ねます。
"uiriamu, sandora desu. watashitachi no konpyu-ta- ga fujuubun na ugoki wo shiteimasu. riyuu wo hakkenshite kuremasenka?" sandora ha tazunemasu.

suggests.

"This is a good idea," says William.

The system administrator and the representative of the software company begin installing the software.

"I think we need to scan the hard drive and restart the system," says the system administrator.

"Look, the antivirus program has detected the presence of malware on the fifth computer. This is undesirable, but there is no significant risk meanwhile," explains Peter.

A call from the sales department.

"William, this is Sandra. Our computers have

"はい、私はその問題に取り組んでいます。"うぃりあむは言います。
"hai, watashi ha sono mondai ni torikundeimasu." Uiriamu ha iimasu.
"あなたは3台のこんぴゅーたーが予防めんてなんすが必要だと言いました。もしかしたらこれがその理由かもしれません。"ぴーたーは言います。
"anata ha sandai no konpyu-ta- ga yoboumentenansu ga hitsuyoudato iimashita. Moshikashitara kore ga sono riyuu kamo shiremasen." pi-ta- ha iimasu.
"かもしれません。私たちはこれらのこんぴゅーたーを確認するべきです。"しすてむ管理者は言います。
"kamoshiremasen. watashitachi ha korera no konpyu-ta- wo kakunin surubeki desu." shisutemu kanrisha ha iimasu.
30分が経過します。
sanjuppun ga keikashimasu.
"実に、2台のこんぴゅーたーのはーどどらいぶにぷろぐらむをいんすとーるするのに十分な容量がありません。でぃすくくりーんあっぷにはいくらかの時間がかかります。3台目のこんぴゅーたーはおふぃすぷろぐらむのあっぷでーとが必要です。"うぃりあむは言います。
Jitsuni, nidai no konpyu-ta- no ha-dodoraibu ni puroguramu wo insuto-ru surunoni juubunna youryou ga arimasen. disukukuri-nappu niha ikurakano jikan ga kakarimasu. sandaime no konpyu-ta- ha ofisupuroguramu no appude-to ga hitsuyou desu." Uiriamu ha iimasu.
"これらの障害を取り除くと、いんすとーるは早くそして上手く始動します。"ぴーたーは言います。

begun to work poorly. Can you find out the reason?" asks Sandra.

"Yes, I'm working on this issue," says William.

"You said that three computers need preventative maintenance. Perhaps this is the reason," says Peter.

"Maybe. We should check these computers," says the system administrator

Half an hour passes.

"Indeed, there is not enough space on the hard drives of the two computers to install the program. Disk cleanup will take some time. The third computer requires office programs updating," says William.

"korera no shougai wo torinozokuto, innsuto-ru ha hayaku soshite umaku shidoushimasu." pi-ta- ha iimasu.

もう1時間経過します。
mouichijikan keikashimasu.

"これはあなたを励すでしょう。私は確認しました、そして全てのこんぴゅーたーが良く動いています。私たちはいんすとーれーしょんを時間内に完了しました。"ぴーたーは言います。
"koreha anata wo hagemasudeshou. watashi ha kakuninshimashita, soshite subete no konpyu-ta- ga yoku ugoiteimasu. watashitachi ha insutore-shon wo jikannai ni kanryou shimashita." pi-ta- ha iimasu.

"教えてください、効率的な守備のために私はどれくらい頻繁にそふとうぇあをあっぷでーとするべきですか？"うぃりあむは尋ねます。
"oshietekudasai, kouritsutekina shubi no tameni watashi ha dorekurai hinpan ni sofutouea wo appude-to surubeki desuka?" uiriamu ha tazunemasu.

"あなたは毎月ぷろぐらむをあっぷでーとする必要があります。"ぴーたーは説明します。
"anata ha maitsuki puroguramu wo appude-to suruhitsuyou ga arimasu." pi-ta- ha setsumeishimasu.

"私たちは今支払いをあなたの銀行口座に送っています。あなたと働けて良かったです。"うぃりあむは言います。
"watashitachi ha ima shiharai wo anata no ginkoukouza ni okutteimasu. anata to hatarakete yokatta desu." uiriamu ha iimasu.

"来年あなたに会えることを望みます。"ぴーたーは

"When we eliminate these drawbacks, the installation will run quickly and successfully," says Peter.

Another hour passes.

"This will cheer you up. I checked, and all the computers are working well. We completed the installation in time," says Peter.

"Tell me, how often should I update this software for effective protection?" asks William.

"You need to update the program every month," explains Peter.

"We are sending your payment to your bank account right now. Good working with you," says William.

"I hope to see you next

<ruby>冗<rt>じょう</rt></ruby><ruby>談<rt>だん</rt></ruby>を<ruby>言<rt>い</rt></ruby>います。

"rainen anata ni aerukoto wo nozomimasu." pi-ta- ha joudan wo iimasu.

"year," jokes Peter.

C

テキストについての質問

1. うぃりあむは<ruby>何<rt>なに</rt></ruby>と<ruby>応答<rt>おうとう</rt></ruby>しますか？
2. <ruby>会社<rt>かいしゃ</rt></ruby>の<ruby>経営陣<rt>けいえいじん</rt></ruby>はどのような<ruby>決定<rt>けってい</rt></ruby>をしましたか？
3. いくつのらいせんすが<ruby>必要<rt>ひつよう</rt></ruby>ですか？
4. <ruby>会社<rt>かいしゃ</rt></ruby>はいつ<ruby>支払<rt>しはら</rt></ruby>いを<ruby>受<rt>う</rt></ruby>け<ruby>取<rt>と</rt></ruby>ることを<ruby>好<rt>この</rt></ruby>みますか？
5. ぴーたーとうぃりあむはどこで<ruby>会<rt>あ</rt></ruby>いますか？
6. <ruby>彼<rt>かれ</rt></ruby>らは<ruby>何<rt>なに</rt></ruby>を<ruby>再起動<rt>さいきどう</rt></ruby>する<ruby>必要<rt>ひつよう</rt></ruby>がありますか？
7. <ruby>彼<rt>かれ</rt></ruby>らは<ruby>何<rt>なに</rt></ruby>をすきゃんする<ruby>必要<rt>ひつよう</rt></ruby>がありますか？
8. あんちうぃるすそふとうぇあは<ruby>何<rt>なに</rt></ruby>を<ruby>発見<rt>はっけん</rt></ruby>しましたか？
9. どのこんぴゅーたーでまるうぇあが<ruby>検出<rt>けんしゅつ</rt></ruby>されましたか？
10. さんどらは<ruby>何<rt>なに</rt></ruby>を<ruby>尋<rt>たず</rt></ruby>ねますか？
11. 3<ruby>台<rt>だい</rt></ruby>のこんぴゅーたーで<ruby>何<rt>なに</rt></ruby>が<ruby>行<rt>おこな</rt></ruby>われるべきですか？
12. <ruby>彼<rt>かれ</rt></ruby>らはぷろぐらむをあっぷでーとするべきですか？

Questions about the text

1. What does William reply?
2. What decision did the company management make?
3. How many licenses are needed?
4. When does the company prefer to receive payments?
5. Where do Peter and William meet?
6. What do they need to restart?
7. What do they need to scan?
8. What did the antivirus software discover?
9. On what computer was the malware detected?
10. What does Sandra ask?
11. What should be done on three computers?
12. Should they update the program?

16

Audio

氷を砕く
Break the ice

アナとお母さんは音楽学校に行くためにタクシーに乗っていました。
アナは"左にまがって…そこの赤信号で止まって、信号が青になるまで待って…今よ、行って！右に曲がって！"と言い続けました。
すると運転手は"その音楽学校への道は知ってるよ"と言いました。
"まあでも喋るのが好きだから、喋り続けるけどね！"とアナは返しました。

Anna and her mom take a taxi to the music school. Anna is speaking to the driver.
"Turn left … stop on the red traffic light … wait 'till the light turns green … Go now! Turn right!" she says.
"I know the way to the music school," the driver says.
"I will speak anyway. I like speaking!" Anna replies.

ana to okāsan wa ongaku gakkō ni iku tameni takushi- ni notteimashita. ana wa hidari ni magatte soko no akashingō de tomatte, shingō ga ao ni naru made matte ima yo, okonatte! migi ni magatte! to iitsuzukemashita. suruto untenshu wa sono ongaku gakkō e no michi wa shitteru yo to iimashita. mā de mo shaberu no ga suki da kara, shaberitsuzukeru kedo ne! to ana wa kaeshimashita.

どの割引を当てにすることができますか？
What discount can we count on?

単語
Words

1. 11、十一 [juuichi] - eleven
2. 4、四 [yon] - four
3. 〜について、近く [〜ni tsuite, chikaku] - about, near
4. 〜になる [〜ni naru] - turn out
5. 〜の間 [〜no aida] - during
6. させる(動詞) [saseru (doushi)] - force *(Verb)*
7. なぜなら [nazenara] - because
8. はっきりする(動詞)、指し示す [hakkiri suru (douhsi), sashishimesu] - specify *(Verb)*, to point out
9. ダメージ [dame-ji] - damage
10. 間違え、欠点 [machigae, ketten] - mistake, flaw
11. 決定する(動詞) [ketteisuru] - decide *(Verb)*
12. 混乱する(動詞)、混合する [konran suru, kongou suru] - confuse *(Verb)*, to mix
13. 昨日 [kinou] - yesterday
14. 書きとめる(動詞)、気づく [kakitomeru (doushi), kizuku] - note *(Verb)*, to notice
15. 招待する(動詞) [shoutai suru] - invite *(Verb)*
16. 詳細、必要な [shousai, shitsuyouna] - details, requisites

17. 状況 [joukyou] - situation
18. 心配して [shinpaishite] - anxiously
19. 正しい [tadashii] - right
20. 接続する(動詞) / 移行する / 取り換える [setsuzoku suru/ ikousuru/ torikaeru] - connect (Verb) / to transfer / to switch
21. 送る、送信する(動詞) [okuru, soushin suru(douhsi)] - send (Verb)
22. 続く(動詞) [tuzuku (doushi)] - continue (Verb)
23. 大きな、豊富な [ookina, houfuna] - large, voluminous
24. 置き換える [okikaeru (doushi)] - replace (Verb)
25. 適切な [tekisetsuna] - appropriate
26. 当てにする(動詞) [ateni suru (douhsi)] - count (Verb)
27. 働く人、従業員 [hataraku hito, juugyouin] - worker
28. 同行する(動詞) [douskou suru(doushi)] - accompany (Verb)
29. 箱 [hako] - box
30. 発送 [hassou] - shipment
31. 不便 [fuben] - inconvenience
32. 普段 [fudan] - usually
33. 聞く(動詞) [kiku (doushi)] - hear (Verb)
34. 便利な、好都合な [benrina, koutsugouna] - convenient
35. 目に見える、見える [meni mieru, mieru] - visible, seen
36. 輸送 [yusou] - transportation
37. 与える(動詞) [ataeru (doushi)] - give (Verb)
38. 量 [ryou] - quantity

B

"こんにちは。みかえると話すことはできますか?"へんりーは尋ねます。
"konnichiha. mikaeru to hanasukoto ha dekimasuka?" henri-ha tazunemasu.

"はい。いいですとも。私はあなたを繋いでいます。"秘書は応答します。
"hai. iidesutomo. watashi ha anata wo tsunaideimasu." hisho ha outoushimasu.

"こんにちは、みかえる。へんりーです。昨日私たちはあなたの製品の大きなばっちを買うことについて話しました。私たちの指導者はあなたの申し出を考えました。私たちはあなたと喜んで

"Hello. Can I speak to Michael?" asks Henry.

"Yes. Sure. I am connecting you," responds the secretary.

"Hello, Michael. This is Henry. Yesterday we talked about buying a large batch of your products. Our leadership considered your offer. We are willing to work with

働きたいです。まーけっとの状況が私たちに早い決定をさせます。"へんりーは説明します。

"konnichiha, mikaeru. henri-desu. kinou watashitachi ha anata no seihin no ookina bacchi wo kaukoto nitsuite hanashimashita. watashitachi no shidousha ha anata no moushide wo kangaemashita. watashitachi ha anatato yorokonde hatarakitai desu. ma-ketto no joukyou ga watashitachi ni hayai kettei wo sasemasu." henri- ha setsumeishimasu.

"私はあなたは正しい決定をしたと思います。私は明日にはあなたにその量のあいてむを売ることができないかもしれません。大きな割引によって、私たちは沢山の注文を受けています。もしあなたが良ければ、私たちは全ての問題を電話で解決できます。"みかえるは応答します。

"watashi ha anata ha tadashii kettei wo shitai to omoimasu. watashi ha ashita niha anatani sonoryou no aitemu wo urukoto ga dekinai kamoshiremasen. ookina waribikiniyotte, watashitachi ha takusan no chuumonwo uketeimasu. moshi anata ga yokereba, watashitachi ha subete no mondai wo denwa de kaiketsu dekimasu." mikaeru ha outoushimasu.

"はい、それは好都合です。今日私はあなたの事務所に行く機会がありません。私たちは2011年もでるを3000ゆにっと、そして新しい物を4000注文したいです。どの割引を当てにすることができますか?"へんりーは尋ねます。

"hai, sore ha koutsugou desu. kyou watashi ha anata no jimusho ni ikukikai ga arimasen. watashitachi ha nisenjuuichinen moderu wo sanzenyunitto, soshite atarashii mono wo yonsen chuumon shitaidesu. Dono waribiki wo

you. The market situation forces us to make decisions quickly," explains Henry.

"I think you made the right decision. Maybe tomorrow I won't be able to sell you that amount of items. Because of the large discounts, we get a lot of orders. If you are comfortable, we can solve all the problems over the phone," Michael responds.

"Yes, it is convenient. Today I don't have the opportunity to come to your office. We want to order three thousand units of two thousand eleven year model and four thousand new ones. What discount can we count on?" asks Henry.

atenisurukoto ga dekimasuka?" henri- ha tazunemasu.

"私たちはあなたに25%の割引を提供することができます。"みかえるは応答します。
"watashitachi ha anata ni nijuugopa-sento no waribiki wo teikyou surukoto ga dekimasu." mikaeru ha outoushimasu.

"良かった。そしたら私たちにあなたの銀行の必要事項を送ることをお願いします。あなたはそれらをふぁっくすまたはめーるで送信することができます。"へんりーは言います。
"yokatta. soshitara watashitachi ni anata no ginkou no hitsuyoujikou wo okurukoto wo onegaishimasu. anata ha sorera wo fakkusu mataha me-ru de soushinsurukoto ga dekimasu."henri- ha iimasu.

"私は必要事項をふぁっくすで送ることを好みます。"みかえるは言います。"watashi ha hitsuyoujikou wo fakkusu de okurukoto wo konomimasu."mikaeru ha iimasu.

10分が経過します。
juppun ga keikashimasu.

"素晴らしいです。私はあなたの必要事項を受け取りました。全てがはっきりと見えます。1時間以内に、私たちはあなたの口座に支払いを送ります。"へんりーは言います。
"subarashii desu. watashi ha anata no hitsuyoujikou wo uketorimashita. subete ga hakkiri to miemasu. Ichijikaninai ni, watashitachi ha anata no kouza ni shiharai wo okurimasu." henri- ha iimasu.

"そうですか、そしたら私たちはあなたの商品を集めて包むことを開始することができます。私

"We can give you a discount of twenty-five percent," Michael responds.

"Good. Then I ask you to send us your banking requisites. You can send them by fax or e-mail," says Henry.

"I prefer to send the requisites by fax," says Michael.

Ten minutes pass.

"Excellent. I have got your requisites. All are clearly visible. Within an hour, we will send the payment to your account," says Henry.

"Well, then we can start to collect and pack your goods. I will call the warehouse right now. Packing takes about three hours," says Michael.

"When can we get the

は倉庫に今電話します。包むのには約3時間かかります。"みかえるは言います。
"soudesuka, soshitara watashitachi ha anata no shouhin wo atsumete tsutsumukoto wo kaishi surukoto ga dekimasu. watashi souko ni ima denwashimasu. Tsutsumunoni ha yaku sanjikan kakarimasu." mikaeru ha iimasu.

"私たちはいつ全ての注文を受け取ることができますか？"へんりーは尋ねます。
"watashitachi ha itsu subete no chuumon wo uketorukoto ga dekimasuka?" henri- ha tazunemasu.

"あなたは注文を今日受け取ることができます。商品はどこに配達されるべきですか？これらは大きな箱です。相応しい場所があると願っていますがどうですか？"みかえるは詳細を言います。
"anata ha chuumon wo kyou uketorukoto ga dekimasu. shouhin ha dokoni haitatsu sareru bekidesuka? korera ha ookina hako desu. fusawashii basho ga aru to negatteimasuga doudesuka?" mikaeru ha shousai wo iimasu.

"私たちの企業のすたっふは普段商品の配達に同行します。彼が目的地をはっきりさせなければなりません。"へんりーは答えます。
"watashitachi no kigyou no sutaffu ha fudan shouhin no haitatsu ni doukoushimasu. kare ga mokutekichi wo hakkiri sasenakereba narimasen." henri- ha kotaemasu.

"それでは今日午後5時にあなたは商品を受け取ります。"みかえるは言います。
"sorede ha kyou gogo goji ni anata ha shouhin wo uketorimasu." Mikaeru ha iimasu.

次の日11時。ゆーろびっと事務所で電話が鳴ります。

"entire order?" asks Henry.

"You can get the order today. Where should the products be delivered? These are large boxes. I hope that you have an appropriate place?" Michael details.

"Our firm's staff person usually accompanies the delivery of goods. He has to specify the destination," answers Henry.

"Then today at five o'clock in the evening you will have the products," says Michael.

Eleven o'clock the next day. The phone rings in the Eurobit office.

"Hello. Please ask Michael to pick up the phone," asks the man.

167

す。
tsuginohi juuichiji. yu-robittojimusho de denwa ga narimasu.

"こんにちは。みかえるに電話を取ってくださいと尋ねてください。"男性は尋ねます。"konnichiha. mikaeru ni denwa wo tottekudasai to tazunetekudasai." dansei ha tazunemasu.

"みかえる、こんにちは。へんりーです。えらーが発生しました。"へんりーは言います。
"mikaeru, konnichiha. henri- desu. era- ga hasseishimashita." henri- ha iimasu.

"何が起こりましたか？"みかえるは心配そうに尋ねます。
"nani ga okorimashitaka?" mikaeru ha shinpaisouni tazunemasu.

"問題は従業員が去年と今年のゆにっとの量を混乱したことです。去年のもでるがひつよう分より1000ゆにっと多かったです。"卸売り会社の代表は言います。
"mondai ha juugyouin ga kyonen to kotoshi no yunitto no ryou wo konranshitakoto desu. kyonen no moderu ga hitsuyouna bun yori senyunitto ookatta desu." oroshiurigaisha no daihyou ha iimasu.

"すぐに気づいて良かったです。今日私たちはこれらのもでるを新しいのと置き換えます。不便をかけて申し訳ありません。"みかえるは謝ります。"これは私たちの従業員の間違いです。"
"suguni kiduite yokatta desu. kyou watashitachi ha korera no moderu wo atarashino to okikaemasu. fuben wo kakete moushiwake arimasen." mikaeru ha ayamarimasu. "kore ha watashitachi no juugyouin no machigai desu."

"Michael, good afternoon. This is Henry. An error has occurred," says Henry.

"What happened?" Michael asks anxiously.

"The problem is that workers confused the quantity of last year's and this year's units. There were a thousand units more of last year's model than we need," says the representative of the wholesale company.

"Good thing you noticed it right away. Today we will replace these models with new ones. My apologies for the inconvenience," Michael apologizes, "This is our employees' mistake."

"Were products damaged during transportation?"

"製品は輸送の間にだめーじを受けましたか？"みかえるは続けます。

"seihin ha yuusou no aidani dame-ji wo ukemashitaka?" mikaeru ha tsudukemasu.

"だめーじはありません。全てが大丈夫です。あなたの電話を待っています、みかえる"へんりーは答えます。

"dame-ji ha arimasen. subete ga daijoubu desu. anata no denwa wo matteimasu. mikaeru." henri- ha kotaemasu.

Michael continues.

"No damage. Everything is OK. Waiting for your call, Michael," Henry answers.

C

テキストについての質問

1. どうしてゆーろびっと会社は沢山注文を受けますか？
2. 卸売り会社は何を注文したいですか？
3. どのような割引をゆーろびっと会社は提供することができますか？
4. へんりーは何を送ることをお願いしますか？
5. どのような方法が必要事項を送るのにふさわ相応しいですか？
6. 製品を包むのにどれくらい時間がかかりますか？
7. すたっふは普段何をしますか？
8. 彼は何をはっきりさせなければなりませんか？

Questions about the text

1. Why does Eurobit company get a lot of orders?
2. What do wholesale buyers want to order?
3. What discount can Eurobit company give?
4. What does Henry ask to send?
5. What is the preferable way for requisites to be sent?
6. How long does it take to package the products?
7. What does the staff person usually do?
8. What does he have to specify?

じゅうぎょういん　ゆそう　まに　こんらん
9. 従業員は輸送の間何を混乱しましたか？
　　おろしう　かいしゃ　だいひょう　なに
10. 卸売り会社の代表は何と
　せつめい
　説明しますか？
　　　だれ　まちが
11. 誰の間違いですか？

9. What did the workers confuse during the shipping?
10. What does the wholesale company representative explain?
11. Whose mistake is it?

17

氷を砕く
Break the ice

　少女は体温計を手に持って座っています。
"何しているの?" と彼女のおとうさんが聞きました。
"釣りしてるんだよ" と彼女は答えました。
"だけど体温計はお医者さんが使うものだよ" と説明しました。
"わかった、じゃあ私はお医者さんね。どうしましたか?" と少女は聞きました。

A little girl is sitting with a toy thermometer in her hand.
"What are you doing?" her daddy asks.
"I am fishing," the girl answers.
"But a thermometer is for a doctor," the daddy explains.
"Okay, I am a doctor. What bothers you?" she asks.

"熱があるんだよね、助けてくれるかな？"

"ごめんなさい、助けられないわ。"

"何で？"

"釣りしてるから"

"I have a fever. Can you help me, please?" the daddy asks her.
"I am sorry. I cannot help you," the girl answers.
"But why, dear?"
"I am fishing."

shōjo wa taionkei o te ni motte suwatteimasu. nani shiteiru no? to kanojo no otōsan ga kikimashita. tsuri shiteru n da yo to kanojo wa kotaemashita. da kedo taionkei wa o isha san ga tsukau mono da yo to setsumeishimashita. wakatta, jā watashi wa o isha san ne. dō shimashita ka? to shōjo wa kikimashita. netsu ga aru n da yo ne, tasuketekureru ka na? gomennasai, tasukerarenai wa. nande? tsuri shiteru kara

カスタムされたプログラム
A custom built program

単語
Words

1. 〜に対して [〜ni taishite] - against
2. について [nitsuite] - about
3. も、また [mo, mata] - also
4. インベントリ、目録 [inbentori-, mokuroku] - inventory
5. カスタム作成 / 個別、個人 [kasutamu seisaku/ kobetsu, kojin] - custom built / individual
6. カテゴリー [kategori-] - category
7. グループ [guru-pu] - group
8. シンプル [shinpuru] - simple

9. ダウンロード [daunro-do] - download
10. ニュース [nyu-su] - news
11. フォーマット [fo-matto] - format
12. 印刷した [printoshita] - printed
13. 開始する(動詞) / をやり始める [kaishisuru (doushi)/ wo yarihajimeru] - start *(Verb)* / to get to
14. 開発者 [kaihatsusha] - developer
15. 確認 [kakunin] - confirmation
16. 含む(動詞) [fukuu (douhsi)] - contain *(Verb)*
17. 記述 [kijutsu] - description
18. 計画 [keikaku] - planning
19. 結果、最低値 [kekka, saiteichi] - result, bottom line
20. 言葉 [kotoba] - word
21. 合計する(動詞) [goukeisuru (doushi)] - sum *(Verb)*
22. 再び、また [futatabi, mata] - again
23. 残り / 残高 [nokori/ zandaka] - remainder / balance
24. 支出 [shishutsu] - expense
25. 取り掛かる、開始する [torikakaru, kaishisuru] - get down to, to start
26. 取り消し、キャンセル [torikeshi, kyanseru] - write-off, cancellation
27. 取得物 [shutokubutsu] - acquisition
28. 処理 / 会計 [shori/ kaikei] - processing / accounting
29. 製品 [seihin] - product
30. 総収入、収入 [soushuunyuu, shuunyuu] - revenue, income
31. 送る、送信する(動詞) [okuru, soushinsuru (doushi)] - send *(Verb)*
32. 電話し直す [denwashinaosu] - call back
33. 答える [kotaeru] - answer
34. 到着 [touchaku] - arrival
35. 動き [ugoki] - movement
36. 売り上げ、認識 [uriage, ninshiki] - sales, realization
37. 普通、標準 [futsuu, hyoujun] - normal
38. 返金、リターン [henkin, rita-n] - return
39. 預金、保存 [yokin, hozon] - saving, preservation
40. 要求する [youkyuusuru] - demand
41. 履歴、ヒストリー [rireki, hisutori-] - history

B

"こんにちは。 私の名前はうぃりあむです。 私はゆーろびっと会社のしすてむ管理者です。 私はぴーたーと話す必要があります。"うぃりあむが秘書に向かって言います。

"konnichiha. watashi no namae ha uiriamu desu. watashi ha yu-robittogaisha no shisutemukanrisha desu. watashi ha pi-ta- to hanasu hitsuyou ga arimasu." uiriamu ga hisho ni mukatteiimasu.

"Hello. My name is William. I am the system administrator for Eurobit company.

I need to speak with Peter," William turns to the secretary.

"彼は現在事務所にいません。彼は1時間後にあなたに電話し直します。"そふとうぇあ会社の秘書は応答します。
"kare ha genzai jimusho ni imasen. kare ha ichijikango ni anata ni denwa shinaoshimasu." sofutoueagaisha no hisho ha outoushimasu.

(1時間後)
(ichijikango)

"おはようございます、うぃりあむ。あなたからまた連絡があって嬉しいです。あんちうぃるすそふとうぇあが正しく動いていることを願います。"ぴーたーは言います。
"ohayougozaimasu, uiriamu. anatakara mata renraku ga atte ureshii desu. anchi uirusu sofutouea ga tadashiku ugoiteirukoto wo negaimasu." pi-ta- ha iimasu.

"はい、もちろん、ぴーたー。私はあなたに他の事柄で頼りたいです。私たちの会社は新しい情報処理しすてむを必要としています。言い換えると、私たちは収入／ししゅつ、商品の動き、そして会社全体の生産企画を全体的に処理出来るようにかすたむされたぷろぐらむが必要です。私たちはあなたの手伝いを当てにすることができますか？"うぃりあむは状況を説明します。
"hai, mochiron, pi-ta-. watashi ha anata ni hoka no kotogara de tayoritaidesu. watashitachi no kaisha ha atarashii jouhoushori shisutemu wo hitsuyouto shiteimasu. iikaeruto, watashitachi ha shuunyuu/shishutsu, shouhin no ugoki,

"He is currently out of his office. He will call you back in an hour," the software company secretary responds.

(An hour later)

"Good morning, William. Glad to hear from you again. Hope the antivirus software is working properly," says Peter.

"Yes, of course, Peter. I want to turn to you on another matter. Our company has a need for a new data processing system. In other words, we need a custom built program, which allows overall processing of revenues/ expenses, the movement of goods, and production planning for the entire company. Can we count on your help?" William explains the situation.

"Yes, we have a group of

soshite kaishazentai no seisankikaku wo zentaitekini shori dekiruyouni kasutamusareta puroguramu ga hitsuyou desu. watashitachi ha anata no tetsudai wo atenisurukoto ga dekimasuka?" uiriamu ha joukyou wo setsumeishimasu.

"はい、私たちは開発者のぐるーぷを持っています。私たちは喜んであなたの問題を解決する事に取り掛かり、そしてあなたの為にしんぷるで便利で、そして効率的なぷろぐらむを作成します。"ぴーたーは答えます。

"hai, watashitachi ha kaihatsusha no guru-pu wo motteimasu. watashitachi ha yorokonde anata no mondai wo kaiketsusuru kotoni torikakari, soshite anata no tameni shinpurude, benride, soshite kouritsuteki na puroguramu wo sakuseishimasu." pi-ta- ha kotaemasu.

"これは良いにゅーすです。"ういりあむは安心しています。"加えて、ぷろぐらむは製品の残り、資産の流れ、そして生産の集計の為の設備を含むべきです。倉庫の集計は別のゆにっとでなければなりません。それは商品の残り、倉庫への新しい製品の到着、取得物、売り上げ、返金、取り消し、そして目録を見せてくれます。重要なぽいんとの一つはぷりんと可能なふぉーむのどきゅめんとやれぽーとをPDFとえくせるふぉーまっとでのだうんろーどと保存です。それとかてごりーと値段ひすとりーが入った値段表です。"彼は説明します。

"kore ha iinyu-su desu." uiriamu ha anshin shiteimasu.

developers. We are happy to get down to resolve your problem and we will create a simple, convenient and effective program for you," Peter answers.

"This is good news," William is glad. "In addition, the program should contain an accounting of remainder products, flow of funds, and supplies for production accounting. The warehouse accounting must stand as a separate unit. It shows the remainders of the goods, the arrival of new products to the warehouse, acquisitions, sales, refunds, write-offs, and the inventory. One of the important points should be downloading and saving printable forms of the documents and reports in PDF and

"kuwaete, puroguramu ha seihin no nokori, shisan no nagare, soshite seisan no shuukei no tame no setsubi wo fukumu bekidesu. souko no shuukei ha betsu no yunittode nakereba narimasen. sore ha shouhin no nokori, souko heno atarashii seihin no touchaku, shuutokubutsu, uriage, henkin, torikeshi, soshite mokuroku wo misetekuremasu. Juuyouna pointo no hitotsu ha purintokanona fo-mu no dokyumento ya repo-to wo PDF to ekuseru fo-mu deno daunro-do to hozon desu. soreto kategori- to nedanhisutori- ga haitta nedanhyou desu." kare ha setsumeishimasu.

"もしこれら全てがぷろぐらむへの要求ならば、それらの記述をめーるで送ってください。"ぴーたーは尋ねます。

"moshi korera subete ga puroguramu heno youkyuunaraba, sorera no kijutsu wo me-ru de okuttekudasai." pi-ta- ha tazunemasu.

"ぴーたー、開発のために必要な時間を見積もることはできますか？"うぃりあむは尋ねます。

"pi-ta-, kaihatsu no tameni hitsuyouna jikan wo mitsumorukoto ha dekimasuka?" uiriamu ha tazunemasu.

"それは通常2から3か月かかります。私がぷろぐらむの為の要求の詳細を処理したら直ぐに、私たちの開発者が仕事を始めます。"ぴーたーは明言します。

"sore ha tsuujou ni kara sankagetsu kakarimasu. watashi ga puroguramu no tame no youkyuu no shousai wo shorishitara suguni, watashitachi no kaihatsusha ga shigoto wo hajimemasu." pi-ta- ha meigenshimasu.

"もし構わなければ、あなたの能力を確認した後に支払いの質問について話し合いましょう。"うぃりあむは結論付けます。

"moshi kamawanakereba, anata no nouryoku wo

Excel formats. Also a price list with the categories and price history," he explains.

"If these are all your requirements for the program, please send their description by email," asks Peter.

"Peter, can you estimate the time that is required for development?" asks William.

"It usually takes about two to three months. As soon as I deal with the details of the requirements for the program, our developers will get to work," Peter clarifies.

"If you do not mind, we shall discuss the question of payment after the confirmation of your abilities," concludes William.

kakuninshita ato ni shiharai no shitsumon ni tsuite hanashiaimashou." uiriamu ha ketsuronzukemasu.

"はい、私は今日の終わりには答えを出すことができます。"ぴーたーは言います。
"hai, watashi ha kyou no owari niha kotae wo dasukoto ga dekimasu." pi-ta- ha iimasu.

"OK, I can give you an answer at the end of the day," says Peter.

C

テキストについての質問

1. ゆーろびっと会社は何が必要ですか？
2. かすたむされたぷろぐらむは何を処理することを可能としますか？
3. ぷろぐらむは何を含むべきですか？
4. 何が別のゆにっとでなければなりませんか？
5. どのようなふぉーまっとでぷりんとされたふぉーむがだうんろーとと保存されるべきですか？
6. ぴーたーは何を尋ねますか？
7. 開発には何か月必要ですか？
8. いつ開発者は仕事に取り掛かれますか？
9. いつ彼らは支払い問題を話し合いますか？

Questions about the text

1. What does the Eurobit company need?
2. What would the custom-built program allow to process?
3. What should the program contain?
4. What must stand as a separate unit?
5. In which formats should printed forms be downloaded and saved?
6. What does Peter ask?
7. How many months does development require?
8. When can developers get to work?
9. When will they discuss the payment issue?

18

Audio

氷を砕く
Break the ice

もう寝る時間だよと言いお父さんは少年を寝室に連れていきました。10分後にお母さんが寝室に入ると、
"お母さん、静かに！お父さん寝てるから"と少年が言いました。

It is time for a little boy to go to bed. The daddy takes him to the bedroom. The mom comes into the bedroom ten minutes later.
"Mommy be quiet, please. Daddy is asleep," the son says.

mō neru jikan da yo to ii otōsan wa shōnen o shinshitsu ni tsureteikimashita. 10 fungo ni okāsan ga shinshitsu ni hairu to, okāsan, shizuka ni! otōsan neteru kara to shōnen ga iimashita.

有利な条件
Advantageous terms

単語
Words

1. 100、百 [hyaku] - one hundred
2. の下 [no shita] - under
3. を取り除く [wo torinozoku] - get rid of
4. インターフェース [inta-fe-su] - interface
5. オプションの / 追加の [opushonno/ tsuikano] - optional / additional
6. ノベルティ [noberuti-] - novelty
7. プレビュー、レビュー [purebyu-, rebyu-] - preview, review
8. メモ、ノート [memo, no-to] - note
9. 加速する(動詞) [kasoku (doushi)] - accelerate *(Verb)*
10. 会話 [kaiwa] - conversation
11. 確信して、あらかじめ決められた [kakushinshite, arakajime kimerareta] - certain, predefined
12. 機能、特徴 [kinou, tokuchou] - feature
13. 起こる(動詞) [okoru (doushi)] - occur *(Verb)*
14. 形づける(動詞) [katachi zukeru (doushi)] - form *(Verb)*
15. 計算する(動詞)、数える/ 考慮する [keisansuru, kazoeru/ kouryosuru] - count *(Verb)* / to consider
16. 考慮した上で [kouryoshitauede] - take into account
17. 合意する(動詞) [gouisuru] - confirm *(Verb)*
18. 最新式の [saishin no] - up to date
19. 作成する(動詞) [sakuseisuru (doushi)] - create *(Verb)*
20. 支出、消費、費用 [shishutsu, shouhi, hiyou] - expenditure

21. 試験 [shiken] - testing
22. 試験された、証明された [shikensareta, shoumeisareta] - tested, proven
23. 自動の [jidouno] - automatic
24. 自動的に [jidoutekini] - automatically
25. 実行する(動詞) [jikkou suru (doushi)] - perform (Verb)
26. 修正された / 改良された [shuuseisareta/ kairyousareta] - modified / improved
27. 処理 [shori] - process
28. 正しく [tadashiku] - correctly
29. 全体 [zentai] - full
30. 誰か / いくつか [dareka/ ikutsuka] - someone / some
31. 短気 [tanki] - impatience
32. 通知する [tsuuchisuru] - inform
33. 展示する(動詞) [tenjisuru(doushi)] - display (Verb)
34. 同様 [douyou] - alike
35. 入手可能な [nyuushukanouna] - affordable
36. 配分 [haibun] - distribution
37. 美しい [utsukushii] - beautiful
38. 評価する(動詞) [hyoukasuru (doushi)] - assess (Verb)
39. 保存する(動詞) [hozonsuru (doushi)] - save (Verb)
40. 毎月の [maitsukino] - monthly
41. 明確な [meikakuna] - specific
42. 役に立つ [yaku ni tatsu] - useful
43. 有利、アドバンテージ [yuuri, adobante-ji] - advantage
44. 予備的に [yobitekini] - preliminarily
45. 予約購読、定期購入[yoyaku kounyuu, teiki kounyuu] - subscription
46. 要求する(動詞) [youkyuusuru (doushi)] - require (Verb)
47. 頼る(動詞) [tayoru (doushi)] - depend (Verb)
48. 利用者 [riyosha] - user
49. 理解する(動詞) [rikaisuru (douhsi)] - understand (Verb)
50. 離れて、別々に [hanarete, betsubetsuni] - apart, separately

B

働く時間の終わりに電話が鳴ります。
Hataraku jikan no owarini denwa ga narimasu.

"こんばんは、うぃりあむ。"ぴーたーは言います。"それは完璧なゆーざーしすてむになります。私たちの開発者はこの仕事を実行する準備ができています。私たちのぷろぐらむの有利な点の1つはぷろぐらむが自動的にあっぷでーとされることで

At the end of the working hours the phone rings.

"Good evening, William," says Peter, "It will be a complete user system. Our developers are ready to perform this task. One of the

"ぴーたーは会話を続けます。"konbanha, uiriamu." pi-ta- ha iimasu. "sore ha kanpekina yu-za-shisutemu ni narimasu. watashitachi no kaihatsusha ha konoshigoto wo jikkousuru junbi ga dekiteimasu. watashitachi puroguramu no yuurinaten no hitotsu ha puroguramu ga jidoutekini appude-to sarerukoto desu." pi-ta- ha kaiwa wo tsudukemasu.

"自動あっぷでーとは素敵な機能です。これは私たちに毎月の費用と時間を節約させます。"うぃりあむは合意します。
"jidouappude-to ha sutekina kinou desu. kore ha watashitachi ni maitsuki no hiyou to jikan wo setsuyaku sasemasu." uiriamu ha gouishimasu.

"私たちの専門家はすでにあなたのぷろぐらむの開発を開始しました。"ぴーたーは言います。
"watashitachi no senmonka ha sudeni anata no puroguramu no kaihatsu wo kaishishimashita." pi-ta- ha iimasu.

"私たちはぷろぐらむに倉庫、売り上げと商品の動きからの収入の処理、生産の費用、様々な期間の生産計画などのいくつかの別々のぶろっくを作成しています。"そふとうぇあ会社の専門家は続けます。
"watashitachi ha puroguramu ni souko, uriage to shouhin no ugokikara no shuunyuu no shori, seisan no hiyou, samazama na kikan no seisankeikaku nadono ikutsukano betsubets u no burokku wo sakusei shiteimasu." sofutoueagaisha no senmonka ha tsudukemasu.

"はい、倉庫のぷろぐらむでは、私たちは残りの製品の集計、新しい製品の倉庫への到着、売り上げと返金を見る必要がありま

advantages of our program will be that the program is automatically updated," Peter continues the conversation.

"Auto update is a great feature. This will save us monthly costs and time," confirms William.

"Our experts already have started to develop your program," says Peter.

"We are creating several separate blocks in the program: warehouse, processing of revenue from sales and goods movement, the cost of production, production planning for different periods," continues the software company specialist.

"Yes. In the warehouse program, we need to see an accounting of product

"はい、倉庫のぷろぐらむでは、私たちは残りの製品の集計、新しい製品の倉庫への到着、売上と返品を見る必要があります。"うぃりあむは追加します。
"hai, souko no puroguramu deha, watashitachi ha nokori no seihin no shuukei, atarashii seihin no souko heno touchaku, uriage to henkin wo miru hitsuyou ga arimasu." uiriamu ha tsuikashimasu.

"私たちは必需品の購入、注文の取り消し、そして商品のいんべんとりーを考慮する必要があると感じます。それは役に立つかもしれません。"ぴーたーは明言します。
"watashitachi ha hitsujuhin no kounyuu, chuumon no torikeshi, soshite shouhin no inbentori- wo kouryosuru hitsuyou ga aruto kanjimasu. sore ha yakunitatsu kamo shiremasen." pi-ta- ha meigenshimasu.

"加えて、値段の履歴を表示し、そして顧客への自動的な配布をもったそれぞれの卸売り業者の買い手のための割引の計算しすてむを作るために、値段りすとを別々に作成する必要があります。"うぃりあむは明言します。
"kuwaete, nedan no rireki wo hyoujishi, soshite kokyaku heno jidoutekina haifu wo motta sorezore no oroshiurigyousha no kaite no tameno waribiki no keisan shisutemu wo tsukurutameni, nedan risuto wo betsubetsu ni sakuseisuru hitsuyou ga arimasu." uiriamu ha meigenshimasu.

"あなたは彼らに新しい製品、ぷろもーしょん、追加の割引を自動的に通知したいですか？ぴーたーは尋ねます。
"anata ha karera ni atarashii seihin, puromo-shon, tsuika no waribiki wo jidouteki ni tsuuchi shitaidesuka?" pi-ta- ha

remainders, the arrival of new products to the warehouse, sales and returns," adds William.

"I believe that we need to consider the purchase of supplies, write-offs, an inventory of goods. It can be useful," clarifies Peter.

"In addition, you need to form price lists separately, to display the price history and to make a calculation system of discounts for each wholesale buyer with automatic distribution to customers," clarifies William.

"Do you want to automatically inform them about new products, promotions, additional discounts?" asks Peter.

"Yes, you understand me

tazunemasu.

"はい、あなたは私を正しく理解しています、ぴーたー。私たちはそれぞれのくらいあんとに最新の情報を時間通りに受け取ってほしいです。"うぃりあむは言います。

"hai, anata ha watashi wo tadashiku rikaishiteimasu, pi-ta-. watashitachi ha sorezore no kuraianto ni saishin no jouhou wo jikandoori ni uketotte hoshiidesu." Uiriamu ha iimasu.

"それはあなたの会社のめーりんぐりすとの定期購読という形で行うことができます。"ぴーたーは申し出ます。

"sore ha anata no kaisha no me-ringurisuto no teikikoudoku toiu katachi de okonaukoto ga dekimasu." pi-ta- ha moushidemasu.

"はい、それは便利になります。"うぃりあむは言います。

"hai, sore ha benri ni narimasu." uiriamu ha iimasu.

"倉庫の集計、収入/支出、生産計画と消費、全てのぶろっくで情報をPDFとえくせるふぉーまっとで閲覧することが可能です。"ぴーたーは明言します。

" souko no shuukei, shuunyuu/shishutsu, seisan kikaku to shouhi, subete no burokku de jouhou wo PDF to ekuserufo-matto de kanransurukoto ga kanou desu," pi-ta- ha meigenshimasu.

"私たちは全ての重要な点を議論しました。開発は3ヶ月以上はかかりません。このぷろじぇくとには私たちの専門家4人が携

correctly, Peter. We want each of our clients to receive up to date information on time," says William.

"It can be done in the form of a subscription to your company mailing list," Peter offers.

"Yes. It will be convenient," notes William.

"Viewing the data in PDF and Excel formats may be available in all blocks: the warehouse accounting, revenues/expenses, production planning and spending," clarifies Peter.

"We have discussed all the important points. The development will take no longer than three months. This project should engage four of our specialists. In

わります。加えて、私たちは利用者にとって使いやすいいんたーふぇーすを作成します。このぷろぐらむを使う能力を早めるに、私たちはあなたに別のゆにっとを試験のために送ることができます。もし何か問題があれば、私たちは開発でそれを取り除きます。"ぴーたーは言います。

"watashitachi ha subete no juuyounaten wo giron shimashita. Kaihatsu ha sankagetsuijou ha kakarimasen. kono purojekuto niha watashitachi no senmonka yonin ga tazusawarimasu. kuwaete, watashitachi ha riyoushani totte tsukaiyasui inta-fe-su wo sakusei shimasu. Kono puroguramu wo tsukau nouryoku wo hayameruni, watashitachi ha anata ni betsuno yunitto wo shiken no tameni okurukoto ga dekimasu. moshi nanika mondai ga areba, watashitachi ha sore wo kaihatsu de torinozokimasu." pi-ta- ha iimasu.

"わかりました。これは良い提案です。それでは2か月後に、私たちは試験済みで、私たちの会社の特徴に合わせて修正された、使う準備のできた情報処理しすてむを受け取ります。私たちの従業員はあのような種類のぷろぐらむを提供してくれる利便性に感謝します。これは仕事をより正確にし、そして時間を節約します。"うぃりあむは言います。

"wakarimashita. kore ha iiteian desu. soredeha nikagetsugo ni, watashitachi ha shiken zumide, watashitachi no kaisha no tokuchou ni awasete shuuseisareta, tsukaujunbi no dekita jouhoushori shisutemu wo uketorimasu. watashitachi no juugyouin ha anoyouna shurui no puroguramu wo

addition we will create a user-friendly interface. To speed up the ability to use this program, we can send you separate units for testing. If there are any complaints, we will already eliminate them in development," says Peter.

"OK. This is a good suggestion. Then in two months, we will receive a ready-to-use data processing system, tested and modified to the peculiarities of our company. Our employees will appreciate the convenience of those kinds of programs provide. This makes the work more accurate and saves time," says William.

teikyoushitekureru ribensei ni kanshashimasu. kore ha shigoto wo yori seikakunishi, soshite jikan wo setsuyakushimasu." uiriamu ha iimasu.

"さて私たちはあなたと値段をはっきりさせる必要があります。そのようなぷろぐらむには事前に決められた値段をがありません。全てはぷろぐらむの明確な詳細に依ります。私たちのこのぷろぐらむの価値の仮見積もりは10万どるです。私は値段はこれよりは高くならないと断言することができます。あなたが私たちの常連の顧客であることとあなたの割引の大きさを考えると、値段は低くなるだけです。"ぴーたーは説明します。

"sate watashitachi ha anata to nedan wo hakkirisaseru hitsuyou ga arimasu. Sonoyouna puroguramu niha jizen ni kimerareta nedan ha arimasen. subete ha puroguramu no meikaku na shousai ni yorimsu. watashitachi no kono puroguramu no kachi no karimitsumori ha juumandoru desu. watashi ha nedan ha koreyori ha takakunaranaito dangensurukoto ga dekimasu. Anata ga watashitachi no jourenno kokyaku dearukoto to anata no waribiki no ookisa wo kangaeruto, nedan ha hikukunaru dake desu." pi-ta- ha setsumei shimasu.

"良かった、ぴーたー。あなたの条件はいつも通り有利です。完成したぷろぐらむを見るのを楽しみにしています。"うぃりあむは言います。

"yokatta, pi-ta-. anata no jouken ha itsumodoori yuuri desu. kanseishita puroguramu wo miruno wo tanoshimini shiteimasu." uiriamu ha iimasu.

"Now we need to clarify the price with you. Such programs do not have a predefined price. Everything depends on the specific details of the program. Our preliminary estimate for the value of this program is one hundred thousand dollars. I can say that the price won't go higher. When we consider that you are our regular customer and the size of your discount, then the price only gets lower," explains Peter.

"Good, Peter. Your terms are advantageous as always. Looking forward to seeing the finished program," says William.

テキストについての質問

1. 開発者は何を実行する準備ができていますか？
2. そふとうぇあはどうあっぷでーとしますか？
3. 専門家は何をすでに始めましたか？
4. ぷろぐらむに作成されたぶろっくは何ですか？
5. 何が考えられる必要がありますか？
6. それぞれの卸売り顧客に何をするべきですか？
7. 全ての顧客は何を時間内に受け取るべきですか？
8. 何人の専門家がこのぷろじぇくとに携わるべきですか？
9. 試験として何が送られますか？
10. 彼らは2か月で何を手に入れますか？
11. ぷろぐらむの見積もり価格は何ですか？

Questions about the text

1. What are developers ready to perform?
2. How does the software update?
3. What have the specialists already started to do?
4. What are the blocks created in the program?
5. What needs to be considered?
6. What should be done for each wholesale customer?
7. What should every customer receive in time?
8. How many experts should be engaged in this project?
9. What can be sent for testing?
10. What do they get in two months?
11. What is the estimated cost of the program?

19

Audio

氷を砕く
Break the ice

お父さんは幼稚園(ようちえん)に行く前(まえ)に娘(むすめ)の着替(きが)えの手伝(てつだ)いをしています。
帽子(ぼうし)をかぶせ、マフラー(まふら)を首(くび)に巻(ま)き付けていた時(とき)です。
"パパ(ぱぱ)、もっときつく巻(ま)いて"と娘(むすめ)は言(い)いました。
お父さんは強(つよ)くマフラー(まふら)を強(つよ)く巻(ま)き直(なお)しました。
"もっときつく！"と再(ふたた)び娘(むすめ)は言(い)いました。
再(ふたた)びマフラー(まふら)を強(つよ)く巻(ま)きました。
"もっときつく！"と娘(むすめ)は言(い)い、お父さんは娘(むすめ)

A daddy is dressing his little daughter for kindergarten. He puts a hat on her head and ties a scarf around her.
"Daddy, stronger," the daughter says.
The dad ties the scarf stronger.
"Stronger, daddy," the daughter says again.
The dad ties the scarf even stronger.
"Daddy, stronger!"
The dad looks attentively

み
を見ました。

"きつすぎじゃない？"とお父さんは娘に聞きます。
"きつすぎ、きつすぎ！"
お父さんは娘からマフラーを外し、彼らは幼稚園へ行きました。

at his daughter.
"May be too strong, dear?" he asks.
"Too strong, daddy, too strong!"
The dad removes the scarf and they go to kindergarten.

otōsan wa yōchien ni iku mae ni musume no kigae no tetsudai o shiteimasu. bōshi o kabuse, mafura- o kubi ni makitsuketeita toki desu. papa, motto kitsuku maite to musume wa iimashita. otōsan wa tsuyoku mafura- o tsuyoku makinaoshimashita. motto kitsuku! to futatabi musume wa iimashita. futatabi mafura- o tsuyoku makimashita. motto kitsuku! to musume wa ii, otōsan wa musume o mimashita. kitsusugi janai? to otōsan wa musume ni kikimasu. kitsusugi, kitsusugi! otōsan wa musume kara mafura- o hazushi, karera wa yōchien e ikimashita.

代表の中国への出張
A representative's trip to China

単語
Words

1. 50、五十 [gojuu] - fifty
2. 〜の中 [〜 no naka] - in
3. あらかじめ [arakajime] - in advance
4. ささいな、マイナーな [sasaina, maina-na] - insignificant, minor

5. むしろ / より早く / きっと～でありそうな [mushiro/ yori hayaku/ kitto ～ de arisouna] - rather / faster / likely
6. ゴール、目標 [go-ru, mokuhyou] - goal, target
7. サインする、署名する(動詞) [sain suru, shomei suru (doushi)] - sign *(Verb)*
8. ルート、方向 [ru-to, houkou] - route, direction
9. 一般の [ippanno] - general
10. 営業マン、ディーラー [eigyouman, di-ra-] - salesman, dealer
11. 気分悪くなる、病気になる [kibun ga warukunaru, byouki ni naru] - be ill, to be sick
12. 議論、話し合い [giron, hanashiai] - discussion
13. 驚く(動詞)、不思議に思う、驚く [odorok (doushi), fushigi ni omou, odoroku] - wonder *(Verb)*, to be surprised
14. 見せる(動詞) [miseru (doushi)] - show *(Verb)*
15. 後で [atode] - later
16. 考える(動詞)、考慮する [kangaeru (doushi), kouryosuru] - consider *(Verb)*
17. 行う(動詞)、携わる [okonau (doushi), tazusawaru] - do *(Verb)*, to engage
18. 時間内に(何かを)行う [jikannai ni (nanika wo) okonau - do (something) in time
19. 取引、売買 [torihiki, baibai] - deal, transaction
20. 出張、旅 [shucchou, tabi] - trip
21. 準備、訓練 [junbi, kunren] - preparation, training
22. 心配する(動詞) [shinpaisuru (doushi)] - worry *(Verb)*
23. 全ての、全部の [subeteno, zenbuno] - all, overall
24. 断言する(動詞) [dangensuru (doushi)] - assert *(Verb)*, to confirm, to approve
25. 難しい、複雑な [muzukashii, fukuzatsuna] - difficult, complicated
26. 認める(動詞) [mitomeru (doushi)] - approve *(Verb)*
27. 保証する(動詞) [hoshousuru (doushi)] - assure *(Verb)*
28. 忘れる [wasureru (doushi)] - forget *(Verb)*
29. 北京 [pekin] - Beijing
30. 未来 [mirai] - future
31. 有名 [yuumei] - popular
32. 予定していない [yotei shiteinai] - unplanned
33. 頼む、要求 [tanomu, youkyuu] - request

B

"みかえる、このめっせーじはあなたのためみたいですよ。私たちの中国のぱーとなーが申し出をふぁっくすしました。"さんどらは言います。
"mikaeru, kono messe-ji ha anata no tame mitai desuyo.

"Michael, this message is likely for you. Our Chinese partners faxed an

watashitachi no chuugoku no pa-tona- ga moushide wo fakkusu shimashita." sandora ha iimasu.

"ありがとうございます。私はそれを私たちのまねーじゃーに見せなければなりません。"みかえるは応答します。

"arigatougozaimasu. watashi ha sore wo watashitachi no mane-ja- ni misenakereba narimasen." mikaeru ha outoushimasu.

まねーじゃーとの会話の後。
mane-ja- tono kaiwa no ato.

"さんどら、私はあなたの助けが必要です。私たちの秘書が病気です。そのため、私たちのまねーじゃーはあなたに私たちの代表の中国への出張の準備を開始してと言っています。"みかえるは言います。

"sandora, watashi ha anata no tasuke ga hitsuyou desu. watashitachi no hisho ga byouki desu. sonotame, watashitachi no mane-ja- ha anatani watashitachi no daihyou no chuugoku heno shucchou no junbi wo kaishishite to itteimasu." mikaeru ha iimasu.

"これは予定されていない出張です!"さんどらは驚いています。

"kore ha yotei sareteinai shucchou desu!" sandora ha odoroiteimasu.

"はい、私たちの中国のぱーとなーは広告の申し出を送ってきました。私たちのまねーじゃーはそれを認め、そして彼はそれは私たちに有利であると主張します。"みかえるは説明します。

"hai, watashitachi no chuugoku no pa-tona- ha koukoku no moushide wo okutte kimashita. watashitachi no mane-ja- ha sore wo mitome, soshite kare ha sore ha watashitachi ni yuuri

offer," says Sandra.

"Thank you. I have to show it to our manager," Michael responds.

After a conversation with the manager.

"Sandra, I need your help. Our secretary is sick. Therefore, our manager asks you to start preparations for our representative's trip to China," says Michael.

"This is an unplanned trip!" Sandra is surprised.

"Yes, our Chinese partners sent us a commercial offer. Our manager approved it, and he claims that it is advantageous for us," explains Michael.

"Who will be the representative from

de aruto shuchoushimasu." mikaeru ha setsumeishimasu.

"誰が私たちの会社の代表になりますか？"さんどらは尋ねます。
"dare ga watashitachi no kaisha no daihyou ni narimasuka?" sandora ha tazunemasu.

"一番ありそうなのは、ぽーるです。彼は交渉の時に自信を持って行動し、そしてはっきりと説得力を持って話すことができます。"みかえるは言います。
"ichiban arisounano ha po-ru desu. kare ha koushou no toki ni jishin wo motte koudoushi, soshite settokuryoku wo motte hanasukoto ga dekimasu." mikaeru ha iimasu.

"けれどもぽーるは中国語を知りません！"さんどらは驚いています。
"keredomo po-ru ha chuugokugo wo shirimasen!" sandora ha odoroiteimasu.

"私たちの通訳が彼と一緒に行きます。彼女は沢山彼を助けることができます。"みかえるは言います。
"watashitachi no tsuuyaku ga kare to isshoni ikimasu. kanojo ha takusan kare wo tasukerukoto ga dekimasu." mikaeru ha iimasu.

"私は彼らの出張の準備のために何をする必要がありますか？"さんどらは尋ねます。
"watashi ha karera no shucchou no junbi no tameni nani wo suru hitsuyou ga arimasuka?" sandora ha tazunemasu.

"私たちは飛行機のちけっとを予約し、そしてほてるでを2部屋予約する必要があります。"みかえるは

our company?" asks Sandra.

"Most likely, it will be Paul. He acts confidently at negotiations and can speak clearly and convincingly," says Michael.

"But Paul does not know Chinese!" Sandra is surprised.

"Our interpreter will go with him. She can help him a lot," says Michael.

"What do I need to do to prepare their trip?" Sandra asks.

"We need to book plane tickets and to book two rooms at a hotel," continues Michael.

"Where will the negotiations take place and when is the

191

続けます。
"watashitachi ha hikouki no chiketto wo yoyakushi, soshite hoteru wo futaheya yoyakusuru hitsuyou ga arimasu." mikaeru ha tsudukemasu.

"交渉はどこで行われますか、そして出張はいつ行われますか?"さんどらは尋ねます。
"koushou ha dokode okonawaremasuka, soshite shucchou ha itsu okonawaremasuka?" sandora ha tazunemasu.

"出張は1週間後に行われる予定です。交渉は北京で行われます。私たちは全てを時間内に行わなければなりません。"みかえるは心配します。
"shucchou ha isshuukango ni okonawareru yotei desu. koushou ha pekin de okonawaremasu. watashitachi ha subete wo jikannai ni okonawanakereba narimasen." mikaeru ha shinpaishimasu.

"私は次のふらいとのちけっとを予約するために航空会社に今日電話をしたいです。今月中国へのちけっとを買うのは難しいです。中国へのるーとは今とても人気です。"さんどらは言います。
"watashi ha tsugino furaito no chiketto wo yoyaku surutameni koukuugaisha ni kyou denwa wo shitai desu. kongetsu chuugoku heno chiketto wo kaunoha muzukashii desu. chuugoku heno ru-to ha ima totemo ninki desu." sandora ha iimasu.

"はい、あなたは正しいです。あらかじめ行う方が良いです。"みかえるは追加します。
"hai, anata ha tadashii desu. arakajime okonauhou ga iidesu."

"trip planned to take place?" asks Sandra.

"The trip is planned to take place in a week. The negotiations will be held in Beijing. We have to do everything on time," Michael worries.

"I want to call the airline today to book their tickets for the next flight. Buying tickets to China is difficult this month. The Chinese route is very popular now," says Sandra.

"Yes, you're right; it's better to do it in advance," adds Michael.

"I sent an inquiry to several Beijing hotels. The answer about room availability should come in an

mikaeru ha tsuikashimasu.

"私はいくつかの北京のほてるに問い合わせを送りました。部屋の利用状況についての答えは1時間後に来るはずです。"さんどらは言います。
"watashi ha ikutsuka no pekin no hoteru ni toiawase wo okurimashita. heya no riyoujoukyou ni tsuite no kotae ha ichijikango ni kuruhazu desu." sandora ha iimasu.

中国のぱーとなーとの今後の交渉についての詳細の議論はまねーじゃーの事務所で進行中です。
chuugoku no pa-tona- tono kongo no koushou ni tsuiteno shousai no giron ha mane-ja- no jimusho de shinkouchuu desu.

"商品のすとっくの残りがささいだということを考えると、私たちはいくつの製品のゆにっとを買うべきですか?"ぽーるはまねーじゃーに訪ねます。
"shouhin no sutokku no nokori ga sasaida toiukoto wo kangaeruto, watashitachi ha ikutsuno seihin no yunitto wo kaubeki desuka?" po-ru ha mane-ja- ni tazunemasu.

"この契約は製品を50,000ゆにっと補充することについてです。"まねーじゃーは応答します。"私たちの出張の目的は大きな商品のばっちを買って良い割引を受けることです。私たちの代表は今後同じ状況で一緒に働く可能性を含んだ1年間の契約書にさいんしなければなりません。"彼は言います。
"kono keiyaku ha seihin wo gomanyunitto hojuu surukotoni tsuite desu." mane-ja- ha outoushimasu. "watashitachi no shucchou no mokuteki ha ookina shouhin no bacchi wo katte ii

hour," says Sandra.

A discussion of details about the future negotiations with the Chinese partners is under way in the manager's office.

"How many units of product should we buy, considering that the remainders of goods in stock are insignificant?" Paul asks the manager.

"This contract should be on the supply of fifty thousand units of the product," responds the manager. "The purpose of our trip is to get a good discount for buying a large batch of goods. Our representative must sign a contract for one year with the possibility of working

waribiki wo ukerukoto desu. watashitachi no daihyou ha kongo onaji joukyou de isshoni hataraku kanousei wo fukunda ichinenkan no keiyakusho ni sain shinakereba narimasen." kare ha iimasu.

"どんな配達時間が私たちにとって好都合ですか？"ぽーるは尋ねます。
"donna haitatsujikan ga watashitachi ni totte koutsugou desuka?" po-ru ha tazunemasu.

"私たちの注文から1か月以内です。また、売り手は自分たちの費用で商品を提供することについての議論を忘れてはいけません。それは普段商品の値段に含まれています。"まねーじゃーは続けます。
"watashitachi no chuumon kara ikkagetsuinai desu. Mata, urite ha jibuntachi no hiyou de shouhin wo teikyousurukoto nitsuite no giron wo wasureteha ikemasen. sore ha fudan shouhin no nedan ni fukumarete imasu." mane-ja- ha tsudukemasu.

"ぽーる、私はあなたを当てにしています。この取引は私たちにとってとても有利です。"まねーじゃーは意見します。
"po-ru, watashitachi ha anata wo ateni shiteimasu. kono torihiki ha watashitachi ni totte totemo yuuri desu." mane-ja- ha ikenshimasu.

"全てに私の能力を最大限につかいます。"ぽーるは保証します。
"subete ni watashi no nouryoku wo saidaigen ni tsukaimasu." po-ru ha hoshoushimasu.

together in the future under the same conditions," he says.

"What products delivery times are convenient for us?" asks Paul.

"No longer than one month after our order. Also, do not forget to discuss that the seller must supply the goods at his own expense. It is usually taken into account in the price of goods," the manager continues.

"Paul, I'm counting on you. This deal is very advantageous for us," notes the manager.

"I will do everything to the best of my abilities," assures Paul.

テキストについての質問

1. 中国のぱーとなーは何をふぁっくすしましたか？
2. まねーじゃーは何を頼みますか？
3. 誰が会社の代表になりますか？
4. ぽーるは交渉でどう動きますか？
5. 彼らは何を予約する必要がありますか？
6. 出張はいつ行われることが予定されていますか？
7. 交渉はどこで行われますか？
8. さんどらは問い合わせをどこに送りましたか？
9. どのような契約書であるべきですか？
10. 私たちの代表は何にさいんしなければなりませんか？
11. 売り手は自分たちの費用で何をするべきですか？
12. ぽーるは何をしますか？

Questions about the text

1. What did the Chinese partners fax?
2. What does the manager request?
3. Who will be the representative of the company?
4. How does Paul act in negotiations?
5. What do they need to book?
6. When is the trip planned to take place?
7. Where will the negotiations take place?
8. Where did Sandra send an inquiry?
9. What kind of contract should it be?
10. What must our representative sign?
11. What should the seller do at his own expense?
12. What will Paul do?

20

Audio

氷を砕く
Break the ice

少年(しょうねん)はお姉(ねえ)ちゃんのマニキュア(まにきゅあ)を注意深(ちゅういぶか)くみていました。
"リンダ(りんだ)、爪(つめ)長(なが)すぎない？"と少年(しょうねん)はお姉(ねえ)ちゃんに伝(つた)えました。
"長(なが)いよね、気(き)に入(はい)った？"と彼女(かのじょ)は言(い)った。
"うん、簡単(かんたん)に木登(きのぼ)り出来(でき)そうだよね！"

A little boy is looking attentively at his elder sister's manicure.
"Linda, your nails are so long," he says to her.
"Yes, they are. Do you like them?" the sister asks.
"Yes, I do. Your nails are cool. You can climb a tree easily!"

shōnen wa o nēchan no manikyua o chūibukaku miteimashita. Rinda, tsumechō suginai? to shōnen wa o nēchan ni tsutaemashita. nagai yo ne, kiniitta? to kanojo wa itta. un, kantan ni ki nobori dekisō da yo ne!

プログラムブロックの試験
Testing of program block

単語
Words

1. けれども / けれども [keredomo/keredomo] - but / though
2. せざるおえない [sezaruoenai] - obliged
3. つるす(動詞) [tsurusu] - hang *(Verb)*, to crash
4. なぜなら [nazenara] - because
5. アップデート [appude-to] - updated
6. アドバイスする(動詞) [adobaisusuru (doushi)] - advise *(Verb)*
7. サーバー [sa-ba-] - server
8. セル、箱 [seru, hako] - cell, box
9. テーブル [te-buru] - table
10. バージョン [ba-jon] - version
11. パラメーター [parame-ta-] - parameters
12. メール [me-ru] - mail
13. ユーザー [yu-za-] - user
14. 間違って [machigatte] - incorrectly
15. 機能 [kinou] - function
16. 極秘の [gokuhino] - confidential
17. 故障、問題 [koshou, mondai] - malfunction, trouble
18. 考慮した上で、考える [kouryoshita uede, kangaeru] - take into account, to consider
19. 再起動する(動詞)、リブートする [saikidousuru (douhsi), ribu-tosuru] - restart *(Verb)*, to reboot
20. 最初は、始め [saisho ha, hajimeni] - initially, first
21. 試す(動詞) [tamesu (doushi)] - try *(Verb)*

22. 試験された [shikensareta] - tested
23. 修正する(動詞) [shuuseisuru (doushi)] - modify (Verb)
24. 尋ねる(動詞) [tazuneru (doushi)] - ask (Verb)
25. 制限 / 上限 [seigen/ jougen] - restriction / limit
26. 倉庫 [souko] - warehouse
27. 追加 [tsuika] - addition
28. 提供する(動詞)、〜を含める [teikyousuru (doushi), 〜 wo fukumeru] - provide (Verb), to include
29. 電子の [denshino] - electronic
30. 動く(動詞) [ugoku (doushi)] - move (Verb)
31. 不正確 [fuseikaku] - inaccuracy
32. 変形 [henkei] - formation
33. 埋める [umeru] - fill out

B

"こんにちは、ういりあむと話をすることはできますか?" 男は尋ねます。
"konnichiha, uiriamu to hanashi wo surukoto ha dekimasuka?" otoko ha tazunemasu.

"はい、もちろん。私は彼に電話することができます。" 秘書は応答します。
"hai, mochiron. watashi ha kare ni denwa surukoto ga dekimasu." hisho ha outoushimasu.

"ぴーたー、私はあなたから連絡がきて嬉しいです。あなたは私たちに何かにゅーすはありますか?" ういりあむは尋ねます。
"pi-ta-, watashi ha anatakara renraku ga kite ureshii desu. anata ha watashitachi ni nanika nyu-su ha arimasuka?" uiriamu ha tazunemasu.

"はい、あります。私たちは試験のためにぷろぐらむぶろっくを1つあなたに送りたいです。これがいんべんとりーこんとろーるです。私たちはそれを始めに

"Hello, can I speak to William?" the man asks.

"Yes, of course. I can call him," responds the secretary.

"Peter, I'm glad to hear from you. Do you have any news for us?" asks William.

"Yes, we do. We want to send you one program block for testing. This is the inventory control. We are developing it first because more flaws and inaccuracies occur in it," explains

開発しています、なぜなら沢山の欠点と誤作動が起こるからです。"ぴーたーは説明します。

"hai, arimasu. watashitachi ha shiken no tameni puroguramu burokku wo hitotsu anata ni okuritai desu. kore ga inbenntori-kontoro-ru desu. watashitachi ha sore wo hajimeni kaihatsu shiteimasu, nazenara takusan no ketten to gosadou ga okorukara desu." pi-ta- ha setsumei shimasu.

"まあ、私はめーるを30分後に確認することができます。もしぷろぐらむがそこにあれば、私はそれをめいんさーばーからしすてむへ起動させます。それからぷろぐらむは事務所の全てのこんぴゅーたーからあくせすすることができます。"うぃりあむは明言します。

"ma, watashi ha me-ru wo sanjuppungo ni kakunin surukoto ga dekimasu. moshi puroguramu ga sokoni areba, watashi ha sore wo meinsa-ba- kara shisutemu he kidou sasemasu. sorekara puroguramu ha jimusho no subete no konpyu-ta- kara akusesu surukoto ga dekimasu." uiriamu ha meigenshimasu.

"私はでーたにあくせすできる事務所にいるゆーざーの輪を制限することを勧めます。それはあなたの会社の極秘情報だと考えられます。"ぴーたーは言います。

"watashi ha de-ta ni akusesudekiru jimusho ni iru yu-za- no wa wo seigensurukoto wo susumemasu. sore ha anata no kaisha no gokuhi jouhou dato kangaeraremasu." pi-ta- ha iimasu.

"警告ありがとうございます。それはとても重要です"うぃりあむは応答します。

"keikoku arigatougozaimasu. sore ha totemo juuyoudesu."

Peter.

"Well, I can check my email in half an hour. If the program is there, I will run it from my main server into the system. The program can then be accessed by all the office computers," clarifies William.

"I advise you to limit the circle of users in the office to whom this data may be accessible. It is considered confidential information for your company," says Peter.

"Thank you for the warning. It is really important," William responds.

Four hours pass. The phone rings in the software company.

"Peter, this is William.

uiriamu ha outoushimasu.

4時間が経過します。そふとうぇあ会社の電話が鳴ります。

yojikan ga keika shimasu. sofutoueagaisha no denwa ga narimasu.

"ぴーたー、うぃりあむです。えくせるあぷりけーしょんに問題があります。問題は様々な期間のてーぶるに正しくでーたが表示されていないことです。倉庫にある残りが自動的に次の月に移動されません。また、返金が会計に計上されておらず、いくつかのせるが埋まっていません。"うぃりあむは言います。

"pi-ta-, uiriamu desu. ekuseru apurike-shon ni mondai ga arimasu. mondai ha samazama na kikan no te-buruni tadashiku de-ta ga hyouji sareteinaikoto desu. souko ni aru nokori ga jidoutekini tsugino tsuki ni idou saremasen. mata, henkin ga kaikei ni keijou sareteorazu, ikutsuka no seru ga umatteimasen." uiriamu ha iimasu.

"わかりました、私たちはこれらの面を修正しなければなりません。私は直ぐに新しいばーじょんをあなたに送ります。"ぴーたーは答えます。

"wakarimashita, watashitachi ha korera no men wo shuusei shinakereba narimasen. watashi ha suguni atarashii ba-jon wo anatani okurimasu." pi-ta- ha iimasu.

1日後、ぴーたーは新しいばーじょんのぷろぐらむと収入/支出の集計ぶろっくを送ります。

ichinichigo, pi-ta- ha atarashii ba-jon no puroguramu to shuunyuu/shishutsu no shuukei burokku wo okurimasu.

"ぴーたー、いんべんとりーの会計ぷろぐらむは良く

We are having trouble with the Excel application. The problem is that the data is not displayed correctly in the tables for different periods. The remainders in the warehouse are not automatically transferred to the next month. Also, returns are not taken into account, some cells are not filled," says William.

"OK, we have to modify these aspects. Soon I will send you a new version," Peter answers.

A day later, Peter sends a new version of the program, and the revenues/expenses accounting block.

"Peter, the inventory accounting program

動いています。けれどもしばらくすると、こんぴゅーたーがくらっしゅし始めました。"うぃりあむは言います。
"pi-ta-, inbentori- no kaikeipuroguramu ha yoku ugoiteimasu. keredomo shibarakusuruto, konpyu-ta- ga kurasshu shihajimemashita." uiriamu ha iimasu.

"私はあなたがさーばーをりぶーとする必要があると思います。もしそれが助けにならないならば、それぞれのこんぴゅーたーを再起動してください。"ぴーたーは勧めます。
"watashi ha anata ga sa-ba- wo ribu-tosuru hitsuyou ga aruto omoimasu. moshi sore ga tasukeni naranainaraba, sorezore no konpyu-ta- wo saikidou shitekudasai." pi-ta- ha susumemasu.

"わかりました、これが助けになることを希望します。"うぃりあむは言います。
"wakarimashita, kore ga tasukeninarukoto wo kiboushimasu." uiriamu ha iimasu.

"うぃりあむ、製造費用機能が良く動いているかどうか確認する必要があります。それは収入/支出集計のぶろっくの中の別のてーぶるに表示されているはずです。"ぴーたーは言います。
"uiriamu, seizouhiyou kinou ga yoku ugoite irunokadouka kakuninsuru hitsuyou ga arimasu. sore ha shuunyuu/shishutsu shuukei no burokku no naka no betsu no te-buru ni hyoujisarete isruhazudesu." pi-ta- ha iimasu.

"数日後に、私たちはあなたに値段表作成のためのしすてむと値段の履歴の表示を試験のために送ることができるようになります。"彼

"works well. But after a while, the computers begin to crash," says William.

"I think you need to reboot the server. If this does not help, then restart each computer," advises Peter.

"OK, I hope this will help," says William.

"William, you need to check whether the production costs function is working OK. It should be displayed in a separate table in the block for revenues/expenses accounting," says Peter.

"In a few days, we will be able to send you a system for price lists generation and the price history display for testing," he continues.

は続けます。

"suujitsugo ni, watashitachi ha anata ni nedanhyou sakusei no tameno shisutemu to nedan no rireki no hyouji wo shiken notameni okurukoto ga dekiruyouni narimasu." kare ha tsudukemasu.

値段表と買い手の為の割引計算のせくしょんが試験されました。しすてむ管理者とぷろぐらまーはしすてむの詳細について再度話し合います。

nedanhyou to kaite no tameno waribiki keisan no sekushon ga shikensaremashita. shisutemukanrisha to purogurama- ha shisutemu no shousaini tsuite saido hanashiaimasu.

"私たちはあっぷでーとした値段表を卸売り顧客に送ろうとしました。けれども割引計算のしすてむが正しく動きません；もしかしたらそれぞれの卸売り顧客のための計算ぱらめーたーが間違ってせっとされているのかもしれません。そして新しい顧客追加のための計算が提供されていません。各大きな卸売り業者の商品の購入の後顧客情報があっぷでーとされると便利になります。"
管理者は説明します。

"watashitachi ha appude-toshita nedanhyou wo oroshiuri kokyaku ni okurouto shimashita. keredomo waribikikeisan no shisutemu ga tadashiku ugokimasen; moshikashitara sorezoreno oroshiuri kokyaku no tameno keisanparame-ta- ga machigatte setto sareteirunokamo shiremsen. soshite atarashii kokyaku tsuika no tameno keisan ga teikyou sareteimasen. kaku ookina oroshiuri gyousha no shouhin no kounyu no ato kokyakujouhou ga appude-to sareruto benrini

The price lists and calculating discounts for buyers sections were tested. The system administrator and the programmer discuss the system details again.

"We tried to send an updated price list to our wholesale customers. But the discount calculation system does not work properly; perhaps the calculation parameters for each wholesale customer are set incorrectly. And calculations for the addition of new customers are not provided. It would be convenient if customer data is updated after each major wholesale purchase," explains the administrator.

narimasu." kanrisha ha setsumeishimasu.

"顧客への自動めーりんぐしすてむの動きはどうですか?"ぴーたーは尋ねます。

"kokyaku heno jidoume-ringu shisutemu no ugoki ha doudesuka?" pi-ta- ha tazunemasu.

"私たちが新しいぷろぐらむを使って値段表を作成し、顧客に送信してからその評価と試験をすることができます。"ういりあむは説明します。

"watashitachi ga atarashii puroguramu wo tsukatte nedanhyou wo sakuseishi, kokyaku ni soushin shitekara sono hyouka to shaken wo surukoto ga dekimasu." uiriamu ha setsumeishimasu.

"わかりました。時間が経つにつれて全体のぷろぐらむを開始することができます。そしたら私たちの開発者があなたの事務所で仕事をし、その場でとらぶるしゅーてぃんぐを実行しなければなりません。"ぴーたーは結論付けます。

"wakarimashita. Jikan ga tatsuni tsurete zentai no puroguramu wo kaishisurukoto ga dekimasu. soshitara watashitachi no kaihatsusha ga anata no jimusho de shigoto wo shi, sonoba de toraburushu-tingu wo jikkou shinakereba narimasen." pi-ta- ha ketsurondukemasu.

"How is the automatic mailing to customers system behaving?" asks Peter.

"It will be possible to assess and test after we create and send the price list to customers using the new program," explains William.

"OK. Over time we will be able to run the entire program. Then our developers will have to work in your office and perform on-site troubleshooting," concludes Peter.

C

テキストについての質問

1. 彼らは試験の為に何を送りたいですか?
2. ぷろぐらむはどこで入手可能ですか?

Questions about the text

1. What do they want to send for testing?
2. Where can the

3. ぴーたーはどの制限(せいげん)を設定(せってい)することを勧(すす)めますか？
4. どのぷろぐらむが問題(もんだい)を抱(かか)えていますか？
5. ぴーたーは1日(にち)で何(なに)を送(おく)りますか？
6. ぴーたーはういりあむに何(なに)を勧(すす)めますか？
7. ういりあむは何(なに)を確認(かくにん)するべきですか？
8. 値段表作成(ねだんひょうさくせい)のためのしすてむはいつ試験(しけん)の為(ため)に送信(そうしん)されますか？
9. しすてむ管理者(かんりしゃ)とぷろぐらまーは何(なに)を話(はな)し合(あ)いますか？
10. どのぱらめーたーが間違(まちが)って設定(せってい)されていますか？
11. 新(あたら)しい顧客(こきゃく)に何(なに)が提供(ていきょう)されていませんか？
12. 開発者(かいはつしゃ)はどこでとらぶるしゅーてぃんぐを行(おこな)いますか？

program be available?
3. Which limit does Peter advise to set?
4. Which program is having trouble?
5. What does Peter send in a day?
6. What does Peter advise William?
7. What should William check?
8. When will the system for generating price lists be sent for testing?
9. What do the system administrator and the programmer discuss?
10. What parameters are set incorrectly?
11. What is not provided for new customers?
12. Where will developers have to troubleshoot?

21

氷を砕く
Break the ice

お母さんは 幼(おさな)い息子(むすこ)に 靴(くつ)を履(は)かせようとしています。
"足(あし)上(あ)げて"と 右足(みぎあし)を持(も)っているお母さん言(い)いました。しかし 彼(かれ)は 逆(ぎゃく)の 足(あし)をあげたのです。
"逆(ぎゃく)の 足(あし)をあげて"とお母さんは 言(い)いましたが また 違(ちが)う 足(あし)をあげました。
"逆(ぎゃく)の 足(あし)をあげて"と 彼女(かのじょ)はもう 一回(いっかい)言(い)いました。

A mom is helping her little son put on his shoes.
"Lift up a foot," she says holding the right shoe. The son lifts a foot, but the mom sees it is the wrong one.
"Lift up the other foot," she says. The son lifts another foot, but the mom sees it is really the wrong one now.
"Lift up the other foot," she says again. The son looks around him in surprise.

息子(むすこ)は辺(あた)りを見渡(みわた)して、驚(おどろ)いたように、"もう足(あし)ないよ！"と答(こた)えました。
"ごめんね、坊(ぼう)や"と言(い)いお母さんは笑顔(えがお)で靴(くつ)を履(は)かせ、"準備(じゅんび)できたよ"と言(い)いました。

"I do not have anymore!" he answers.
"I am sorry, dear," the mom smiles, putting the shoes on. "Now you are set!"

okāsan wa osanai musuko ni kutsu o hakaseyou to shiteimasu. ashi agete to migiashi o motteiru okāsan iimashita. shikashi kare wa gyaku no ashi o ageta no desu. gyaku no ashi o agete to okāsan wa iimashita ga mata chigau ashi o agemashita. gyaku no ashi o agete to kanojo wa mō ichi kai iimashita. musuko wa atari o miwatashite, odoroita yōni, mō ashi nai yo! to kotaemashita. gomen ne, bōya to ii okāsan wa egao de kutsu o hakase junbi dekita yo to iimashita.

北京
Beijing

単語
Words

1. 40、四十 [yonjuu] - forty
2. 7日、七日 [nanoka] - seventh
3. 〜の向かいに、〜の前に [〜no mukaini, 〜no maeni] - across from / in front of
4. 〜の前 [〜no mae] - before
5. きれい [kirei] - clean
6. さまざまな [samazamana] - various
7. したがって、ここから [shitagatte, kokokara] - hence / from here

8. エレベーター [erebe-ta-] - elevator
9. タクシー [takushi-] - taxi, cab
10. テクノロジー [tekunoroji-] - technology
11. パスする(動詞) [pasusuru (doushi)] - pass (Verb)
12. パノラマ式の [panoramashikino] - panoramic
13. ビジネス [bijinesu] - business
14. ビジネスカード [bijinesuka-do] - business card
15. フライト [furaito] - flight
16. 愛する [aisuru (doushi)] - love (Verb)
17. 安心、嬉しい、喜ばしい [anshin, ureshii, yorokobashii] - glad, happy, joyful
18. 位置する [ichisuru] - be located, located
19. 一部 [ichibu] - part
20. 右の、右に [migino, migini] - to the right
21. 運ぶ(動詞) [hakobu (doushi)] - carry (Verb)
22. 影響する(動詞) [eikyousuru (douhshi)] - influence (Verb)
23. 横、側 [yoko, soba] - side
24. 横になる / ベッドに入る、寝る [yokoni naru/ beddo ni hairu, neru] - lay down / to go to bed
25. 回転する(動詞) [kaitensuru(doushi)] - turn (Verb), to rotate
26. 外国 [gaikoku] - foreign
27. 革新的な [kakushintekina] - innovative
28. 基本 [kihon] - basic
29. 帰る、戻る(動詞) [kaeru, modoru (doushi)] - return (Verb)
30. 休む、休養、休憩する(動詞)、リラックスする [yasumu, kyuuyou, kyuukeisuru, rirakkusu suru] - rest, recreation (Verb), to relax
31. 空港、[kuukou] - airport
32. 迎える(動詞) [mukaeru (doushi)] - welcome (Verb), to greet
33. 結局は、最後は [kekkyoku ha, saigo ha] - eventually, at last
34. 建てられた、建設された [taterareta, kensetsusareta] - built
35. 建築上の [kenchikujouno] - architectural
36. 建築物 [kenchikubutsu] - architecture
37. 鍵 [kagi] - key
38. 交換 [koukan] - exchange
39. 工学、エンジニアリング [kougaku, enjiniaringu] - engineering
40. 行く(動詞)、へ向かう [iku (doushi), he mukau] - go (Verb), to head
41. 高層建築 [kousoukenchiku] - highrise
42. 高速 / 早い [kousoku, hayai] - high speed / fast
43. 左の、左に [hidarino, hidarini] - to the left
44. 残る(動詞) [nokru (douhsi)] - stay (Verb)
45. 支払われた [shiharawareta] - paid
46. 止まる(動詞) [tomaru (doushi)] - stop (Verb)
47. 視界、景色 [shikai, keshiki] - view
48. 事業欲 [jigyouyoku] - entrepreneurship
49. 車 [kuruma] - car
50. 取る(動詞) [toru (doushi)] - take (Verb)
51. 出る、出発する [deru, shuppatsusuru] - go out, to leave
52. 上手く、成功して [umau, seijoushite] - successfully

53. 食事する(動詞) [shokujisuru (doushi)] - dine (Verb)
54. 人々 [hitobito] - people
55. 数字、番号 [suuji, nanba-] - number
56. 正午 [shougo] - noon
57. 説明する(動詞) [setsumeisuru (doushi)] - explain (Verb)
58. 素晴らしい [subarashii] - amazing
59. 壮大な、豪華な [soudaina, goukana] - magnificent, gorgeous
60. 早い [hayai] - early
61. 大きな、巨大な [ookina, kyodaina] - huge
62. 知らせる(動詞) [shiraseru (doushi)] - acquaint (Verb)
63. 知られている [shirareteiru] - known
64. 地域の [chiikino] - regional
65. 着陸する(動詞) [chakurikusuru (doushi)] - land (Verb)
66. 中央 [chuuou] - central
67. 注文 [chuumon] - order
68. 伝統的な [dentoutekina] - traditional
69. 登る(動詞) [noboru (doushi)] - climb (Verb)
70. 統括会社、ヘッドクオーター [toukatsugaisha, heddokuo-ta-] - headquarter
71. 動かす、動く [ugokasu, ugoku] - move
72. 道 [michi] - path
73. 道路 [douro] - road
74. 得る、学ぶ [toru, manabu] - acquire
75. 南の [minamino] - southern
76. 入口 [iriguchi] - entrance
77. 配達する(動詞) [haitatsusuru (doushi)] - deliver (Verb)
78. 疲れさせる(動詞) [tsukaresaseru (doushi)] - tire (Verb)
79. 物 [mono] - thing
80. 歩く(動詞) [aruku] - walk (Verb)
81. 法人 [houji] - corporation
82. 満足できる、楽しい [manzokudekiru, tanoshii] - pleasant
83. 眠る(動詞) [nemuru (doushi)] - sleep (Verb)
84. 名づける、名前をあげる [nazukeru, namae wo ageru] - name
85. 名声 [meisei] - fame
86. 友達 [tomodachi] - friend
87. 予約した [yoyakushita] - booked
88. 与える、渡す(動詞) [ataeru, watasu (doushi)] - give (Verb)

B

飛行機は上手く北京に着陸しました。正午ごろに、ゆーろびっと会社代弁者のぽーるは北京空港の建物に入り、そこで中国の会社の代表のでみんぐとしゃんりーと出会います。彼らはお互いを暖かく迎

The plane successfully landed in Beijing airport. Around noon, Eurobit company spokesman Paul enters the building of the Beijing airport, where he

えます。
hikouki ha umaku pekin ni chakuriku shimashita. shougogoro ni, yu-robittogaisha daibensha no po-ru ha pekin kuukou no tatemono ni hairi, sokode chuugoku no kaisha no daihyou no demingu to shanri- to deaimasu. karera ha otagai wo atatakaku mukaemasu.

"ぽーる、ほてるに行く前に、私たちはあなたに私たちの事務所を見せ、そして交渉の正確な時間を設定したいです。"彼らは提案します。

"po-ru, hoteru ni ikumae ni, watashitachi ha anatani watashitachi no jimusho wo mise, soshite koushou no seikaku na jikan wo setteishitai desu." karera ha teianshimasu.

"良いですね。私はこの機会を貰えたことをとても嬉しく思います。私は初めて北京にいます。"ぽーるは答えます。

"iidesune. watashi ha kono kikai wo moraetakoto ni totemo ureshiidesu. watashi ha hajimete pekin ni imasu." po-ru ha kotaemasu.

"車が空港への主要な入り口の近くで私たちを待ってます。"しゃんりーは言います。

"kuruma ga kuukou heno shuyou na iriguchi no chikaku de watashitachi wo matteimasu." shanri- ha iimasu.

"空港から町の中央への旅は高速道路で40分かかります。"でみんぐが説明します。

"kuukou kara machi no chuuou heno tabi ha kousokudouro de yonjuppun kakarimasu." demingu ga setsumeishimasu.

車は町の主要な道を進みます。ぽーるは最新の工学てくのろじーによって建築され

is met by representatives of the Chinese company Deming and Shanley. They greet each other warmly.

"Paul, before going to the hotel, we want to show you our office and set the exact time for negotiations," they suggest.

"Good. I am very happy to have this opportunity. I am in Beijing for the first time," answers Paul.

"The car is waiting for us near the main entrance to the airport," says Shanley.

"The trip from the airport to the city center takes forty minutes on the highway," explains Deming.

The car goes down the main street of the city. Paul sees the magnificent highrise buildings constructed according to

た壮大な高層建築物を見ます。
kuruma ha machi no shuyou na michi wo susumimasu. poru ha saishin no kougaku tekunoroji- ni yotte kenchikusareta soudai na kousoukenchikubutsu wo mimasu.

"私たちは中央びじねす地区に向かっています。ここにはもだんな建築物があります。中国の伝統的な建築物は町の他の地域で見ることができます。"でみんぐは言います。
"watashitachi ha chuuou bijinesuchiku ni mukatteimasu. kokoni ha modan na kenchikubutsu ga arimasu. chuugoku no dentouteki na kenchikubutsu ha machi no hoka no chiiki de mirukoto ga dekimasu." demingu ha iimasu.

"びじねすせんたーへの道は町の主要地区を通り抜けます。私たちは喜んであなたを案内します。今私たちは北京のびじねすせんたーを通り抜けます。ここのは数多くのしょっぴんぐもーる、美しいもだんな建物、そして様々な法人の地域統括会社があります。"でみんぐは続けます。
"bijinesusenta- heno michi ha machi no shuyouchiku wo toorinukemasu. watashitachi ha yorokonde anata wo annaishiasu. ima watashitachi ha pekin no bijinesusenta- wo toorinukemasu. Kokko niha kazuooku no shoppingmoru, utsukushii modanna tatemono, soshite samazamana houjin no chiikitoukatsugaisha ga arimasu." demingu ha tsudukemasu.

"伝統的な財務せんたーは北京財務通りで、それはふしんめんとふちぇんめんの2つの地域に

the latest engineering technologies.

"We're heading to the Central Business District. There are modern architectural buildings here. China's traditional architecture can be seen in another part of the city," says Deming.

"The road to the business center passes through the central part of the city. We are happy to show it to you. Now we drive through the business center of Beijing. There are a large number of shopping malls, beautiful modern buildings, and the regional headquarters of various corporations," continues Deming.

"The traditional financial center is Beijing Financial Street, it is located in two areas: Fusinmen and Fuchenmen. Many banks

位置します。沢山の銀行と財務会社がここに位置します。右は主要銀行の建物です。"しゃんりーは指し示します。
"dentouteki na zaimusenta- ha pekinzaimudoori desu, soreha fushinmen to fuchenmen no futatsu no chiiki ni ichishimasu. takusan no ginkou to zaimugaisha ga koko ni ichishimasu. migi ha shuyouginkou no tatemono desu." shanri- ha sashishimeshimasu.
"私は北京は革新的な事業欲の中心として知られて来ていると知っています。"ぽーるは言います。
"watashi ha pekin ha kakushinteki na jigyouyoku no chuushin toshite shiraretekiteiruto shitteiimasu." po-ru ha iimasu.
"はい、沢山の外国と中国の革新的な会社はここで働いています。"でみんぐは言います。
"hai, takusan no gaikoku to chuugoku no kakushinteki na kaisha ha koko de hataraiteimasu." demingu ha iimasu.
車は左に曲がりそして巨大な建物への入り口の前で止まります。
kuruma ha hidari ni magari soshite kyodaina tatemono heno iriguchi no mae de tomarimasu.
"この建物の中には、びじねすせんたーと私たちの会社の事務所があります。"しゃんりーは続けます。
"kono tatemono no nakaniha, bijinesusenta- to watashitachi no kaisha no jimusho ga arimasu." shanri- ha tsudukemasu.
ぱーとなーたちは高速えれべーたーに入り、そし

and financial companies are located here. To your right is the building of a major bank," Shanley points out.

"I know that Beijing is becoming better known as a center of innovative entrepreneurship," says Paul.

"Yes, many foreign and Chinese innovative companies work here," says Deming.

The car turns left and stops in front of the entrance to a huge building.

"In this building, there are a business center and our company office," Shanley continues.

The partners enter the high-speed elevator and go up to the twenty-fifth floor.

"It has a beautiful view of

て25階に上がります。
pa-tona-tachi ha kousokuerebe-ta- ni hairi soshite nijuugokai ni agarimasu.

"町の南側の美しい景色が見えます。"でみんぐは言いそしてぱのらま式の窓に近づくようぽーるに勧めます。
"machi no minamigawa no utsukushi keshiki ga miemasu." demingu ha ii soshite panoramashiki no mado ni chikadukuyou po-ru ni susumemasu.

"あなたの町の素晴らしい建築物はとても美しいです。"ぽーるは言います。
"anata no machi no subarashii kenchikubutsu ha totemo utsukushii desu." po-ru ha iimasu.

"はい。中国の人は美しいものを全て愛しそして感謝します。"でみんぐは嬉しそうに応答します。
"hai. chuugoku no hito ha utsukushiimono wo subete aishi soshite kanshashimasu." demingu ha ureshisou ni outoushimasu.

彼らは事務所に入り、交渉を指揮するすたっふと会い、そしてびじねすかーどを交換しました。karera ha jimusho ni hairi, koushou wo shikisuru sutaffu to ai, soshite bijinesuka-do wo koukanshimashita.

"私たちは交渉を明日11時に行うことを提案します。この時間までには、交渉の進路に影響するかもしれない全ての基本的な物は解決されます。そして今彼らはあなたをふらいとの後休むことができる、ほて

---

the southern part of the city," says Deming and offers Paul to approach the panoramic window.

"Your city's amazing architecture is very beautiful," says Paul.

"Yes. The Chinese people love and appreciate everything beautiful," Deming responds happily.

They walk into the office, meet with the staff who will conduct the negotiations, and exchange business cards.

"We offer to hold negotiations tomorrow at eleven o'clock. By this time, all the basic things that can influence the course of the negotiations will be solved. And now they will take you to your hotel, where you can rest after the flight," says the Chinese company

るに連れて行きます。"中国の会社の代表は言います。
"watashitachi ha koushou wo ashita juuichiji ni okonaukoto wo teian shimasu. kono jikanni madeniha, koushou no shinro ni eikyou surukamoshirenai subeteno kihontekina mono ha kaiketsusaremasu. soshite ima karera ha anata wo furaito no ato yasumukoto ga dekiru, hoteru ni tsureteikimasu." chuugoku no kaisha no daihyou ha iimasu.

たくしーは壮大な中国世界ほてるの入り口の前に止まります。
Takushi-ha soudai na chuugoku sekai hoteru no iriguhi no mae ni tomarimasu.

ぽーるは管理者に近づきます。彼は彼の為に予約されている部屋があるかか尋ねます。
po-ru ha kanrisha ni chiakazukimasu. kare kare no tame ni yoyakusareteiru heya ga aruka tazunemasu.

"この部屋は今月の7日に予約されて支払われました。この情報を確認してください。"ぽーるは言います。
"kono heya ha kongetsu no nanoka ni yoyaku sarete shiharawaremashita. kono jouhou wo kakunin shitekudasai." po-ru ha iimasu.

"全て問題ありません。あなたは自分の部屋に行くことが可能です。ぽーたーがあなたの荷物を部屋の中に運びます。楽しんで休んで下さい。"管理者は言いそしてぽーるに鍵を渡します。
"subete mondai arimasen. anata ha jibun no heya ni ikukoto ga kanoudesu. po-ta- ga anata no nimotsu wo heya no naka ni hakobimasu. tanoshin de yasunde kudasai." kanrisha ha ii soshite po-ru ni kagi wo watashimasu.

representative.

The taxi stops in front of the entrance of the magnificent China World Hotel.

Paul approaches the administrator. He asks whether there is a room booked for him.

"This room was booked and paid for on the seventh of this month. Please confirm this information," asks Paul.

"Everything is all right. You can go up to your room. The porter will carry your luggage into your room. Enjoy your rest," says the administrator and gives the keys to Paul.

"Finally, I can relax!" says Paul when he is alone in his room.

He is pleased with the clean and comfortable

"やっと、休むことができる！"部屋で一人の時にぽーるは言います。
"yatto, yasumukotoga dekiru!" heya de hitori no toki ni po-ru ha iimasu.

彼はきれいで心地の良い部屋に満足しています。ほてるの中のさーびすの質も良いです。
kare ha kirei de kokochi no ii heya ni manzoku shiteimasu. hoteru no naka no sa-bisu no shitsu mo iidesu.

しばらくした後、ぽーるは食事の為に出発します。彼はぽーたーから通りの向かいに良いかふぇがあることを習います。夕飯の後、ぽーるはほてるの周りを歩くことを決めます。夜8時に、彼は部屋に戻ります。ぽーるは疲れています。彼は大事な日の前によく休むためにべっどに早く入ります。
shibarakushitaato, po-ru ha shokuji no tame ni shuppatsu shimasu. kare ha po-ta- kara toori no mukai ni ii kafe ga arukoto wo naraimasu. yuushoku no ato, po-ru ha hoteru no mawari wo arukukoto wo kimemasu. yoru hachiji ni, kare ha heya ni modorimasu. po-ru ha tsukareteimasu. kare ha daiji na hi no mae ni yoku yasumutame ni beddo ni hayaku hairimasu.

room. The quality of service in the hotel is also good.

After a while, Paul leaves to dine. He learns from the porter that there is a nice cafe across the street. After dinner, Paul decides to take a walk around the hotel. At eight o'clock in the evening, he returns to the room. Paul is tired. He goes to bed early to have a good rest before an important day.

C

テキストについての質問

1. 飛行機はどこに着陸しましたか？
2. ぽーるは何に入りますか？

Questions about the text
1. Where did the plane land?
2. What does Paul enter?
3. Where does the car wait?

3. 車はどこで待っていますか？
4. 空港から町の中央に行くためにはどのくらいかかりますか？
5. ぽーるは何を見ますか？
6. 町の中央地域で何が通り抜けますか？
7. 北京財務通りはどこにありますか？
8. 主要銀行の建物はどこにありますか？
9. ぱーとなーはどこに行きますか？
10. 町のどこの地域の美しい景色がありますか？
11. 彼らはいつ交渉することを申し出ましたか？
12. たくしーはどのほてるの前に止まりますか？
13. 良いかふぇはどこにありますか？

4. How long does it take to drive from the airport to the city center?
5. What does Paul see?
6. What passes through the central part of the city?
7. Where is Beijing Financial Street?
8. Where is the building of a major bank?
9. Where do the partners go?
10. Of what part of the city is there a beautiful view?
11. When do they offer to negotiate?
12. In front of what hotel does the taxi stop?
13. Where is there a good cafe?

氷を砕く
Break the ice

"誰が一番好きだい？"とエマのおばあちゃんは聞きました。
"コーラ、リンゴ"
"違うよ、人の話をしてるんだよ"とおばあちゃん。
"私は人間は食べないよ、くまさんチョコは食べるけどね？"

dare ga ichibansuki dai? to Ema no o bāchan wa kikimashita. ko-ra, ringo chigau yo, hito no hanashi o shiteru n da yo to o bāchan. watashi wa ningen wa tabenai yo, kuma san choko wa taberu kedo ne?

"Dear, who do you like the most?" little Emma's granny asks.
"I like cola and apples," the girl answers.
"No, dear. I mean people," the granny says.
"I do not eat people. May it be just a chocolate bear?" the girl asks.

交渉
The negotiations

単語
Words

1. 〜の間 [〜no aida] - between
2. スピーチ [supi-chi] - speech
3. プロデューサー、メーカー、製造業者 [purodu-sa-, mēkā, seizō gyōsha] - producer, maker, manufacturer
4. 案内する(動詞) [annaisuru (doushi)] - escort *(Verb)*
5. 移動する(動詞) [idousuru] - transfer *(Verb)*
6. 一年の、年間 [ichinenno, nenkan] - annual
7. 外部の [gaibuno] - external
8. 活動 [katsudou] - activity
9. 記述された [kijutsu sareta] - described
10. 義務 [gimu] - obligation
11. 議論の [gironno] - controversial
12. 合法 [gouhou] - legal
13. 参加者、メンバー [sankasha, menba-] - participant, member
14. 賛成した [sanseishita] - agreed
15. 賛成する(動詞)、和解する [sansei suru (doushi), wakaisuru] - agree *(Verb)*, to reconcile
16. 残り [nookri] - the rest
17. 事例 [jirei] - case
18. 持ってくる(動詞) [mottekuru (doushi)] - bring *(Verb)*
19. 主題 [shudai] - subject
20. 守る、保証する(動詞)、固定する [mamoru, hoshousuru (doushi), koteisuru] - secure *(Verb)*, to set down
21. 祝う(動詞) [iwau (doushi)] - congratulate *(Verb)*
22. 正しい / 保証 [tadashii, hoshou] - right / guarantee

23. 相互利益、ウィンウィン [sougorieki, uinuin] - mutually beneficial, win-win
24. 増加する [zoukasuru] - increase
25. 待っている、予想、予期、期待 [matteiru, yosou, yoki, kitai] - waiting, anticipation, expectation
26. 長い [nagai] - long
27. 統合 [tougou] - joint
28. 同意、契約 [doui, keiyaku] - agreement
29. 発見された [hakkensareta] - found
30. 反映された、反射された [haneisareta, hanshasareta] - reflected
31. 費用のかからない [hiyou no kakaranai] - inexpensive
32. 部門 [bumon] - department
33. 変化 [henka] - change
34. 容認できる [younin dekiru] - acceptable
35. 要求されていない [youkyuu sareteinai] - unclaimed
36. 力強く [chikarazuyoku] - strongly
37. 連絡を取る(動詞) [renraku wo toru (doushi)] - contact *(Verb)*

B

ぽーるは事務所に到着します。秘書が彼を迎えそして会議室へ案内します。でみんぐと通訳がそこで彼を待っています。少し後、残りの交渉の参加者が入ってきます。彼らはお互いを迎えます。中国のぱーとなーが交渉を始めます。

po-ru ha jimusho ni touchaku shimasu. hisho ga kare wo mukae soshite kaigishitsu he annaishimasu. demingu to tsuuyaku ga sokode kare wo matteimasu. sukoshi ato, nokori no koushou no sankasha ga haittekimasu. karera ha otagai wo mukaemasu. chuugoku no pa-tona- ga koushou wo hajimemasu.

"この交渉の目的は長くて有益な協定です。"中国の会社の代表は始めます。彼は続けます:"私たちはゆーろびっとと1年以上取引をしてきました、そして

Paul arrives at the office. A secretary meets him and escorts him into the meeting room. Deming and an interpreter wait for him there. A minute later, the rest of the negotiations participant come in. They greet each other. The Chinese partners start the negotiations.

"The purpose of our negotiations is a long and beneficial partnership," begins the representative of the

"この交渉の目的は長くて有益な協定です。"中国の会社の代表は始めます。彼は続けます:"私たちはユーロビットと一年以上取引をしてきました、そして私たちの統合活動はお互いの会社に有益であると信じています。なので、今年私たちはあなたに新しい取引の条件を提供したいです。"

"kono koushou no mokuteki ha nagakute yuueki na kyoutei desu." chuugoku no kaisha no daihyou ha hajimemasu. kare ha tsudukemasu: "watashitachi ha yu-robitto to ichinenijou torihiki wo shitekimashita, soshite watashitachi no tougoukatsudou ha otagai no kaisha ni yuueki dearu to shinjiteimasu. nanode, kotoshi watashitachi ha anatani atarashii torihiki no jouken wo teikyou shitaidesu."

"私たちはめじゃーな商品の製造業者です。生産量の増加に伴い、私たちの会社は購入の際のゆにっとの数を増加させることを提案します。割引率が10%増加するためこれらの条件は有利です。"外国の取引会社の社長は彼らを説得します。

"watashitachi ha meja- na shouhin no seizougyousha desu. seisanryou no zouka ni tomonai, watashitachi no kaisha ha kounyuu no sai no yunitto no kazu wo zouka saserukoto wo teianshimasu. waribekiritsu ga juppa-sento zoukasuru tame korera no jouken ha yuuridesu." gaikoku no torihikigakisha no shachou ha karera wo settokushimasu.

ぽーるは彼のためにすぴーちを翻訳する通訳の話を聞きます。

po-ru ha kare no tame ni supi-chi wo honyakusuru tsuuyaku no hanashi wo kikimasu.

"けれどもこのけーすでは、私たちはあなたの

Chinese company. He continues: "We have been trading with Eurobit for over a year, and we believe our joint activities are beneficial to both companies. So this year we want to offer you new trade terms."

"We are a major goods manufacturer. Due to the increase in our production volume, our company proposes to increase the number of units in a purchase. These conditions are advantageous because the discount rate is increased by ten percent," the head of the foreign trade department convinces them.

Paul listens to the interpreter who translates the speech for

製品の購入のいんたーばるを増加させなければなりません。私たちはより沢山の製品を同じ期間に売ることはできません。それらの製品は要求されないままかもしれません。あなたはどのような年間取引量を期待していますか？"ぽーるは尋ねます。彼の目的は購入の量を増価させることなく割引を受けることです。

"keredomo kono ke-su deha, watashitachi ha anata no seihin no kounyu no inta-baru wo zouka sasenakereba narimasen. watashitachi ha yori takusan no seihin wo onaji kikan ni urukoto ha dekimasen. sorera no seihin ha youkyuu sarenaimama kamoshiremasen. anata ha donoyouna nenkantorihikiryou wo kitaishite imasuka?" po-ru ha tazunemasu. kare no mokuteki ha kounyu no ryou wo zoukasaseru kotonaku waribiki wo uketorukoto desu.

通訳はぽーるのすぴーちを伝えます。
tsuuyaku ha po-ru no supi-chi wo tsutaemasu.

"私たちはあなたの会社との年間取引量を3%増加させることを期待します。"部長は続けました。
"watashitachi ha anatano kaisha tono nenkan torihikiryou wo sanpa-sento zouka saserukoto wo kitaishimasu." buchou ha tsudukemashtia.

"それは私たちの会社に容認できる内容だと思います。けれども、購入のいんたーばるを20日に増加させなければなりません。"ぽーるは答えます。
"sore ha watashitachi no kaisha ni younindekiru naiyoudato omoimasu. keredomo, kounyuu no inta-baru wo

him.

"But in this case, we will have to increase the intervals between the purchases of your products. We cannot sell more products in the same period of time. They may stay unclaimed. What annual trade volume do you you expect?" asks Paul. His goal is to get a discount without increasing the volume of purchases too much.

The interpreter conveys Paul's speech.

"We expect to increase the annual trade volume with your company by three percent," continued the head of the department.

"I think it is acceptable to our company. However, we must increase the interval

nijuunichikan ni zouka sasenakereba narimasen." po-ru ha kotaemasu.

"わかりました、私たちには私たちの会社に相互に利益のある計画があります。"中国の会社の代表は答えます。

"wakarimashita, watashitachi niha watashitachi no kaisha ni sougo ni rieki no aru keikaku ga arimasu." chuugoku no kaisha no daihyou ha kotaemasu.

"配達の状況は同じままですか?"ぽーるは尋ねます。

"haitatsu no joukyou ha onajimama desuka?" po-ru ha tazunemasu.

"はい。配達の状況は同じままです。これは最も高くなく信頼できる方法です。"中国の会社の代表は答えます。

"hai. haitatsu no joukyou ha onajimama desu. kore ha mottomo takakunaku shinyoudekiru houhou desu." chuugoku no kaisha no daihyou ha kotaemasu.

"教えてください、私は私の会社の経営陣に連絡を取り、そして重要な点を整理することはできますか?"ぽーるは尋ねます。

"oshietekudasai, watashi ha watashi no kaisha no keieijin ni renraku wo tori, soshite juuyouna ten wo seiri surukoto ha dekimasuka?" po-ru ha tazunemasu.

"はい、あなたは彼らと国際電話で連絡を取ることができます。どれくらいかかりますか?"中国のぱーとなーは尋ねます。

"hai, anata ha karera to kokusaidenwa de renraku wo torukoto ga dekimasu. dorekurai kakarimasuka?" chuugoku no pa-tona- ha tazunemasu.

between purchases to twenty days," answers Paul.

"OK, we have a mutually beneficial work scheme for our companies," responds the Chinese company representative.

"Do the delivery conditions remain the same?" asks Paul.

"Yes. The delivery conditions remain the same. This is the most inexpensive and reliable way," responds the Chinese company representative.

"Tell me please, can I contact my company management and coordinate important points?" asks Paul.

"Yes, you can contact them on the international line. How long will it take you?"

"全てが上手くいけば、1時間も必要ありません。待ってくれてありがとうございます。"ぽーるは答えます。

"subete ga umakuikereba, ichijikan mo hitsuyouarimasen. mattekurete arigatougozaimasu." po-ru ha kotaemasu.

ゆーろびっと会社の経営陣と話した後。

yu-robittogaisha no keieijin to hanashita ato.

"私の経営陣は協定の新しい条件を受け入れます。私たちはぽじてぃぶな決定をする準備ができています。"ぽーるは中国のぱーとなーに言います。

"watashi no keieijin ha kyoutei no atarashii jouken wo ukeiremasu. watashitachi ha pojitibu na kettei wo suru junbi ga dekiteimasu." po-ru ha chuugoku no pa-tona- ni iimasu.

"もし全ての論争問題が解決し同意されれば、私たちは解決方を契約上で法的化し、それを実行するための方法とたいむらいんを調整できます。"弁護士が申し出ます。

"moshi subete no ronsou mondai ga kaiketsushi doui sarereba, watashitachi ha kaiketsuhou wo keiyakujou de houtekikashi, sore wo jikkou surutameno houhou to taimurain wo chousei dekimasu." bengoshi ga moushidemasu.

"同意のどの部分が団体の権利と義務を反映しますか?"ぽーるは尋ねます。

"doui no dono bubun ga dantai no kenri to gimu wo hanei shimasuka?" po-ru ha tazunemasu.

"義務、権利そして契約の条件に応諾す

ask the Chinese partners.

"If all goes well, I need no more than an hour. Thank you for waiting," answers Paul.

After speaking with the Eurobit company management.

"My management accepts the new terms of collaboration. We are ready to make a positive decision," says Paul to the Chinese partners.

"If all controversial issues are resolved and agreements are found, we can legalize our solutions in a contract, reconcile the methods and timelines for its implementation," offers a lawyer.

"What part of the agreement reflects the rights and obligations of the parties?" asks Paul.

ることの管理については2つ目の部分に記述されています。それらは変わっていません。変更は契約者に対して作られます。"弁護士は説明します。

"gimu, kenri soshite keiyaku no jouken ni oudaku surukoto no kanri nitsuite ha futateume no bubun ni kijutsu sareteimasu. sorera ha kawatteimasen. henkou ha keiyakusha ni taishite tukuraremasu." bengoshi ha setsumeishimasu.

"おめでとうございます。私たちはあなたの会社と引き続き働けて満足しています。"外国の取引部長は言います。

"omedetougozaimasu. watashitachi ha anata no kaisha to hikitsuduki hataraketa manzokushiteimasu." gaikoku no torihikibuchou ha iimasu.

"The obligations, rights and the control of compliance with the terms of the contract are described in the second part. They remain unchanged. Changes are made to the subject of the contract," explains the lawyer.

"Congratulations. We are pleased to continue working with your company," says the head of the foreign trade department.

C

テキストについての質問

1. 誰がぽーると会いますか？
2. 誰が交渉を始めますか？
3. 交渉の意図は何ですか？
4. 中国の会社は今年何を提供したいですか？
5. 割引のぱーせんてーじはどのくらい増加しますか？
6. 年間取引量はどれくらい増加しますか？

Questions about the text

1. Who meets Paul?
2. Who starts the negotiations?
3. What is the purpose of the negotiations?
4. What does the Chinese company want to offer this year?
5. How much does the percentage of the discount rate increase?
6. How much does the annual trade volume increase?

7. 部長（ぶちょう）は何（なに）を当（あ）てにしていますか？
8. ぽーるはどうやって彼（かれ）の会社（かいしゃ）の経営陣（けいえいじん）に連絡（れんらく）を取（と）りますか？
9. ゆーろびっと会社（かいしゃ）はどのような決定（けってい）を行（おこな）いますか？
10. 法律家（ほうりつか）は何（なに）を調整（ちょうせい）することを提案（ていあん）しますか？
11. 契約（けいやく）の2つ目（め）の部分（ぶぶん）には何（なに）が記述（きじゅつ）されていますか？

7. What does the head of the department count on?
8. How can Paul contact his company management?
9. What decision does Eurobit company management make?
10. What does the lawyer propose to reconcile?
11. What is described in the second part of the contract?

23

氷を砕く
Break the ice

幼(おさな)いフィン(ふぃん)はよく両親(りょうしん)にオウムか金魚(きんぎょ)を買(か)ってくれるようにお願(ねが)いしていました。両親(りょうしん)はいつも、家(いえ)にいる猫(ねこ)が傷付(きずつ)けてしまうと言(い)います。フィン(ふぃん)の猫(ねこ)はとても大(おお)きいのです。ある日(ひ)、フィン(ふぃん)が友達(ともだち)のジャン(じゃん)の家(いえ)を訪(たず)ねた時(とき)のことです。フィン(ふぃん)は小(ちい)さな動物(どうぶつ)を見(み)つけ、こう言いました。

Little Finn often asks his mom and dad to buy him a parrot or a fish. But they usually say their cat can hurt them. Finn's cat is very big. One time Finn goes to visit his friend Jan. Jan is five years old. Finn sees a small animal at Jan's home.

"何これ、ネズミ？"
"違うよ、フェレットだよ"とジャンは言いました。
ジャンのフェレットと猫は一緒に遊び始めました。
"ジャンの猫はジャンのフェレットを食べると思う？"とフィンは質問しました。
"食べないよ"とジャン。
"じゃあ、フェレットが猫を食べると思う？"とフィンはもう一回聞きました。
"食べないと、彼らは戯れているだけだよ"とジャンは答えました。
"ねえ、ママ！うちも猫を飼えるよ！"とフィンは彼のお母さんに言いました。"フェレットと猫はお互いのことを食べたりしないよ！"

"Is this a rat?" Finn asks Jan.
"No, it is not. It is a ferret," Jan answers. At this moment Jan's ferret and cat start playing together.
"Can your cat eat your ferret?" Finn asks Jan.
"No, it cannot," Jan answers.
"Can your ferret eat your cat?" Finn asks Jan again.
"No, they only play together," Jan answers.
"Wow! Mom, we can buy a ferret!" Finn says to his mom. "A ferret and a cat cannot eat each other!"

osanai fyin wa yoku ryōshin ni ōmu ka kingyo o kattekureru yōni onegaishiteimashita. ryōshin wa itsumo, ie ni iru neko ga kizutsuketeshimau to iimasu. fyin no neko wa totemo ōkii no desu. aru hi, fyin ga tomodachi no Jan no ie o tazuneta toki no koto desu. fyin wa chiisana dōbutsu o mitsuke, kō iimashita. nani kore, nezumi? chigau yo, fyeretto da yo to Jan wa iimashita. Jan no fyeretto to neko wa issho ni asobi hajimemashita. Jan no neko wa Jan no fyeretto o taberu to omou? to fyin wa shitsumonshimashita. tabenai yo to Jan. jā, fyeretto ga neko o taberu to omou? to fyin wa mō ichi kai kikimashita. tabenai to, karera wa tawamureteiru dake da yo to Jan wa kotaemashita. nē, mama! uchi mo neko o kaeru yo! to fyin wa kare no okāsan ni iimashita. fyeretto to neko wa otagai no koto o tabe tari shinai yo!

インストール
The installation

単語
Words

1. それでは、そのため、あれ [sore deha, sonotame, are] - so, that
2. ソフトウェア [sofuouea] - software
3. デバッグする(動詞)、取り除く [debaggu suru (doushi), torinozoku] - debug *(Verb)*
4. ブロックする(動詞) [burokkusuru (doushi)] - block *(Verb)*
5. プログラマー [puroguramaa] - programmer
6. モニターする(動詞)、監視する [monita-suru (doushi), kanshisuru] - monitor *(Verb)*, to watch
7. 扱う(動詞)、うまく処理する [atsukau (doushi), umakushorisuru] - handle *(Verb)*, to cope
8. 一緒に [isshoni] - together
9. 皆 [minna] - guys
10. 起こる(動詞) [okoru (doushi)] - happen *(Verb)*
11. 駆り立てる(動詞) [karitateru (douhsi)] - prompt *(Verb)*
12. 見る(動詞) / スキャンする [miru (doushi)/ sukyansuru] - look *(Verb)* / to scan
13. 実体のある、かなりの [jittai no aru, kanarino] - substantial
14. 取り除く(動詞) [torinozoku (doushi)] - remove *(Verb)*, to delete, to take off
15. 手に入れる [te ni ireru] - obtain

227

16. 少し [sukoshi] - little
17. 上手く、成功して [umaku, sekoushite] - successfully
18. 心配する(動詞) [shinpaisuru] - worry (Verb)
19. 成功する(動詞) / 管理する [seikousuru (doushi)/ kanrisuru] - succeed (Verb) / to manage
20. 掃除する(動詞) [soujisuru (doushi)] - clean (Verb)
21. 争い [arasoi] - conflict
22. 誰も [daremo] - no one
23. 日本語 [nihongo] - Japanese
24. 普段 / 良く知っている [fudan, yokushittiru] - usual / familiar
25. 本当、訂正 [hontou, teisei] - true, correct
26. 余分の [yobunno] - extra
27. 両立しがたい、合わない [ryouritsu shigatai, awanai] - incompatibility
28. 話す(動詞) - talk (Verb) / to reflect

B

"こんにちは、うぃりあむ。ぴーたーです。私たちの専門家は明日ぷろぐらむの開発を完成させます。彼らはあなたの事務所に行きぷろぐらむを開始そして調整しなければなりません。"ぴーたーは言います。

"konnichiha, uiriamu. pi-ta- desu. watashitachi no senmonka ha ashita puroguramu no kaihatsu wo kanseisasemasu. karera ha anata no jimusho ni iki puroguramu wo kaishi soshite chousei shinakereba narimasen." pi-ta- ha iimasu.

"もちろん。私は彼らと会う準備ができています、そして一緒に働くことができます。"うぃりあむが応答します。

"mochiron. watashi ha karerato au junbi ga dekiteimasu, soshite issho ni hatarakukoto ga dekimasu." uiriamu ga goutoushimasu.

ぷろぐらまーがゆーろびっと事務所に来て仕事を開始します。事務所のすたっふはこんぴゅーたーをし

"Hello, William. This is Peter. Our specialists will finalize the program development tomorrow. They have to come to your office to run and tune up the program," says Peter.

"Of course. I am ready to meet them, and together we can work on this," William responds.

The programmers come to the Eurobit office and start working. The office staff cannot use their computers in the usual

ばらく普段通りに使うことができません。
purograma- ga yu-robittojimusho ni kite shigoto wo kaishishimasu. jimusho no sutaffu ha konpyu-ta- wo shibaraku fudandoori ni tsukaukoto ga dekimasen.

"3時間以内に、ぷろぐらまーはいんべんとりーの集計と収入/支出の集計のための新しいぷろぐらむをでばっぐします。私達はそれぞれのこんぴゅーたーの動きを監視する必要があります。どのようなぷろぐらむも開始させないでください。"うぃりあむはお願いします。
"sanjikaninaini, purograma- ha inbentori- no shuukei to shuunyuu/shisyutsu no shuukei no tameno atarashii puroguramu wo debaggu shimasu. watashitachi ha sorezore no konpyu-ta- no ugoki wo kanshisuru hitsuyou ga arimasu. donoyouna puroguramu mo kaishi sasenaide kudasai." uiriamu ha onegaishimasu.

"私達はこんぴゅーたーのさーばーにぷろぐらむのだうんろーどを開始します。始めにここでどう動くか確認します。もし全てが上手く行ったら、私達はそれを全てのこんぴゅーたーにだうんろーどします。"ぷろぐらまーが言います。
"watashitachi ha konpyu-ta- no sa-ba- ni puroguramu no daunro-do wo kaishishimasu. hajimeni kokode dou ugokuka kakuninshimasu. moshi subete ga umaku ittara, watashitachi ha sore wo subete no konpyu-ta- ni daunro-doshimasu." purograma- ga iimasu.

"うぃりあむ、あなたはどれくらいの頻度でさーばーをりぶーとし、掃除しますか?"ぷろぐらまーは尋ねます。
"uiriamu, anata ha dorekurai no hindo de sa-ba- wo ribu-

way for a while.

"Within three hours, the programmers will debug the new program for inventory accounting and accounting of the revenues/ expenses. We need to monitor the work of each computer. I ask you not to run any programs," asks William.

"We are starting to download the program to the company's server. First we are checking how it works here. If everything goes well, we will download it to all the computers," the programmers say.

"William, how often do you reboot and clean your server?" asks the programmer.

"Periodically," clarifies William.

"William, and how does

toshi, soujishimasuka?" purogurama- ha tazunemasu.

"定期的にします。"うぃりあむは明言します。
"teikitekini shiamsu." uiriamu ha meigenshimasu.

"うぃりあむ、そしてあなたのあんちうぃるすそふとうぇあはどう動きますか?"ぷろぐらまーは続けます。
"uiriamu, soshite anata no anchi uirusu sofutouea ha dou ugokimasuka?" purogurama- ha tsudukemasu.

"あっぷでーとの後、いい状態で動いています。何か問題がありますか?"うぃりあむは心配します。
"appude-to no ato, ii joutai de ugoiteimasu. nani ka mondai ga arimasuka?" uiriamu ha shinpaishimasu.

"いくつか問題があると思います。私達はそふとうぇあをいんすとーるするのに問題を抱えています。それらは新しいそふとうぇあとあんちうぃるすが両立しがたいことに関係しています。あんちうぃるすがそれをまるうぇあだと認識しています。"ぷろぐらまーは説明します。
"ikutsuka mondai ga aruto omoimasu. watashitachi ha sofutouea wo insuto-rusuru noni mondai wo kakaete imasu. sorera ha atarashii sofutouea to anchi uirusu ga ryouritsu shigataikoto ni kankeishiteimasu. anchi uirusu ga sre wo maruuea dato ninshiki shiteimasu." purogurama- ha setsumeishimasu.

"それではぷろぐらむ同士の争いがあるのですか?あんちうぃるすが新しいぷろぐらむをぶろっくしていますか?"うぃりあむは尋ねます。
"soredeha puroguramu doushi no arasoi ga aruno desuka? Anchi uirusu ga atarashii puroguramu wo burokku shiteimasuka?" uiriamu ha tazunemasu.

your antivirus software work?" continues the programmer.

"After the upgrade, it has been behaving well. Is something wrong?" William worries.

"I think there are some problems. We are having trouble installing the software. They are related to the incompatibility of the antivirus with the new software. The antivirus perceives it as malware," explains the programmer.

"So is there a conflict of programs? Is the antivirus blocking the new program?" asks William.

"Yes, that is right. I think we won't be able to handle it ourselves. The problem is in the peculiarities of the

"はい、それは正しいです。私たちはそれを自分たちでは扱えないと思います。問題はあんちういるすの特徴にあります。私はどうしてこれが起こるのか分かりません。"ぷろぐらまーは言います。
"hai, sore ha tadashii desu. watashitachi ha sore wo jibuntachi deha atsukaenai to omoimasu. mondai ha anchi uirusu no tokuchou ni arimasu. watashi ha doushite kore ga okoruno ka wakarimasen." purogurama- ha iimasu.

"あなたは何をする予定ですか?"うぃりあむは尋ねます。
"anata ha nani wo suru yotei desuka?" uiriamu ha tazunemasu.

"あんちうぃるすそふとうぇあの開発会社に連絡を取ることが必須です。彼らが問題を解決する手伝いをしてくれるはずです。"ぷろぐらまーは言います。
"anchi uirusu sofutouea no kaihatsugaisha ni renraku wo torukoto ga hissu desu. Karera ga mondai wo kaiketsusuru tetsudai wo shitekureru hazudesu." purogurama- ha iimasu.

彼らは日本の開発会社にめーるで連絡を取ります。彼らの専門家は何をする必要があるのか、そしてあんちうぃるすそふとうぇあの何の制限を取り除く必要があるのか提案します。そしたらそれは争いなく新しいそふとうぇあを受け入れることができるでしょう。
karera ha nihon no kaihatsugaisha ni me-ru de renraku wo torimasu. karera no senmonka ha nani wo suru hitsuyou ga arunoka, soshite anchi uirusu sofutouea no nanno seigen wo torinozoku hitsuyou ga arunoka teianshimasu. soshitara sore

antivirus. I do not understand how this could happen," says the programmer.

"What are you going to do?" asks William.

"It is necessary to contact the development company of the antivirus software. They should help us to resolve this issue," the programmers say.

They contact the Japanese development company by e-mail. Their experts suggest what is needed to be done and what limitations of antivirus software must be removed. Then it will be able to accept new software without conflict.

"We managed to clarify one small but significant point. After its

ha arasoinaku atarashii sofutouea wo ukeirerukoto ga dekirudeshou.

"私たちは1つの小さいけれども重要な点をはっきりさせることができました。この除去の後、いんすとーるは滑らかに行くはずです。"ぷろぐらまーは言います。

"watashitachi ha hitotsu no chiisaikeredomo juuyouna ten wo hakkiri saserukoto ga dekimashita. kono jokyo no ato, insuto-ru ha nameraka ni ikuhazu desu." purogurama- ha iimasu.

"さーばーへのあぷりけーしょんのいんすとーるは今のところ通常通りに行われています。約30%あっぷろーどされました。"しばらくした後にぷろぐらまーが言います。

"sa-ba- heno apurike-shon no insuto-ru ha imanotokoro tsuujoudoori ni okonawareteimasu. yaku sanjuppa-sento appuro-do saremashita." shibarakushitaato ni purogurama-ga iimasu.

"おおよそ、どれくらいかかりますか？"うぃりあむは尋ねます。

"ooyoso, dorekurai kakarimasuka?" uiriamu ha tazunemasu.

"約40分かかるはずです。"ぷろぐらまーは言います。

"yaku jonjuppun kakaruhazu desu." purogurama- ha iimasu.

"皆、おめでとうございます。さーばーへのいんすとーるは成功しました！さてそれぞれのこんぴゅーたーで個別に作業を続けることができます。"彼は続けます。

" mina, omedetougozaimasu. sa-ba- heno insuto-ru ha seikoushimashita! sate sorezore no konpyu-ta- de kobetsu ni sagyou wo tsudukerukoto ga dekimasu." kare ha

elimination, the installation should go smoothly," says the programmer.

"The installation of the application on the server is going normally so far. About thirty percent uploaded," says the programmer after a while.

"How long should it take, approximately?" asks William.

"It should take about forty minutes," says the programmer.

"Congratulations, guys. The installation on the server went successfully! Now we can continue our work with each computer individually," he continues.

"Sandra, you are low on disk space. You need to scan and delete

tsudukemasu.

"さんどら、あなたのでぃすくすぺーすが少ないです。あなたは不必要なぷろぐらむをすきゃんし、削除する必要があります。"うぃりあむは言います。
"sandora, anata no disukusupe-su ga sukunai desu. anata ha fuhitsuyou na puroguramu wo sukyanshi, sakujosuru hitsuyou ga arimasu." uiriamu ha iimasu.

"みかえる、いんすとーるはあなたのこんぴゅーたーで進行中です。どのようなどきゅめんとも開かないでください。"しすてむ管理者は続けます。
"mikaeru, insuto-ru ha anata no konpyu-ta- de shinkouchuu desu. donoyouna dokumento mo hirakanaide kudasai." shisutemukanrisha ha tsudukemasu.

"新しいそふとうぇあが5台のこんぴゅーたーにいんすとーるされました。他の全てのこんぴゅーたーでいんすとーるが完了したら、ぷろぐらむ全体の試験を開始します。"ぷろぐらまーは言います。
"atarashii sofutouea ga godai no konpyu-ta- ni insuto-ru saremashita. hoka no subete no konpyu-ta- de insuto-ru ga kanryoushitara, puroguramu zentai no shaken wo kaishishimasu." purogurama- ha iimasu.

C

テキストについての質問

1. どうして専門家が事務所に来なければなりませんか？
2. 何を事務所すたっふは普段通りに行えませんか？
3. ぷろぐらまーは新しいそふとうぇあのでばっ

unnecessary programs," asks William.

"Michael, the installation is under way on your computer. Do not open any documents," continues the system administrator.

"The new software is installed on five computers. When the installation is complete on the rest of computers, we start testing the entire program," says the programmer.

Questions about the text

1. Why do the specialists have to come to the office?
2. What cannot the office staff do in the usual way?
3. How many hours will

ぐに何時間かけますか？

4. あっぷぐれーどの後あんちういるすそふとはどのような状態ですか？

5. 新しいそふとうぇあのいんすとーるの問題は何と関係していますか？

6. あんちういるすそふとは何をぶろっくしますか？

7. ぷろぐらまーは誰に連絡を取りますか？

8. 日本の会社の専門家は何を提案しますか？

9. ぷろぐらむをいんすとーるするのにどれくらいかかりますか？

10. さんどらは何をすきゃんそして削除する必要がありますか？

11. ぷろぐらまーはいつぷろぐらむの試験を開始しますか？

the programmers spend debugging the new software?

4. How has the antivirus software been behaving after the upgrade?

5. To what are the new software installation problems related?

6. What does the antivirus software block?

7. Whom do the programmers contact?

8. What do the Japanese company experts suggest?

9. How long does it take to install the program?

10. What does Sandra need to scan for and delete?

11. When do the programmers start testing the program?

24

Audio

氷を砕く
Break the ice

　幼い女の子と彼女のお母さん、お父さん、おばあちゃんが家にいます。彼らはテレビでグラミー賞を見ていました。受賞者はみんなに感謝をしていました。その後、家族は夕食を食べました。
 "お母さん、綺麗なコップをくれてありがとう。おばあちゃん、ハンバーガーを作ってくれてありがとう。

A little girl, her mom, her dad and her granny are at home. They are watching Grammy Awards live on TV. Winners thank everybody many times. Later the family has supper.
"Thank you, mommy, for giving me a clean cup," the little girl says, "thank you granny for making a hamburger for me! Thank

お父さん、お祈りしてくれてありがとう。"と 幼い女の子は言いました。みんなありがとう！

you, daddy, for wishing me a good appetite! Thank you everybody!"

osanai onnanoko to kanojo no okāsan, otōsan, o bāchan ga ie ni imasu. karera wa terebi de Gurami-Shō o miteimashita. jushōsha wa minna ni kansha o shiteimashita. sonogo, kazoku wa yūshoku o tabemashita. okāsan, kireina koppu o kurete arigatō. o bāchan, hanba-ga- o tsukuttekurete arigatō. otōsan, oinorishitekurete arigatō. to osanai onnanoko wa iimashita. minna arigatō!

品質と値段は正しいレートです
The quality and price have the right ratio

単語
Words

1. 〜について [〜ni tsuite] - about
2. 〜のおかげで [〜no okagede] - thanks to
3. その代わりに、見返りに、代わりとして [sono kawarini, mikaerini, kawari toshite] - instead, in return, as a replacement
4. もうすぐ [mousugu] - almost
5. アクティブ、活動的 [akutibu, kappatsuteki] - active
6. レート、割合 [re-to, wariai] - ratio
7. 一致する、調和する [icchisuru, chouwasuru] - in accord, harmoniously

8. 印をつけた、登録された [shirushi wo tsuketa, touroku sareta] - marked, registered
9. 応答する(動詞) [outousuru (doushi)] - respond (Verb)
10. 義務的な [gimutekina] - obligatory
11. 欠点のある [ketten no aru] - defective
12. 賛成する(動詞) [sanseisuru (doushi)] - agree (Verb)
13. 指標、指示するもの [shihyou, shijisurumono] - indicator
14. 支店 [shiten] - branch
15. 時間内に [jikannaini] - in time
16. 出現する(動詞) [shutsugensuru (doushi)] - appear (Verb)
17. 申し訳ありません [moushiwake arimasen] - Sorry
18. 成功した、ラッキーな [seikoushita, rakki-na] - successful, lucky
19. 増加する(動詞)、育つ [zoukasuru (doushi), sodatsu] - increase (Verb), to grow
20. 断片、破片 [danpen, hahen] - piece, unit
21. 注文 [chuumon] - order
22. 売った [utta] - sold
23. 発見する(動詞) [hakkensuru (doushi)] - find (Verb)
24. 不足 / 損失 [fusoku, sonshitsu] - shortage / loss
25. 変換 [koukan] - exchange
26. 変更する(動詞) [henkousuru (doushi)] - change (Verb)
27. 戻る [modoru] - back
28. 欄、コラム [ran, koramu] - column

B

2か月が過ぎます。ゆーろびっと会社はまーけっとであくてぃぶです。会社の製品は大いに要求されています。顧客が言うように、"あなたの製品の品質と値段は正しいれーとです。"

nikagetsu ga sugimasu. yu-robittogaisha ha ma-ketto de akutibu desu. kaisha no seihin ha ookini youkyuu sareteimasu. kokyaku ga iuyouni, "anata no seihin no hinshitsu to nedan ha tadashii re-to desu."

彼らの新しいそふとうぇあは時間内に顧客の要求に応答することを可能とします。

karera no atarashii sofutouea ha jikannai ni kokyaku no youkyuu ni outousurukoto wo kanou to shimasu.

彼らの新しいそふとうぇあは時間内に顧客

Two months passes. Eurobit company is active on the market. The company's products are in great demand. As customers say, "The quality and price of your products have the right ratio."

Their new software allows them to react to customers' requests just in time.

の要求に応答することを可能とします。
顧客は値段の変更と新しいおふぁーを自動的にめーるで受け取ります。今彼らは必須で適切な情報を受け取りそして時間を節約します。
kokyaku ha nedan no henkou to atarashii ofa- wo jidouteki ni me-ru de uketorimasu. ima karera ha hissu de tekisetsuna jouhou wo uketori soshite jikan wo setsuyakushimasu.

"さんどら、先月の生産と残りの結果を見せてください。"まねーじゃーは言います。
"sandora, sengetsu no seisan to nokori no kekka wo misete kudasai." mane-ja- ha iimasu.

"それらはあなたのこんぴゅーたーの集計ぷろぐらむにある、製造ふぉるだの中です。"さんどらは応答します。
"sorera ha anata no konpyu-ta- no shuukei puroguramu ni aru, seizouforuda no naka desu." sandora ha outoushimasu.

倉庫にある在庫と前2か月で売られたゆにっとの数をどこで見ることができますか？"まねーじゃーは尋ねます。
"souko ni aru zaiko to mae nikagetsu de urareta yunitto no kazu wo dokode mirukoto ga dekimasuka?" mane-ja- ha tazunemasu.

"在庫、完成した商品の流れと動き、そして購入は倉庫いんべんとりーふぉるだにあります。合計欄でそれらを見るととても便利です。"さんどらは説明します。

The customers receive price changes and new offers automatically by e-mail. Now they just receive the necessary and relevant information and save time.

"Sandra, show me the last month's results for the production and remainders," asks the manager.

"They are on your computer in the accounting program, in the Production folder," Sandra responds.

"Where can I see the remainders by warehouse and the number of units sold in the last two months?" asks the manager.

"The remainders, the flow and the movement of finished goods, and

"zaiko, kanseishita shouhin no nagare to ugoki, soshite kounyuu ha souko inbentori- foruda ni arimasu. goukeiran de sorera wo miruto totemo benri desu." sandora ha setsumeishimasu.

"生産と卸売りのえりあでの指標が著しく増加したことが見て取れます。私たちはより沢山の顧客を獲得しています。"まねーじゃーは嬉しそうに意見します。

"seisan to oroshiuri no eria deno shihyou ga ichijirushiku zoukashitakoto ga mitetoremasu. watashitachi ha yori takusan no kokyaku wo kakutoku shiteimasu." mane-ja- ha ureshisou ni ikenshimasu.

"はい、新しいぷろぐらむのおかげで、私たちの支店は製造部門と一体して、より多く働きます。彼らは商品の動きをより効率的に追跡します。彼らは小さな卸売りろっとの買い手の要求に早く応答します。"さんどらは追加します。

"hai, atarashii puroguramu no okagede, watashitachi no shiten ha seizoubumon to ittaishite, yori ooku hatarakimasu. karera ha shouhin no ugoki wo yori kouritsuteki ni tsuisekishimasu. karera ha chiisana oroshiuri rotto no kaite no youkyuu ni hayaku outoushimasu." sandora ha tsuikashimasu.

"つまり、倉庫を管理することは今、より簡単です。ほとんど不足が無いと見て取れます。これは良い結果です。"まねーじゃーは言います。

"tsumari, souko wo kanrisurukoto ha ima yori kantan desu. hotondo fusoku ga nai to mitetoremasu. kore ha iikekka desu." mane-ja- ha iimasu.

purchases are in the Warehouse Inventory folder. It is very convenient to see them in the Total column," explains Sandra.

"I see that the indicators in the areas of the production and wholesale increased significantly. We are acquiring more customers," notes the manager happily.

"Yes, thanks to our new program, our branches operate more in accord with the manufacturing division. They follow the movement of goods more efficiently. They respond quickly to the demands of small wholesale lots buyers," adds Sandra.

"So, controlling the warehouse is now much easier. I see we have

"ここに少量の商品が見えます。それらは先月から通過してきました。これは何ですか？"
彼は尋ねます。

"koko ni shouryou no shouhin ga miemasu. sorera ha sengetsukara tsuukashitekimashita. kore ha nandesuka?" kare ha tazunemasu.

"はい。欠点のある製品がここに登録されています。私達は先月20個そして今月10個を配達の時に発見しました。"さんどらは説明します。

"hai. ketten no aru seihin ga kokoni touroku sareteimasu. watashitachi ha sengetsu nijukko soshite kongetsu jukko wo haitatsu no toki ni hakkenshimashita." sandora ha setsumeishimasu.

"ぽーるは私たちの中国のぱーとなーに連絡を取り、そして欠点のあるゆにっとの返金または交換を取り付ける必要があります。"まねーじゃーは意見します。

"po-ru ha watashitachi no chuugoku no pa-tona- ni renraku wo tori, soshite kettennoaru yunitto no henkin mataha koukan wo toritsukeru hitsuyou ga arimasu." mane-ja- ha ikenshimasu.

"わかりました、今彼にそれについて知らせることができます。"さんどらは応答します。

"wakarimashita, ima kare ni sorenitsuite shiraserukoto ga dekimasu." sandora ha outoushimasu.

"ぽーる、あなたは私たちの中国のぱーとなーに連絡を取り、そして欠点のある製品につい

almost no shortages. This is a good result," says the manager.

"I see here a small amount of goods. They pass from previous month. What is this?" he asks.

"Yes. Defective products are registered here. We found twenty pieces last month and ten pieces this month in the delivery," explains Sandra.

"Paul must contact our Chinese partners and arrange a refund or exchange of the defective units," the manager comments.

"OK, I can let him know about it now," Sandra responds.

"Paul, you need to contact our Chinese partners and inform

て通知する必要があります。"さんどらはまねーじゃーの命令を伝えます。
"po-ru, anata ha watashitachi no chuugoku no pa-tona- ni renraku wo tori, soshite ketten no aru seihin ni tsuite tsuuchisuru hitsuyou ga arimasu." sandora ha mane-ja- no meirei wo tsutaemasu.

"them about the defective products," Sandra conveys the manager's instruction.

"わかりました。できるだけ早くそれを行います。"ぽーるは応答します。
"wakarimashita. dekirudake hayaku okonaimasu." po-ru ha outoushimasu.

"OK. I'll do this as quickly as possible," Paul responds.

1時間後、ぽーるは中国の会社の代表のでみんぐに連絡を取ります。
ichijikango, po-ru ha chuugoku no kaisha no daihyou no demingu ni renraku wo torimasu.

An hour later, Paul contacts Deming, the representative of the Chinese company.

"こんにちは、でみんぐ。ぽーるです。私は商品の品質について質問があります。前2つのまとまりで、30個の欠点のあるゆにっとを発見しました。私たちはあなたにそれらを送り、そして良いものに交換したいです。"ぽーるは説明します。
"konnichiha, demingu. po-ru desu. watashi ha shouhin no hinshitsu ni tsuite shitsumon ga arimasu. mae futatsu no matomari de, sanjukko no ketten no aru yunitto wo hakkenshimashita. watashitachi ha anata ni sorera wo okuri, soshite iimono ni koukanshitai desu." po-ru ha setsumeishimasu.

"Good afternoon, Deming. This is Paul. We have a question about the quality of goods. In the last two parties, we found thirty defective units. We want to send them to you, and exchange them for good ones," explains Paul.

"ごめんなさい、ぽーる。あなたはそれを倉庫にとっておいていいです。欠点のある製品の代わりとして私たちは次のばっちと一緒に30個の追加の

"I'm very sorry, Paul. You can keep them in the warehouse. We will send

241

ゆにっとを送ります。そして私たちは次のばっちの全ての保証を3か月伸ばします。けれども欠点のあるゆにっとはある一定のぱーせんてーじで時々製品の大きなばっちの中にあります。特定の量の欠点のあるゆにっとが蓄積した時、あなたの会社はそれらを送り返すことができます。"でみんぐは申し出ます。
"gomennasai, po-ru. anata ha sore wo souko ni totteoite iidesu. ketten no aru seihin no kawari toshite watashitachi ha tsugi no bacchi to issho ni sanjukko no tsuika no yunitto wo okurimasu. soshite watashitachi ha tsugi no bacchi no subete no hoshou wo sankagetsu nobashimasu. keredomo ketten no aru yunitto ha aru ittei no pa-sente-ji de tokidoki seihin no ookina bacchi no nakani arimasu. tokutei no ryou no ketten no aru yunitto ga chikuseki shitatoki, anata no kaisha ha sorera wo okurikaesukoto ga dekimasu." demingu ha moushidemasu.

"私は賛成します。あなたの解決策はより都合が良いです。良い一日を！"ぽーるは言います。
"watashi ha sanseishimasu. anata no kaiketsusaku ha yori tsugou ga iidesu. iiichinichi wo!" po-ru ha iimasu.

C

テキストについての質問

1. 顧客は会社の製品について何と言いますか？
2. 新しいそふとうぇあは何をすることを可能としますか？

Questions about the text

1. What do customers say about the company's products?
2. What does the new software allow doing?

3. 全ての顧客はどうやって新しいおふぁーを受け取りますか？
4. どのふぉるだが在庫、完成した商品の流れそして動きを含んでいますか？
5. どのえりあで指標が増加しましたか？
6. 何の要求に支店は早く応答しますか？
7. 先月の配達で何が発見されましたか？
8. ぽーるは誰に連絡を取るべきですか？
9. ぽーるは何について中国のぱーとなーに通知するべきですか？
10. 中国の会社の代表の名前は何ですか？
11. 中国の会社は次のばっちと一緒に何を送りますか？
12. どのくらい保証期間は増加しますか？

3. How do all customers receive new offers?
4. What folder contains the remainders, the flow and the movement of finished goods?
5. In what areas did the indicators increase?
6. To what demands do branches respond quickly?
7. What was found in last month's delivery?
8. Who must Paul contact?
9. About what should Paul inform the Chinese partners?
10. What is the name of the Chinese company representative?
11. What does the Chinese company send with the next batch?
12. By how much does the warranty period increase?

25

Audio

氷を砕く
Break the ice

お母さんが仕事が終えて帰宅すると、息子が駆け寄ってきて抱きしめながらおかえりと言いました。
"ママ、なんか変な感じがするの"と息子はお母さんに言いました。
"どうしたの？どんな感じ？"とお母さんは聞き返します。
すると"分からない"と息子。
"言ってごらん？"と答えを聞き出そうとしています。

A mom comes home from work. Her little son runs up to her, greeting her with a hug.
"Mom, I feel something," he says.
"What do you feel, dear?" the mom asks.
"I do not know," he answers.
"What do you feel? Say it to me," she presses him for an answer.
"It is love," the little son

"これは多分、愛だ"と息子はお母さんに囁きました。 whispers to his mom.

okāsan ga shigoto ga oete kitakusuru to, musuko ga kakeyottekite dakishime nagara okaeri to iimashita. mama, nan ka henna kanji ga suru no to musuko wa okāsan ni iimashita. dō shita no? donna kanji? to okāsan wa kikikaeshimasu. suru to wakaranai to musuko. itte goran? to kotae o kikidasou to shiteimasu. kore wa tabun, ai da to musuko wa okāsan ni sasayakimashita.

取締役会の会議
The board of directors meeting

単語
Words

1. アプリケーション、使う [apurike-shon, tsukau] - application, use
2. エリア、領域、地域 [eria, ryouiki, chiiki] - area, region
3. バランス(シート) [baransushi-to] - balance (sheet)
4. マージン / 在庫 [ma-jin/ zaiko] - margin / stock
5. ムード [mu-do] - mood
6. メンテナンス [mentenansu] - maintenance
7. レポート [repo-to] - report
8. 一年の [ichinenno] - annual
9. 一般的 [ippanteki] - general
10. 回転率 [kaitenritsu] - turnover
11. 開ける(動詞) [akeru (doushi)] - open *(Verb)*

12. 拡大する(動詞) [kakudaisuru (doushi)] - expand (Verb)
13. 革新 [kakushin] - innovation
14. 楽天主義 [rakutenshugi] - optimism
15. 合理的な [gouritekina] - rational
16. 作られた、終わった [tsukurareta, owatta] - made, done
17. 支払い [shiharai] - payment
18. 持ち上げる、増加する(動詞) [mochiageru, zoukasuru (doushi)] - raise (Verb)
19. 持ってくる(動詞) [mottekuru (doushi)] - bring (Verb)
20. 手に取る(動詞)、持つ [tenitoru (doushi), motsu] - have (Verb)
21. 祝う(動詞) [iwau (doushi)] - celebrate (Verb)
22. 消費する(動詞)、費やす [shouhisuru (doushi), tsuiyasu] - expend (Verb), to spend
23. 心、精神 [kokoro, seishin] - spirit
24. 成長 [seichou] - growth
25. 製造、生産 [seizou, seisan] - manufacturing, production
26. 創立する(動詞) [souritsu suru (doushi)] - establish (Verb)
27. 導く(動詞)、持ってくる [michibiku (doushi), mottekuru] - lead (Verb), to bring
28. 認識 [ninshiki] - realization
29. 能力 [nouryoku] - skill
30. 比較する [hikakusuru] - comparing
31. 費用効果のある [hiyoukouka no aru] - cost effective
32. 評議会、委員会(監督の) [hyougikai, iinkai (kantokuno)] - council, board (of directors)
33. 分配する、配る [bunpaisuru, kubaru] - distribute
34. 法人 [houjin] - corporate
35. 魅力 [miryoku] - attraction
36. 予想、予測、視点 [yosou, yosoku, shiten] - prospect, perspective
37. 利益 [rieki] - profit

B

ゆーろびっと会社で取締役会の会議が予定されています。彼らは去年の結果を議論し、そして来年の予想を検討します。
CEO, COO, CCOそしてCFOが一年のれぽーとを作成します。

yu-robittogaisha de torishimariyakkai no kaigi ga yotei sareteimasu. karera ha kyonen no kekka wo gironshi, soshite rainen no yosou wo kentou shimasu. CEO, COO, CCO soshite CFO ga ichinen no repo-to wo sakuseishimasu.

"新しい会計しすてむのおかげで、すたっふはよ

The board of directors meeting is scheduled at Eurobit company. They discuss last year's results and build up next year prospects. The CEO, the COO, the CCO, and the CFO make annual reports.

"Thanks to the new

り効率的に時間を配分しそして会社のりそーすを節約します。今私たちの会社は新しい企画を維持する余裕があります。"CEOは言います。

"atarashii kaikeishisutemu no okagede, sutaffu ha yori kouritsuteki ni jikan wo haibunshi soshite kaisha no riso-su wo setsuyaku shimasu. ima watashitachi no kaisha ha atarashii kikaku wo ijisuru yoyuu ga arimasu." CEO ha iimasu.

"今私たちの会社はより沢山の支店を開く能力があります。来年、私たちは他の地域で3つの支店を開く予定です。"彼は続けます。

"ima watashitachi no kaisha ha yori takusan no shiten wo hiraku nouryoku ga arimasu. rainen, watashitachi ha hoka no chiiki de mittsuno shiten wo hiraku yotei desu." kare ha tsudukemasu.

"去年を経て、顧客の数が倍になりました。製品の回転率の増加は利益の増加を導きます。私たちの会社は革新の実行によりまーけっとで効率的に働きます。せーるすまねーじゃーは素晴らしい結果を見せます。彼らは新しい顧客を引き付けるために効率的にぷれぜんてーしょんを行い、ぱーとなーとのつながりを構築する能力を持ち、彼らに私たちの会社と協力することに興味を抱かせます。"こまーしゃるまねーじゃーは

accounting system, the staff allocates time more efficiently and saves the company's resources. Now our company can afford to maintain new projects," says the CEO.

"Now our company has the ability to open more branches. Next year, we plan to open three branches in another region," he continues.

"Over the past year, the number of customers has doubled. Increasing the turnover of products leads to an increased profit. Our company works effectively on the marketplace through the implementation of innovations. The sales managers show excellent results. They effectively make presentations to attract new customers, have the ability to establish contact with

言います。

"kyonen wo hete, kokyaku no kazu ga bai ni narimashita. seihin no kaitenritsu no zouka ha reiki no zouka wo michibikimasu. watashitachi no kaisha ha kakushin no jikkouniyori ma-ketto de kouritsuteki ni hatarakimasu. se-rusu mane-ja- ha subarashii kekka wo misemasu. karera ha atarashii kokyaku wo hikitsukerutame ni kouritsuteki ni purezente-shon wo okonai, pa-tona- tono tsunagari wo kouchikusuru nouryoku wo mochi, karera ni watashitachi no kaisha to kyouryoku surukoto ni kyoumi wo idakasemasu." koma-sharumane-ja- ha iimasu.

"製造の結果は去年と比べてより良い結果を示します。私たちのえんじにあの開発のおかげで、私たちは製品の製造の為の素材をより経済的に使うことができます。私たちの倉庫は今相当な製品のまーじんを持っています。"おぺれーてぃんぐ事務所の所長が言います。

"seizou no kekka ha kyonen to kurabete yoriyoi kekka wo shimeshimasu. watashitachi no enjinia no kaihatsu no okagede, watashitachi ha seihin no seizou no tame no sozai wo yori keizaiteki ni tsukaukoto ga dekimasu. watashitachi no souko ha ima soutou na seihin no ma-jin wo motteimasu." opere-tingu jimusho no shochou ga iimasu.

"私たちの会社は顧客からの良いふぃーどばっくにより知名度を得ています。"PRまねーじゃーは言います。

"watashitachi no kaisha ha kokyakukara no ii fi-dobakku niyori chimeido wo eteimasu." pi-a-rumane-ja- ha iimasu.

"年間の利益のれぽーとは黒字を示しています。利益の合計量は生産の拡大と従業員への支払いの増加を可能とします

partners, make them interested in collaborating with our company," notes the commercial manager.

"Manufacturing shows better results compared to last year. Thanks to our engineers' developments, we can use materials for the products' manufacturing more economically. Our warehouses have now a substantial margin of products," says the Chief Operating Officer.

"Our company is gaining prominence due to the good feedback from our customers," says the PR-manager.

"The annual profit report shows a positive balance. The total amount of profit allows us to expand production and increase payments to

。"財務事務所の所長が言います。
"nekan no rieki no repo-to ha kuroji wo shimeshiteimasu. rieki no goukeiryou ha seisan no kakudai to juugyouin heno shiharai no zouka wo kanouto shimasu." zaimujimusho no shochou ga iimasu.

スタッフによって行われた仕事の有力な結果は彼らを良いムードにさせ、そして仕事で楽観的な見通しを立て、そして法人の精神を成長させます。
sutaffu niyotte okonawareta shigoto no yuuryoku na kekka ha karera wo ii mu-donisase, soshite shigoto de rakkantekina mitooshi wo tate, soshite houjin no seishin wo seichousasemasu.

our employees," says the Chief Financial Officer.

The positive results of the work done by the staff put them in a good mood and an optimistic outlook at work, and raised the corporate spirit.

テキストについての質問 / Questions about the text

1. ゆーろびっと会社ではどのような会議が予定されていますか？
2. 誰が一年のれぽーとを作成しますか？
3. 新しい会計しすてむを適用することは何を可能としますか？
4. 来年支店をいくつ開く予定ですか？
5. 何が生産の回転率を増加させますか？
6. 誰が仕事で素晴らしい結果を示しますか？
7. 倉庫は何を持っていますか？

1. What meeting is scheduled in the Eurobit Company?
2. Who makes the annual reports?
3. What does applying the new accounting system allow?
4. How many branches are they planning to open next year?
5. What causes an increase in production turnover?
6. Who shows excellent results in their work?
7. What do the

8. せーるすまねーじゃーは何を効率的に行いますか？

9. 年間利益れぽーとは何を示しますか？

8. What do the sales managers do effectively?

9. What does the annual profit report show?

***

日英辞書
Japanese-English dictionary

(〜に)興味を持つ / 興味を持たせる [kyoumi wo motsu / kyoumi wo motaseru] - get (be) interested / to interest
(商品の)バッチ、一部 [(shouhin no) bacchi, ichibu] - batch (of goods)
(専門)領域、プロフィール [(senmon)ryouiki, purofi-ru] - area (of specialization), profile
(料金が)無料 [(ryoukin ga) muryou] - free (of charge)
〜〜のために / 〜となるように / 〜するために [〜no tameni / 〜tonaruyouni / 〜surutameni] - to / so that / in order
〜から [〜kara] - from
〜から構成される / 〜と同等の [〜kara kouseisareru / 〜to doutouno] - consist of / be equal to
〜することができる、〜できる [〜surukoto ga dekiru, 〜dekiru] - be able, can
〜だけ [〜dake] - only
〜だった [〜datta] - was
〜でない [〜de nai] - not
〜で来る [〜de kuru] - come by
〜と / 〜で [〜to / 〜de] - with / at
〜なる(動詞) [〜naru (doushi)] - be *(Verb)*
〜に [〜ni] - to
〜について、近く [〜ni tsuite, chikaku] - about, near
〜になった(動詞) [〜ni natta (doushi)] - became *(Verb)*
〜になる(動詞) [〜ni naru (doushi)] - become *(Verb)*
〜によって [〜ni yotte] - by
〜に対して [〜ni taishite] - against
〜に適している(期間や状況に) [〜ni tekishiteiru (kikan ya joukyouni)] - be suitable (about terms or conditions)
〜のおかげで [〜no okagede] - thanks to
〜のため [〜no tame] - for
〜の上 [〜no ue] - on
〜の中 [〜 no naka] - in

〜の前 [〜no mae] - before
〜の向かいに、〜の前に [〜no mukaini, 〜no maeni] - across from / in front of
〜の間 [〜no aida] - between, during
〜も [〜mo] - also
〜を除いて [〜wo nozoite] - without
〜以外、〜を除いて [〜igai, 〜wo nozoite] - except, besides, but
1、一 [ichi] - one
10、十 [juu] - ten
100、百 [hyaku] - one hundred
1000、千 [sen] - thousand
11、十一 [juuichi] - eleven
12、十二 [juuni] - twelve
15、十五 [juugo] - fifteen
2、二 [ni] - two
20、二十 [nijuu] - twenty
2番 [niban] - second
2番目の [nibanmeno] - secondary
3、三 [san] - three
30、三十 [sanjuu] - thirty
30分 [sanjuppun] - half an hour
3番 [sanban] - third
4、四 [yon] - four
40、四十 [yonjuu] - forty
5、五 [go] - five
50、五十 [gojuu] - fifty
7、七 [nana] - seven
7日、七日 [nanoka] - seventh
8、八 [hachi] - eight
9、九 [kyuu] - nine
IT スペシャリスト、IT 専門家 [IT supesharisuto, IT senmonka] - IT-specialist, IT-professional
アイデア [aidea] - idea
アクティブ、活動的、活発 [akutibu, kappatsuteki] - active
あげる(動詞) [ageru (doushi)] - give *(Verb)*
アップデート、リニュー [appude-to, rinyuu] - update, renew

アドバイスする(動詞) [adobaisusuru (doushi)] - advise (Verb)
あなた [anata] - you
あなたの [anatano] - your
アプリケーション、使う [apurike-shon, tsukau] - application, use
アプローチ(動詞) [apuro-chi (doushi)] - approach (Verb)
アメ [ame] - candy
アメリカ女性 [amerikajosei] - American woman
あらかじめ [arakajime] - in advance
ありがとうございます [arigatougozaimasu] - thank you
あれ [are] - that
アンチウィルスソフト [anchi uirusu sofutowea] - antivirus software
アンチウィルスソフトウェア [anchi uirusu sofutouea] - antivirus software
いいえ [iie] - no
イギリス人、英国人 [igirisujin, eikokujin] - Englishman, British
イギリス女性 [igirisujosei] - British woman
いくつか、何個か [ikutsuka, nankoka] - a few, several, some
いくら(いくつ) [ikutsu (ikura)] - how much (many)
イタリアの、イタリア人 [itariano, itariajin] - Italian
いつ [itsu] - when
インターネット [inta-netto] - Internet
インターフェース [inta-fe-su] - interface
インベントリ、目録 [inbentori-, mokuroku] - inventory
ウィルスの [uirusuno] - viral
ウェブデザイン [uebudezain] - Web designer
エラー [era-] - error
エリア、領域、地域 [eria, ryouiki, chiiki] - area, region
エレベーター [erebe-ta-] - elevator
エンジニア [enjinia] - engineer
オーダー、注文 [o-da-, chuumon] - order
オープンに [o-punnni] - openly
オフィス、事務所 [ofisu, jimusho] - office
オプションの / 追加の [opushonno / tsuikano] - optional / additional
お金 [okane] - money
お願い、どうぞ [onegai, douzo] - please
カード [ka-do] - card
かかる(動詞) [kakaru (doushi)] - cost (Verb)
かかる [kakaru] - cost
カスタム作成 / 個別、個人 [kasutamu seisaku / kobetsu, kojin] - custom built / individual
カタログ [katarogu] - catalog
カテゴリー [kategori-] - category
カフェ [kafe] - cafe
カンファレンス、会議 [kanferensu, kaigi] - conference
キーボード [ki-bo-do] - keyboard
ギリシャの、ギリシャ人 [girishano, girishajin] - Greek
きれい [kirei] - clean
キロメートル [kirome-toru] - kilometer
クライアント、顧客 [kuraianto, kokyaku] - client, customer
グループ [guru-pu] - group
けれども / けれども [keredomo / keredomo] - but / though
コーヒー [ko-hi-] - coffee
ゴール、目標 [go-ru, mokuhyou] - goal, target
ここ [koko] - here
このような / こんな [konoyouna / konna] - such / so
コピー / サンプル [kopi- / sanpuru] - copy / sample
コピー機 [kopi-ki] - copy machine, Xerox, copier
コマーシャル広告 [koma-sharu koukoku] - commercial advertising
これ [kore] - this
これは〜です [kore ha 〜 desu.] - here is
こんにちは！ [konnichiha!] - Hello!
コンピューター [konpu-ta-] - computer
サーバー [sa-ba-] - server
サービス [sa-bisu] - service

サインする、署名する(動詞) [sain suru, shomei suru (doushi)] - sign (Verb)
ささいな、マイナーな [sasaina, maina-na] - insignificant, minor
させる(動詞) [saseru (doushi)] - force (Verb)
さまざまな [samazamana] - various
さようなら！ [sayounara!] - Goodbye!
さらにもっと [saranimotto] - much more
サンプル [sanpuru] - sample
シート / 表、一覧、リスト [shi-to / hyou, ichiran, risuto] - sheet / list
シールド [shi-rudo] - shield
しかし、けれども [shikashi, keredomo] - but
システム [shisutemu] - system
したがって、ここから [shitagatte, kokokara] - hence / from here
してもよい [〜shitemoyoi] - may, can
しばらくの間、短い間 [shibaraku no aida, mijikaiaida] - for a while, for a short time
シンプル [shinpuru] - simple
ずいぶん前、昔 / 長く [zuibun mae, mukashi / nagaku] - long ago / for long
スキャンする(動詞) [sukyan suru (doushi)] - scan (Verb)
すぐ [sugu] - soon
スタッフ、社員 [sutaffu, shainn] - staff, personnel
すでに、もう / また / 同じ [sudeni, mou / mata / onaji] - already / again / same
スピーチ、プレゼンテーション [supi-chi, purezente-shon] - speech, presentation
スペインの [supeinno] - Spain
スペイン女性 [supeinjosei] - Spanish woman
する(動詞)、行う、作る [〜suru (doushi), okonau, tsukuru] - do (Verb), to perform, to make
〜する必要がある、〜しなければならない [〜suru hitsuyou ga aru, 〜shinakereba naranai] - must, to have to
セクション / ブロック [sekushon / burokku] - section / block
せざるおえない [sezaruoenai] - obliged

セットアップ、インストール、設置する、置く [setto appu, insuto-ru, secchisuru, oku] - set up, to install, to put, to place
セル、箱 [seru, hako] - cell, box
そこ [soko] - there
そして、それから、と [soshite, sorekara, to] - then, and
その代わりに、見返りに、代わりとして [sono kawarini, mikaerini, kawari toshite] - instead, in return, as a replacement
その間に / 〜まで [sonoaidani / 〜made] - meanwhile / until
ソフトウェア、プログラム [sofutouea, puroguramu] - software, program
それ [sore] - it
それぞれ、皆 [sorezore, mina] - each, everybody
それでは、そのため、あれ [sore deha sonotame, are] - so, that
たいてい、ほとんど [taitei, hotondo] - almost
ダウンロード [daunro-do] - download
ダウンロードする(動詞) / ロードする [daunro-do- suru / ro-dosuru] - download (Verb) / to load
タクシー [takushi-] - taxi, cab
タスク、仕事 [tasuku,shigoto] - task
ダメージ [dame-ji] - damage
チケット [chiketto] - ticket
つまり、そして [tsumari, soshite] - so, then
つるす(動詞) [tsurusu] - hang (Verb), to crash
で / いつ [de / itsu] - at / when
で / の上 [de / no ue] - by / on
ディスク [disuku] - disk
ディレクトリー [direkutori-] - directory
テーブル [te-buru] - table
テクノロジー [tekunoroji-] - technology
デザイン、開発 [dezain, kaihatsu] - design, development
デバッグする(動詞)、取り除く [debaggu suru (doushi), torinozoku] - debug (Verb)
ドア [doa] - door
ドイツ [doitsu] - Germany

ドイツ語、ドイツの、ドイツ人 [doitsugo, doitsuno, doitsujin] - German
どうして [douhsite] - why
どうやって [douyatte] - how
どこ / どこから [doko / doko kara] - where / from where
とても [totemo] - very
ドル [doru] - dollar
どれ [dore] - which
なぜなら [nazenara] - because
について [nitsuite] - about
ニュース [nyu-su] - news
ネットワーク [nettowa-ku] - network
ノード [no-do] - node
ノベルティ [noberuti-] - novelty
の下 [no shita] - under
〜の中 [〜 no naka] - in
バージョン [ba-jon] - version
パートナー、仲間、協力者 [pa-tona-, nakama, kyouryokusha] - partner
はい [hai] - yes
バイヤー、買い手 [baiya-, kaite] - buyer
パスする(動詞) [pasusuru (doushi)] - pass (Verb)
ハッカー [hakka-] - hacker
はっきり、明確、理解できる [hakkiri, meikaku, rikaidekiru] - clear, understandable
はっきりする(動詞)、指し示す [hakkiri suru (douhsi), sashishimesu] - specify (Verb), to point out
はっきりと、明らかに [hakkirito, akirakani] - clearly
パッケージ、包み、バッチ [pakke-ji, tsutsumi, bacchi] - package, parcel, batch
パノラマ式の [panoramashikino] - panoramic
はまる(動詞)、合う / アレンジする [hamaru (doushi), au / arenjisuru] - suit (Verb) / to arrange
パラメーター [parame-ta-] - parameters
バランス(シート) [baransushi-to] - balance (sheet)

ビジネス、企業 [bijinesu, kigyou] - business, enterprise
ビジネスカード [bijinesuka-do] - business card
ビジネスセンター [bijinesusenta-] - business-center
ファイル / フォルダ [fairu / foruda-] - file / folder
ファイルにまとめる(動詞) [fairu ni matomeru] - file (Verb)
ファックス [fakkusu] - fax
フォーマット、フォーム [fo-matto, fo-mu] - format, form
フォーム、用紙 [fo-mu, youshi] - form
フライト [furaito] - flight
プラスチック [purasuchikku] - plastic
フランスの、フランス人 [furansuno, furansujin] - French, Frenchman
フランス女性 [furansujosei] - French woman
フランス語、フランスの、フランス人 [furansugo, furansuno, furansujin] - French
プリンター [purinta-] - printer
プレゼンテーション [purezente-shon] - presentation
プレビュー、レビュー [purebyu-, rebyu-] - preview, review
プログラマー [purogurama-] - programmer
プログラム [puroguramu] - program
プロジェクト、企画 [purojekuto, kikaku] - project
ブロックする(動詞) [burokkusuru (doushi)] - block (Verb)
プロデューサー、メーカー、製造業者 [purodu-sa-] - producer, maker, manufacturer
ポジティブ [pojitibu] - positive
ホテル [hoteru] - hotel
マーケット [ma-ketto] - market
マージン / 在庫 [ma-jin / zaiko] - margin / stock
マウス [mauseu] - mouse
まだ [mada] - yet
または [mataha] - or

マネージャー、管理者 [mane-jya-, kanrisha] - manager
ムード [mu-do] - mood
むしろ / より早く / きっと〜でありそうな [mushiro / yori hayaku / kitto 〜 de arisouna] - rather / faster / likely
メール [me-ru] - mail
メッセージ [messe-ji] - message
メモ、ノート [memo, no-to] - note
メンテナンス [mentenansu] - maintenance
も、また [mo, mata] - also
もうすぐ [mousugu] - almost
もし [moshi] - if
モダン、現代の [modan, gendaino] - modern
もちろん [mochiron] - of course
モデル [moderu] - model
モニター [monita-] - monitor
モニターする(動詞)、監視する [monita-suru (doushi), kanshisuru] - monitor *(Verb)*, to watch
やっと、最後に [yatto, saigoni] - finally
ユーザー [yu-za-] - user
ユニット、単位 [yunitto, tani] - unit
よく [yoku] - often
よく考え抜いた [yoku kangaenui ta] - thoughtful
より、更に [yori, sarani] - more
よりシンプルな、より簡単な [yori shinpuruna, yori kantanna] - simpler, easier
よりも [yorimo] - instead
より低い / 低い、下 [yori hikui / hikui, shita] - lower / below
より便利に [yori benrini] - more convenient
より安い [yori yasui] - cheaper
より少ない [yorisukunai] - less
より有益な [yori yuuekina] - more profitable
より自信を持って [yori jishin wo motte] - more confidently
より良い [yoriyoi] - better
より詳細に [yorishousaini] - more detailed
より説得力のある [yori settokuryoku no aru] - more convincing
より速い、より早い [yorihayai, yorihayai] - faster
より高い / の上 [yori takai / no ue] - higher / above
より高価な [yori koukana] - more expensive
ライセンスのある、認証された [raisensu no aru, nintei sareta] - licensed, certified
ライン、線 [rain, sen] - line
リーダー、社長 [ri-da-, shachou] - leader, head
リーダーシップ [ri-da-shippu] - leadership
リニューアル [rinyu-aru] - renewal
ルート、方向 [ru-to, houkou] - route, direction
レート、割合 [re-to, wariai] - ratio
レポート、報告 [repo-to, houkoku] - report
ロシア語、ロシアの、ロシア人 [roshiago, roshiano, roshiajin] - Russian
〜をより好む(動詞)、〜をより望む [〜 wo yori konomu (doushi), 〜 wo yori nozomu] - prefer *(Verb)*
を取り除く [wo torinozoku] - get rid of
を必要とする [hitsuyouto suru] - be in need
〜を超えて、〜の上 [〜wo koete, 〜no ue] - over, above
一定の、絶えず続く [itteino, taezu tuzuku] - constant
一年の、年間 [ichinenno, nenkan] - annual
一度に、すぐに、てきぱきして [ichidoni, suguni, tekipakishite] - at once, right away, promptly
一緒に [isshoni] - together
一致する(動詞)、調和する [icchisuru (doushi), chouwasuru] - match *(Verb)*, to correspond, in accord, harmoniously
一般の [ippanno] - general
一般的 [ippanteki] - general
一部 [ichibu] - part
上げる(動詞) [ageru (doushi)] - raise *(Verb)*
上手く、成功して [umaku, sekoushite] - successfully
上手に、うまく [jyouzuni, umaku] - tactfully, well

不便 [fuben] - inconvenience
不正確 [fuseikaku] - inaccuracy
不足 / 損失 [fusoku, sonshitsu] - shortage / loss
与える、渡す(動詞) [ataeru, watasu (doushi)] - give (Verb)
両立しがたい、合わない [ryouritsu shigatai, awanai] - incompatibility
中国 [chuugoku] - China
中国女性 [chuugokujosei] - Chinese woman
中国語、中国の、中国人 [chuugokugo, chuugokuno, chuugokujin] - Chinese
中央 [chuuou] - center, central
中心、主要な [chuushin, shuyou na] - main, major
主題 [shudai] - subject
予備的に [yobitekini] - preliminarily
予定、計画、摂生 [yotei, keikaku, sessei] - plan, schedule, regimen
予定していない [yotei shiteinai] - unplanned
予想、予測、視点 [yosou, yosoku, shiten] - prospect, perspective
予算 [yosan] - budget
予約した [yoyakushita] - booked
予約する(動詞) [yoyaku suru (doushi)] - book (Verb)
予約購読、定期購入 [yoyaku kounyuu, teiki kounyuu] - subscription
予防メンテナンス [yobou mentenansu] - preventative maintenance
争い [arasoi] - conflict
事例 [jirei] - case
事務所 [jimusho] - office
事務所の [jimusho] - of the office
事業家 [jigyouka] - Entrepreneur
事業欲 [jigyouyoku] - entrepreneurship
交換 [koukan] - exchange
交渉 [koushou] - negotiations
人々 [hitobito] - people
人間 / 人 [ningen / hito] - human / man
今 [ima] - now
今日 [kyou] - today

仕事、取引 [bijinesu, torihiki] - business, deal
仕事を始める(動詞) [shigoto wo hajimeru (doushi) / modoru] - turn (Verb) to / to return
他の [hoka no] - other
代理店 [dairiten] - agency
代表、メンバー [daihyou, menba-] - delegate, member, representative
企業 [kigyou] - enterprise
休む、休憩する(動詞)、リラックスする、休養 [yasumu, kyuukeisuru, rirakkusu suru, kyuuyou] - rest (Verb), to relax, recreation
会う(動詞) / 紹介する [au (doushi) / shoukaisuru] - meet (Verb) / to introduce
会社、企業 [kaisha, kigyou] - company, firm, enterprise
会社の、組織の [kaishano, soshikino] - corporate
会計 [kaikei] - accounting
会計士 [kaikeishi] - accountant
会話 [kaiwa] - conversation
会議、ミーティング [kaigi, mi-tingu] - meeting
会議室 [kaigishitsu] - conference room
伝統的な [dentoutekina] - traditional
位置する、〜にある [ichisuru, 〜ni aru] - be located, located, located, is
低い [hikui] - low
何 / あれ / どれ [nani / are / dore] - what / that / which
何もない [nanimo nai] - nothing
余分に払う [yobun ni harau] - pay extra
余分の [yobunno] - extra
作られた、終わった [tsukurareta, owatta] - made, done
作成する(動詞) [sakuseisuru (doushi)] - create (Verb)
使う(動詞) [tsukau (doushi)] - use (Verb)
価値、重要性 [juuyousei] - value, significance
便利な、好都合な [benrina, koutsugouna] - convenient

保存する(動詞) / 保つ / 保管する [hozonsuru (doushi) / tamotsu / hokansuru] - save (Verb) / to keep / to store
保管する(動詞) [hokansuru (doushi)] - store (Verb)
保証する(動詞) [hoshousuru (doushi) / hoshousuru] - assure (Verb), guarantee (Verb)
修正された / 改良された [shuuseisareta / kairyousareta] - modified / improved
修正する(動詞) [shuuseisuru (doushi)] - modify (Verb)
倉庫 [souko] - warehouse
値段、レート [nedan, re-to] - price, rate
値段表、値段のリスト [nedanhyou, nedan no risuto] - price list
働く(動詞) [hataraku (doushi)] - work (Verb)
働く人、従業員 [hataraku hito, juugyouin] - worker
優れた、良い、元気 [sugureta, yoi, genki] - good
免許、ライセンス [menkyo, raisensu] - license
入る(動詞)、〜に入る [hairu (doushi), 〜ni hairu] - enter (Verb), to go in, to get into
入口 [iriguchi] - entrance
入手可能な [nyuushukanouna] - affordable
全て [subete] - all, full
全ての、全部の [subeteno, zenbuno] - all, overall
全体 [zentai] - full
公共の場、公共の [koukyou no ba, koukyou no] - public
内容 [naiyou] - content
再び、また [futatabi, mata] - again
再起動する(動詞)、リブートする [saikidousuru (douhsi), ribu-tosuru] - restart (Verb), to reboot
冗談を言う(動詞) [jyoudan wo iu (doushi)] - joke (Verb)
処理 / 会計 [shori / kaikei] - process, processing / accounting
処理する、一掃 [shorisuru (doushi), issou] - process (Verb), processing, clearance

出る、出発する、去る [deru (doushi), shuppatsusuru, saru] - exit (Verb), go out, to leave
出席する [shussekisuru] - be present
出張、旅 [shucchou, tabi] - trip
出現する(動詞) [shutsugensuru (doushi)] - appear (Verb)
分 [fun] - minute
分配する、配る [bunpaisuru, kubaru] - distribute
利用者 [riyosha] - user
利益、もうけ [rieki, mouke] - profit, benefit
利益の無い [rieki no nai] - unprofitable
到着 [touchaku] - arrival
到着する(動詞) [touchakusuru (doushi)] - arrive (Verb)
制限 / 上限 [seigen / jougen] - restriction / limit
削減する(動詞)、切る [sakugensuru (doushi), kiru] - reduce (Verb), to cut
前の、前回の [maeno, zenkaino] - previous
割り当てる(動詞) [wariateru (doushi)] - assign (Verb)
割引 [waribiki] - discount
創立する(動詞) [souritsu suru (doushi)] - establish (Verb)
力強く [chikarazuyoku] - strongly
加えて、更に [kuwaete, sarani] - additionally, further
加える、追加する(動詞) [kuwaeru, tuikasuru(doushi)] - add (Verb)
加速する(動詞) [kasoku (doushi)] - accelerate (Verb)
助ける(動詞)、役立つ [tasukeru (doushi), yakudatsu] - help (Verb)
励ます(動詞) [hagemasu (doushi)] - cheer (Verb)
効率的、効力、能率的 [kouritsuteki, kouryoku, nouritsuteki] - efficient, effective
動かす、動く [ugokasu, ugoku] - move
動き [ugoki] - movement
動く(動詞) [ugoku (doushi)] - move (Verb)
動機付ける(動詞)、やる気になる [doukizukeru (doushi), yarukininaru] - motivate (Verb)

257

勤勉な、熱心な、勉強好きな [kinbenna, nesshinna, benkyouzukina] - diligent, studious
北京 [pekin] - Beijing
十分 [juubun] - enough
十分でない [juubun de nai] - not enough
協力、提携 [kyouryoku, teikyou] - collaboration, cooperation
協力する(動詞) [kyouroku suru (doushi)] - cooperate (Verb)
南の [minamino] - southern
印をつけた、登録された [shirushi wo tsuketa, touroku sareta] - marked, registered
印刷した [printoshita] - printed
印刷する(動詞)、プリント [insatsu suru (doushi), purinto suru] - print (Verb)
危険 [kiken] - danger
卸売り [oroshiuri] - wholesale
厳しい [kibishii] - strict
参加 [sanka] - participation
参加する(動詞) [sankasuru (doushi)] - participate (Verb), to take part
参加者、メンバー [sankasha, menba-] - participant, member
参照、調査する、評判 [sanshou, chousasuru, hyouban] - reference, review
参照する(動詞)、仕事をする [sanshou suru(doushi), shigoto wo suru] - refer (Verb) / to turn to
友達 [tomodachi] - friend
反対にする [hantai ni suru] - reverse
反対意見、意見の不一致 [hantai iken, iken no fuicchi] - disagreement
反映された、反射された [haneisareta, hanshasareta] - reflected
取り掛かる、開始する [torikakaru, kaishisuru] - get down to, to start
取り消し、キャンセル [torikeshi, kyanseru] - write-off, cancellation
取り除く(動詞) [torinozoku (doushi)] - eliminate (Verb), remove (Verb), to delete, to take off
取る(動詞) [toru (doushi)] - take (Verb)

取引、広告、宣伝、売買 [torihiki, koukou, senden, baibai] - trading, commercial, deal, transaction
取引する(動詞) [torihiki suru (doushi)] - trade (Verb)
取得物 [shutokubutsu] - acquisition
受け入れる(動詞) [ukeireru (doushi)] - accept (Verb) / to take
受け取る(動詞) / 了解する [uketoru (doushi) / ryoukaisuru] - receive (Verb) / to perceive
口座、アカウント [kouza, akaunto] - account
古い [furui] - old
可能である、もしかしたら [kanou dearu, moshikashitara] - possible, perhaps
右の、右に [migino, migini] - to the right
合意する(動詞) [gouisuru] - confirm (Verb)
合法 [gouhou] - legal
合理的な [gouritekina] - rational
合計する(動詞) [goukeisuru (doushi)] - sum (Verb)
同僚、従業員 [douryou, jyuugyouin] - coworker, employee
同意、契約 [doui, keiyaku] - agreement
同様 [douyou] - alike
同行する(動詞) [douskou suru(doushi)] - accompany (Verb)
名づける、名前をあげる [nazukeru, namae wo ageru] - name
名声 [meisei] - fame
含む(動詞) [fukuu (douhsi)] - contain (Verb)
品質、質 [hinshitsu, shitsu] - quality
商品、製品 [shouhinn, seihin] - goods, products
商業 [shougyou] - trade
商業の、コマーシャル [shougyouno, koma-sharu] - commercial
問題 [mondai] - problem
喜び、楽しみ [yorokobi, tanoshimi] - pleasure
営業マン、ディーラー [eigyouman, di-ra-] - salesman, dealer
回転する(動詞) [kaitensuru(doushi)] - turn (Verb), to rotate

回転率 [kaitenritsu] - turnover
国 [kuni] - country
国際的な [kokusaitekina] - international
地図、マップ [chizu, mappu] - map
地域の [chiikino] - regional
地方、地域 [chihou, chiiki] - district
埋める [umeru] - fill out
基本 [kihon] - basic
報告する(動詞) [houkoku suru (doushi)] - report *(Verb)*
場所 [basho] - place
増加する(動詞)、増える、育つ [zoukasuru (doushi), fueru, sodatsu] - increase *(Verb)*, to grow
壊す [kowasu] - break
壮大な、豪華な [soudaina, goukana] - magnificent, gorgeous
売った [utta] - sold
売り上げ、認識 [uriage, ninshiki] - sales, recognition
売る(動詞) [kau (doushi) / uru (doushi)] - sell *(Verb)*, sale
変化 [henka] - change
変形 [henkei] - formation
変換 [koukan] - exchange
変更する(動詞) [henkousuru (doushi)] - change *(Verb)*
外国 [gaikoku] - foreign
外部の [gaibuno] - external
夜 [yoru] - evening, night
大きい、巨大 [ookii, kyodai] - big, large
大きくない、小さい [ookikunai, chiisai] - not big, small
大きさ、サイズ [ookisa, saizu] - size
大きな、巨大な、豊富な [ookina, kyodaina, houfuna] - huge, large, voluminous
天気 [tenki] - weather
失敗、衝突 [shippai, shoutotsu] - failure, crash
契約、契約書 [keiyaku, keiyakusho] - contract
女性 [josei] - woman
好き [suki (doushi)] - like *(Verb)*

学ぶ(動詞)、知るようになる、勉強する [manabu (doushi), shiruyouni naru, benkyousuru] - learn *(Verb)*, to get to know, to study
守る(動詞)、保証する(動詞)、固定する [mamoru (doushi), hoshousuru (doushi), koteisuru] - defend *(Verb)*, secure *(Verb)*, to set down
守備、保護 [shubi, hogo] - defense, protection
安い [yasui] - cheap
安全に / 頼りになるように、壊れることなく [anznni, tayorininaru youni, kowarerukoto naku] - safely / reliably
安心、嬉しい、喜ばしい [anshin, ureshii, yorokobashii] - glad, happy, joyful
完了する(動詞) [kanryou suru (doushi)] - complete *(Verb)*
定期刊行の [teikikankouno] - periodical
実体のある、かなりの [jittai no aru, kanarino] - substantial
実行 [zikkou] - execution
実行する(動詞) [jikkou suru (doushi)] - perform *(Verb)*
客、ゲスト [kyaku, gesuto] - guest
容認できる [younin dekiru] - acceptable
専門家 [senmonka] - specialist
尋ねる、聞く(動詞) [tazuneru, kiku (doushi)] - ask *(Verb)*
導く(動詞) / リードする、指揮を執る、持ってくる [michibiku (doushi) / ri-dosuru, shiki wo toru, mottekuru] - lead *(Verb)*, to conduct, to control, to bring
小さい [chiisai] - small
少々、少し、ちょっと [shoushou, sukoshi, chotto] - slightly, a bit, a little bit
少し [sukoshi] - little
少ない [sukuna] - less
展示する(動詞) [tenjisuru(doushi)] - display *(Verb)*
展覧会 [tenrankai] - exhibition
履歴、ヒストリー [rireki, hisutori-] - history
工場、施設 [koujou, shisetsu] - factory, plant

工学、エンジニアリング [kougaku, enjiniaringu] - engineering
左の、左に [hidarino, hidarini] - to the left
希望する(動詞)、願う、期待する [kibou suru (doushi), negau, kitaisuru] - hope (Verb) / to expect
帰る、戻る(動詞) [kaeru, modoru (doushi)] - return (Verb)
常に、いつも [tsuneni, itsumo] - always
年 [nen] - year
広い、広々とした [hiroi, hirobirotoshita] - spacious, roomy
広告、宣伝 [koukoku, senden] - advertising
延長 [enchou] - extension
建てられた、建設された [taterareta, kensetsusareta] - built
建てる(動詞) [tateru(doushi)] - build (Verb)
建物 [tatemono] - building
建築上の [kenchikujouno] - architectural
建築物 [kenchikubutsu] - architecture
建設、建物、構造 [kensetsu, tatemono, kouzou] - construction, structure
強い [tsuyoi] - strong
強いられる [shiirareru] - be forced
当てにする(動詞) [ateni suru (douhsi)] - count (Verb)
当座預金(口座) [touzayokin (kouza)] - checking (account)
形づける(動詞) [katachi zukeru (doushi)] - form (Verb)
影響する(動詞) [eikyousuru (douhshi)] - influence (Verb)
役に立つ [yakunitatsu] - useful
役職、地位 [yakushoku - position, post
彼 [kare] - he
彼ら、彼女ら、それら [karera, kanojyora, sorera] - they
彼女 [kanojyo] - she
待つ(動詞) [matsu (doushi)] - wait (Verb)
待っている、予想、予期、期待 [matteiru, yosou, yoki, kitai] - waiting, anticipation, expectation
待合室 [machiaishitsu] - waiting room
後 [ato] - after

後で / 後 [atode / ato] - later / after
後に残る(動詞)、遅くなる [ato ni nokoru (doushi), osokunaru] - linger (Verb), to be late
従順な [juujunna] - obedient
得る、学ぶ [toru, manabu] - acquire
心 、精神 [kokoro, seishin] - spirit
心地が良い [kokochi ga ii] - comfortable
心配して [shinpaishite] - anxiously
心配する(動詞) [shinpaisuru (doushi)] - worry (Verb)
必ずしも、やむをえず、避けられない [kanarazushimo, yamuoezu, sakerarenai] - necessarily, unavoidably
必要、必須 [hitsuyou, hissu] - need, necessary
忘れる [wasureru (doushi)] - forget (Verb)
忙しい [isogashii] - busy
応答する(動詞) [outousuru (doushi) - respond (Verb)
急いで [isoide] - quickly
急ぐ(動詞) [isogu (doushi)] - hurry (Verb), to rush
恐らく [osoraku] - probably
悪く、不十分に [waruku, fujuubunni] - badly, poorly
悪意のある [akui no aru] - malicious
情報 [jyouhou] - information
愛する [aisuru (doushi)] - love (Verb)
感謝する(動詞) [kansha suru (doushi)] - thank (Verb)
慎重に [shinchouni] - carefully
成功した、ラッキーな [seikoushita, rakki-na] - successful, lucky
成功する(動詞) / 管理する [seikousuru (doushi) / kanrisuru] - succeed (Verb) / to manage
成長 [seichou] - growth
戦略 [senryaku] - strategy
戻る [modoru] - back
所有する [shoyuu suru] - own
手に入れる [te ni ireru] - obtain
手に取る(動詞)、持つ [tenitoru (doushi), motsu] - have (Verb)

手短に、要するに [temijikani, yousuruni] - briefly, in short
手紙 [tegami] - letter
払う(動詞) [harau (doushi)] - pay (Verb)
扱う(動詞)、うまく処理する [atsukau (doushi), umakushorisuru] - handle (Verb), to cope
招待する(動詞) [shoutaisuru (doushi)] - invite (Verb)
拡大する(動詞) [kakudaisuru (doushi)] - expand (Verb)
持ち上げる、増加する(動詞) [mochiageru, zoukasuru (doushi)] - raise (Verb)
持つ(動詞) / エスコート [motsu (doushi) / esuko-to] - hold (Verb) / to escort
持つ、持っていく(動詞) [motsu, motteiku (doushi)] - take (Verb)
持っている、所有する(動詞) [motteiru, shoyuusuru (doushi)] - have (Verb)
持ってくる(動詞) [mottekuru (doushi)] - bring (Verb)
指名した、任命した、指定した [shimeishita, ninmeishita, shiteishita] - appointed
指名する(動詞) 、任命する、指定する [shimeisuru (douishi), ninmeisuru, shiteisuru] - appoint (Verb)
指揮する(動詞)、導く [shikisuru(doushi), michibiku] - conduct (Verb), to lead
指標、指示するもの [shihyou, shijisurumono] - indicator
挑戦する(動詞)、試す [chousen suru(doushi), kokoromiru] - try (Verb)
掃除 / 清掃 [souji, seisou] - cleaning / clearing
掃除する(動詞) [soujisuru (doushi)] - clean (Verb)
接続する(動詞) / 移行する / 取り換える [setsuzoku suru / ikousuru / torikaeru] - connect (Verb) / to transfer / to switch
提供する(動詞)、〜を含める、申し出る [teikyousuru (doushi), 〜 wo fukumeru, moushideru] - provide (Verb), to include, offer (Verb)

提案する(動詞)、勧める、アドバイスする(動詞) [teiansuru (doushi), susumeru, adobaisusuru] - advise (Verb), suggest (Verb), to offer
携わる(動詞) [tazusawaru (doushi)] - engage (Verb) (in an activity)
支出、消費、費用 [shishutsu, shouhi, hiyou] - expenditure, expense
支店 [shiten] - branch
支払い [shiharai] - payment
支払われた [shiharawareta] - paid
故障、問題 [koshou, mondai] - malfunction, trouble
教える(動詞) [oshieru (doushi)] - teach (Verb)
数字、番号 [suuji, bangou] - number
断片、破片 [danpen, hahen] - piece, unit
断言する(動詞) [dangensuru (doushi)] - assert (Verb), to confirm, to approve
新しい、目新しい [atarashii, metarashii] - new, novel
方法 [houhou] - method, way
日 [hi] - day
日本 [nihon] - Japan
日本語 [nihongo] - Japanese
早い [hayai] - early
明日 [asu] - tomorrow
明確な [meikakuna] - specific
明示する(動詞) [meijisuru] - specify (Verb), to itemize
昨日 [kinou] - yesterday
昼食、夕食 [chuushoku, yuushoku] - lunch, dinner
時々 [tokidoki] - sometimes
時間、締め切り日 [jikan, shimekiribi] - hour, time, due date
時間に正確な [jikan ni seikakuna] - punctual
時間内に(何かを)行う [jikannai ni (nanika wo) okonau] - do (something) in time
時間内に [jikannaini] - in time
時間通りに、時間内に [jikandoorini, jikannai ni] - in time

261

普段 / 良く知っている [fudan, yokushittiru] - usual, usually / familiar
普通、標準 [futsuu, hyoujun] - normal
暑い [atsui] - hot
暖かい [atatakai] - warm
更に、より [sarani, yori] - more
更に複雑な / 難しい [sarani fukuzatsuna, muzukashii] - more complex / difficult
書きとめる(動詞)、気づく [kakitomeru (doushi), kizuku] - note (Verb), to notice
書く(動詞) [kaku (doushi)] - write (Verb)
書類、文書 [shoryi, bunsho] - document
最も [mottomo] - most
最初、始め、1番 [saisho, hajime, ichiban] - first
最初は、始め [saisho ha, hajimeni] - initially, first
最後 [saigo] - last
最新の [saishinno] - the newest
最新式の [saishin no] - up to date
最良の、最高、最も [sairyouno, saikou, mottomo] - best
月 [tsuki] - month
月曜日 [getsuyoubi] - Monday ['mʌndei]
有利、アドバンテージ [yuuri, adobante-ji] - advantage
有名 [yuumei] - popular
有益な、有利な、もうかる [yuuekia, yurina, moukaru] - profitable, advantageous, lucrative
有線の、接続した、繋がった [yuusen no, setuzokushita, tsunagatta] - wired, connected
望ましくない [nozomashikunai] - undesirable
朝 [asa] - morning
期間、時間、フェーズ [kikan, jikan, fr-zu] - period, time, phase
木曜日 [mokuyoubi] - Thursday
未来 [mirai] - future
本当、訂正 [hontou, teisei] - really, true, correct
本当に、とても [hontouni, totemo] - really

来る(動詞)、到着する [kuru (doushi), touchakusuru] - come (Verb), to arrive
来る [kuru] - will be
案内する(動詞) [annaisuru (doushi)] - escort (Verb)
棚 [tana] - shelve
極秘の [gokuhino] - confidential
楽天主義 [rakutenshugi] - optimism
横、側 [yoko, soba] - side
横になる / ベッドに入る、寝る [yokoninaru / beddo ni hairu, neru] - lay down / to go to bed
機材、設備 [kizai, setsubi] - equipment
機能、特徴 [kinou, tokuchou] - function, feature
欄、コラム [ran, koramu] - column
欠点のある [ketten no aru] - defective
次 [tsugi] - next
欲しい(動詞) [hoshii (doushi)] - want (Verb)
止まる(動詞)、留まる [tomaru (doushi), todomaru] - stop (Verb) / to stay
正しい / 保証 [tadashii, hoshou] - right / guarantee
正しく [tadashiku] - correctly
正午 [shougo] - noon
正確な、精密な [saikakuna, seimitsuna] - exact, precise
歩く(動詞) [aruku] - walk (Verb)
残す(動詞) [nokosu (doushi)] - leave (Verb)
残り / 残高 [nokori / zandaka] - remainder / balance
残り [nookri] - the rest
残る(動詞) [nokru (douhsi)] - stay (Verb)
毎月の [maitsukino] - monthly
比較する [hikakusuru] - comparing
気づく(動詞) [kizuku (doushi)] - notice (Verb)
気分悪くなる、病気になる [kibun ga warukunaru, byouki ni naru] - be ill, to be sick
水曜日 [suiyoubi] - Wednesday
求める(動詞) [motomeru (doushi)] - require (Verb)

決定する(動詞) [ketteisuru (doushi)] - decide (Verb)
決意する(動詞)、定義する [ketsuisuru (doushi), teigisuru] - determine (Verb), to define
沢山、多くの [takusan, ookuno] - many, a lot of
法人 [houji / houjin] - corporation, corporate
法律家、弁護士 [houritsuka, bengoshi] - lawyer, attorney
注文 [chuumon] - order
注文する(動詞)、予約する [chuumonsuru, yoyakusuru] - order (Verb), to book
洗練 [senen] - refinement
活動 [katsudou] - activity
消費する(動詞)、費やす [shouhisuru (doushi), tsuiyasu] - expend (Verb), to spend
混乱する(動詞)、混合する [konran suru, kongou suru] - confuse (Verb), to mix
渡す、あげる(動詞) [watasu, ageru (doushi)] - give (Verb)
満足して、喜んで [manzokushite, yorokonde] - pleased
満足できる、楽しい [manzokudekiru, tanoshii] - pleasant
源、リソース [minamoto, reso-su] - resource
準備、訓練 [junbi, kunren] - preparation, training
準備する、用意する [junbisuru, youisuru] - ready
火曜日 [kayoubi] - Tuesday
点、その時 [ten, sonotoki] - point, moment
物 [mono] - thing
特別 [tokubetsu] - special
状況、状態、期間 [joukyou, joutai, kikan] – condition / occasion, situation, term
率、パーセンテージ [ritsu, pa-sente-ji] - percent
理由 [riyuu] - reason
理解する(動詞) [rikaisuru (douhsi)] - understand (Verb)
用意、準備 [youi, jyunnbi] - ready
用意する(動詞) [youisuru (doushi)] - prepare (Verb)
申し訳ありません [moushiwake arimasen] - Sorry
男性 [dansei] - man
町 [machi] - city
疑問 [gimon] - question
疲れさせる(動詞) [tsukaresaseru (doushi)] - tire (Verb)
発売、開始 [hatsubai, kaishi] - launch, startup
発展 [hatten] - development
発行する(動詞)、置く [hakkousuru (doushi), oku] - issue (Verb), to place
発見された [hakkensareta] - found
発見する(動詞)、確認する / 明確にする [hakkensuru (doushi), kakunin suru / meikakunisuru] - find (Verb), find out / to clarify
発送 [hassou] - shipment
登る(動詞) [noboru (doushi)] - climb (Verb)
皆 [minna] - guys
目に見える、見える [meni mieru, mieru] - visible, seen
直す(動詞) [naosu(doushi)] - correct (Verb)
相互利益、ウィンウィン [sougorieki, uinuin] - mutually beneficial, win-win
相応している、適している [souou shiteiru, tekishiteiru] - appropriate
相談する (動詞) [soudansuru (doushi)] - consult (Verb)
真面目な、重要な [majimena, juuyouna] - serious
眠る(動詞) [nemuru (doushi)] - sleep (Verb)
着陸する(動詞) [chakurikusuru (doushi)] - land (Verb)
知らせる(動詞) [shiraseru (doushi)] - acquaint (Verb)
知られている [shirareteiru] - known
知る(動詞) [shiru (doushi)] - know (Verb)
短気 [tanki] - impatience
砂糖 [satou] - sugar
硬い [katai] - hard
確かである [tashika dearu] - sure

確信して、あらかじめ決められた [kakushinshite, arakajime kimerareta] - certain, predefined
確認 [kakunin] - confirmation
確認する(動詞)、調査する [kakuninsuru (doushi), chousasuru] - check (Verb), to examine
祝う(動詞) [iwau (doushi)] - celebrate (Verb), congratulate (Verb)
私 [watashi] - I
私たち [watashitachi] - we
私たちの [watashitachi no] - our
私の [watashi no] - mine, my
秘書 [hisho] - secretary
移動する(動詞) [idousuru] - transfer (Verb)
空港, [kuukou] - airport
窓 [mado] - window
競争者 [kyousousha] - competitor
答える(動詞) [kotaeru (doushi)] - answer (Verb)
管理、制御、監督 [kanri, seigyo, kantoku] - control, supervision
管理する(動詞)、リードする [kanrisuru (doushi), ri-dosuru] - manage (Verb), to lead
管理者 [kanrisha] - administrator
箱 [hako] - box
約束された、有望な、期待できる、考え方 [yakusokusareta, yuunouna, kangaekata] - promising, perspective
紅茶 [koucha] - tea
紙 [kami] - paper
素晴らしい、優秀な、大変良い [subarashii, yuushuuna, taihen yoi] - excellent, amazing
紹介する(動詞) [shoukaisuru (doushi) - introduce (Verb)
終わり [owari] - end
終わる(動詞) / 〜に入る / (契約書に)サインする [owaru (doushi) / 〜ni hairu / (keiyakushi ni) sain suru] - conclude (Verb), finish (Verb) / to enter / to sign (a contract)
経済学者 [keizaigakusha] - economist
経過する(動詞) [tsuukasuru] - pass (Verb)
経験 [keiken] - experience
経験した、経験のある [keikenshita, keiken no aru] - experienced
結局は、最後は [kekkyoku ha, saigo ha] - eventually, at last
結果、最低値 [kekka, saiteichi] - result, bottom line
統合 [tougou] - joint
統括会社、ヘッドクオーター [toukatsugaisha, heddokuo-ta-] - headquarter
続く(動詞) [tuzuku (doushi)] - continue (Verb)
緊急に [kinkyuuni] - urgently
総収入、収入 [soushuunyuu, shuunyuu] - revenue, income
総支配人、取締役、指導者 [soushihainin, torishimariyaku, shidousha] - general manager, director
緑 [midori] - green
繋ぐ、接続 [tsunagu, setsuzoku] - connect
置き換える [okikaeru (doushi)] - replace (Verb)
署名する(動詞)、サインする [shomeisuru (doushi), sainsuru] - sign (Verb)
美しい [utsukushii] - beautiful
義務 [gimu] - obligation
義務的な [gimutekina] - obligatory
考える(動詞)、〜だと思う、熟考する、考慮する [kangaeru (doushi), 〜dato omou, jyukkosuru, kouryosuru] - think (Verb), to contemplate, consider (Verb)
考慮した上で、考える [kouryoshita uede, kangaeru] - take into account, to consider
聞く(動詞) [kiku (doushi)] - hear (Verb), listen (Verb)
職業、業務 [shokugyou, gyoumu] - profession, occupation
背の高い、高い [se no takai, takai] - tall, high
能力、可能性、機会 [nouryoku, kanousei, kikai] - ability, possibility, opportunity, skill
自信をもって [jishin wo motte] - confidently
自動の [jidouno] - automatic
自動的に [jidoutekini] - automatically

自由 [jiyuu] - free
興味 [kyoumi] - interest
興味深い、面白い [kyoumibukai, omoshiroi] - interesting
航空会社、エアライン [koukuu gaisha, earain] - airline
良い、素敵 [yoi, suteki] - nice
良く知られた、有名な [yokushirareta, yuumeina] - wellknown, famous
色 [iro] - color
若い [wakai] - young
英語、イギリスの、イギリス人 [eigo, igirisuno, igirisujinno] - British, English
著しく、ずいぶん、とても [ichijirushiku, zuibun, totemo] - significantly, considerably, much
融資する(動詞) [yuushisuru (doushi)] - finance *(Verb)*
行う(動詞)、携わる [okonau (doushi), tazusawaru] - do *(Verb)*, to engage
行く(動詞)、へ向かう [iku (doushi), he mukau] - go *(Verb)*, to head
行われる、通り過ぎる [okonawareru, toorisugiru] - take place, to pass
行動、アクション [koudou, akushon] - action
表にする(動詞) [hyounisuru] - list *(Verb)*
表現する(動詞) [hyougensuru (doushi)] - express *(Verb)*
製品 [seihin] - product, products
製図 [seizu] - drawing
製造、生産 [seizou, seisan] - manufacturing, production
製造設備、製造ライン [seizousetsubi, seizourain] - manufacturing facilities, production lines
複数 [fukusuu] - multiple
複雑 [fukuzatsu] - complex
要求、需要 [youkyuu, juyou] - demand, requirement
要求されていない [youkyuu sareteinai] - unclaimed
要求する(動詞) [youkyuusuru (doushi)] - demand, require *(Verb)*

見せる(動詞) [miseru (doushi)] - show *(Verb)*
見る(動詞)、会う、スキャンする [miru (doushi), aru, sukyansuru] - see *(Verb)*, view *(Verb)*, to watch *(Verb)*, to look *(Verb)*, look *(Verb)* / to scan
視界、景色 [shikai, keshiki] - view
親切、良い [shinsetsu, yoi] - kind, good
解決する、理解する [kaiketsusuru, rikaisuru] - figure out
解決策 [kaiketsusaku] - solution
言う(動詞)、教える [iu (doushi), oshieru] - tell *(Verb)*
言葉 [kotoba] - word
言語 [gengo] - language
計画 [keikaku] - planning, scheme
計画する(動詞) [keikakusuru (doushi)] - plan *(Verb)*
計算する(動詞)、数える / 考慮する [keisansuru, kazoeru / kouryosuru] - count *(Verb)* / to consider
記事、論文 [kiji, ronbun] - article
記者 [kisha] - journalist
記述 [kijutsu] - description
記述された [kijutsu sareta] - described
訪ねる [tazumeru] - visit
訪問者 [houmonsha] - visitor
設定、セットアップ [settei, settoappu] - set up
設定する、チューニング [setteisuru, chuningusuru] - setting, tuning
設置 [secchi] - installation
許す(動詞)、言い訳をする [yurusu (doushi), iiwake wo suru] - excuse *(Verb)*
許可する(動詞) [kyokasueu (doushi)]] - allow *(Verb)*
評価する(動詞)、尊重する(動詞)、感謝する [hyoukasuru (doushi), souchou suru (doushi), kansha suru] - assess *(Verb)*, value *(Verb)*, to appreciate
評判 [hyouban] - reputation
評議会、委員会(監督の) [hyougikai, iinkai (kantokuno)] - council, board (of directors)
試す(動詞) [tamesu (doushi)] - try *(Verb)*

試験 [shiken] - testing
試験された、証明された [shikensareta, shoumeisareta] - tested, proven
話す(動詞)、発表する [hanasu (doushi), happyou suru] - speak (Verb), talk (Verb) / to reflect, to present
詳細 / じっくり、徹底的に / アイテム / 必要な [shousai / jikkuri, tetteitekini / aitemu /, shitsuyouna] - detail, details, / thoroughly / item / requisites
詳細な [shousaina] - detailed
認める(動詞) [mitomeru (doushi)] - approve (Verb)
認識 [ninshiki] - realization
説得する(動詞) [settoku suru (doushi)] - persuade (Verb)
説得力のある [settokuryoku no aru] - convincing
説得力を持って [settokuryoku wo motte] - persuasively
説明する(動詞) [setsumeisuru (doushi)] - explain (Verb)
読む(動詞) [yomu (doushi)] - read (Verb)
誰 [dare] - who
誰か / いくつか [dareka / ikutsuka] - someone / some
誰の [dareno] - whose
誰も [daremo] - no one
調整する(動詞)、修正する [chousei suru (doushi), shuuseisuru] - adjust (Verb), to tune
調査する(動詞)、見る [chousasuru (doushi), miru] - examine (Verb), to view
謝る(動詞)、謝罪する - apologize (Verb)
議論、話し合い [giron, hanashiai] - discussion
議論する(動詞)、話し合う [gironsuru (doushi), hanashiau] - discuss (Verb)
議論の [gironno] - controversial
象徴する(動詞)、代表する [shouchou suru, daihyou suru] - represent (Verb)
財務 [zaimu] - financial
貨物 [kamotsu] - cargo
責任、責務 [sekinin, sekimu] - responsibility, duty

責任のある [sekinin no aru] - responsible, liable
買う(動詞) [kau (doushi)] - buy (Verb)
費用 [hiyou] - expense
費用のかからない [hiyou no kakaranai] - inexpensive
費用効果のある [hiyoukouka no aru] - cost effective
資料 [shiryou] - material
資産、財産 [shisan, zaisan] - funds, means
賛成した [sanseishita] - agreed
賛成する(動詞)、和解する [sansei suru (doushi), wakaisuru] - agree (Verb), to reconcile
質、品質、クオリティ [shitsu, hinshitsu, kuoriti-] - quality
質問、問い合わせ [shitsumon, toiawase] - inquiry
購入、買う [kounyuu, kau] - purchase, buy
購入する(動詞) [kounyuusuru (doushi)] - purchase (Verb)
走る(動詞) [hashiru (doushi)] - run (Verb)
起こる(動詞)、発生する [okoru (doushi), hassei suru] - happen (Verb), to occur (Verb)
車 [kuruma] - car
輸送 [yusou] - transportation
迎える(動詞) [mukaeru (doushi)] - welcome (Verb), to greet
近い [chikai] - near, close
近所の [kinjyono] - neighboring
返金、リターン [henkin, rita-n] - return
追加 [tsuika] - addition
追加した [tsuikashita] - added
送る、送信する(動詞) [okuru, soushinsuru (doushi)] - send (Verb)
通して、徹底して、後に(一定時間) [toushite, tetteishite, goni (itteijikan) - through, in (a certain time)
通常、普通、普段 [tsuujyou, futsuu, fudan] - regular, normal
通知する [tsuuchisuru] - inform
通訳 [tsuuyaku] - interpreter
速い、早い [hayai, hayai] - fast

連絡を取る(動詞) [renraku wo toru (doushi)] - contact (Verb)
週 [shuu] - week
遂行する(動詞)、実行する [suikou suru (doushi)、jikkou suru] - accomplish, execute
遅い [osoi] - slow
運ぶ、抱える(動詞) [hakobu, kakeru (doushi)] - carry (Verb)
過ぎた / 最後の [suugita / saigono] - past / last
道、道路、外 [michi, douro, soto] - path, street, outside
道路 [douro] - road
違い [chigai] - difference
違う [chigau] - different
適切な [tekisetsuna] - appropriate
部屋 [heya] - room
部門、部 [bumon, bu] - department, division
配分 [haibun] - distribution
配達、供給 [haitatsu, kyoukyuu] - delivery, supply
配達する(動詞) [haitatsusuru (doushi)] - deliver (Verb)
重要 [juuyou] - important
重要な、著しく [juuyouna, ichijirushiku] - significant
量 [ryou] - quantity, volume
金属の [kinzokuno] - metallic
金曜日 [kinyoubi] - Friday
銀行 [ginkou] - bank
銀行業 [ginkougyou] - banking
鍵 [kagi] - key
長い [nagai] - long
閉じる(動詞) [toziru (doushi)] - close (Verb)
開ける(動詞) [akeru (doushi)] - open (Verb)
開催する [kaisai suru] - take place
開始から、始めから [kaishikara, hajimekara] - from the start, from the beginning, first
開始する(動詞) / をやり始める / 始める [kaishisuru (doushi) / wo yarihajimeru / hajimeru] - start (Verb) / to get to / to begin

開発する(動詞) [kaihatsusuru (doushi)] - develop (Verb)
開発者 [kaihatsusha] - developer
間違え、欠点 [machigae, ketten] - mistake, flaw
間違って [machigatte] - incorrectly
関係、フィードバック [kankei, fi-dobakk] - relation, feedback
階 [kai] - floor
障害、不利 [shougai, furi] - drawback, disadvantage
集める(動詞)、収集する [atsumeru (doushi), shuushuu suru] - collect (Verb), gather (Verb)
雑誌 [zasshi] - magazine
離す [hanasu] - separate
離れて、別々に [hanarete, betsubetsuni] - apart, separately
難しい、複雑な [muzukashii, fukuzatsuna] - difficult, complicated
雨 [ame] - rain
電子の [denshino] - electronic
電話 [denwa] - phone
電話し直す [denwashinaosu] - call back
電話する(動詞) / 名前をつける [denwasuru (doushi) / namae wo tsukeru] - call (Verb), ring / to name
革新 [kakushin] - innovation
革新的な [kakushintekina] - innovative
預金、保存 [yokin, hozon] - saving, preservation
頼む、要求 [tanomu, youkyuu] - request
頼りになる [tayorininaru] - reliable
頼る(動詞) [tayoru (doushi)] - depend (Verb)
題名、名前 [daimei, namae] - title, name
飛ぶ(動詞) [tobu (doushi)] - fly (Verb)
飛行機 [hikouki] - plane, airplane
食事する(動詞) [shokujisuru (doushi)] - dine (Verb)
駅 [eki] - station
駆り立てる(動詞) [karitateru (douhsi)] - prompt (Verb)

驚く(動詞)、不思議に思う、驚く [odorok (doushi), fushigi ni omou, odoroku] - wonder *(Verb)*, to be surprised
高い [takai] - high
高くない [takakunai] - inexpensive
高価、(値段が) 高い [kouka, (nedan ga) takai] - expensive
高層建築 [kousoukenchiku] - highrise

高速 / 早い [kousoku, hayai] - high speed / fast
魅力 [miryoku] - attraction
鳴らす(動詞)、呼ぶ [narasu, yobu] - ring *(Verb)*, to call

英日辞書
English-Japanese dictionary

a few, several - いくつか、何個か [ikutsuka, nankoka]
ability, possibility, opportunity - 能力、可能性、機会 [nouryoku, kanousei, kikai]
able, can - 〜することができる、〜できる [〜surukoto ga dekiru, 〜dekiru]
about, near - 〜について、近く [〜ni tsuite, chikaku]
accelerate (*Verb*) - 加速する (動詞) [kasoku (doushi)]
accept (*Verb*) / to take - 受け入れる (動詞) [ukeireru (doushi)]
acceptable - 容認できる [younin dekiru]
accompany (*Verb*) - 同行する (動詞) [douskou suru (doushi)]
accord, harmoniously - 一致する、調和する [icchisuru, chouwasuru]
account - 口座、アカウント [kouza, akaunto]
accountant - 会計士 [kaikeishi]
accounting - 会計 [kaikei]
acquaint (*Verb*) - 知らせる (動詞) [shiraseru (doushi)]
acquire - 得る、学ぶ [toru, manabu]
acquisition - 取得物 [shutokubutsu]
across from / in front of - 〜の向かいに、〜の前に [〜no mukaini, 〜no maeni]
action - 行動、アクション [koudou, akushon]
active - アクティブ、活動的 [akutibu, kappatsuteki]
activity - 活動 [katsudou]
add (*Verb*) - 加える、追加する (動詞) [kuwaeru, tuikasuru (doushi)]
added - 追加した [tsuikashita]
addition - 追加 [tsuika]
additionally, further - 加えて、更に [kuwaete, sarani]
adjust (*Verb*), to tune - 調整する (動詞)、修正する [chousei suru (doushi), shuuseisuru]
administrator - 管理者 [kanrisha]

advance - あらかじめ [arakajime]
advantage - 有利、アドバンテージ [yuuri, adobante-ji]
advertising - 広告、宣伝 [koukoku, senden]
advise (*Verb*) - 提案する、勧める、アドバイスする (動詞) [teiansuru, susumeru, adobaisusuru (doushi)]
affordable - 入手可能な [nyuushukanouna]
after - 後 [ato]
again - 再び、また [futatabi, mata]
against - 〜に対して [〜ni taishite]
agency - 代理店 [dairiten]
agree (*Verb*), to reconcile - 賛成する (動詞)、和解する [sansei suru (doushi), wakaisuru]
agreed - 賛成した [sanseishita]
agreement - 同意、契約 [doui, keiyaku]
airline - 航空会社、エアライン [koukuu gaisha, earain]
airport - 空港, [kuukou]
alike - 同様 [douyou]
all - 全て [subete]
all, overall - 全ての、全部の [subeteno, zenbuno]
allow (*Verb*) - 許可する (動詞) [kyokasueu (doushi)]]
almost - たいてい、ほとんど、もうすぐ [taitei, hotondo, mousugu]
already / again / same - すでに、もう / また / 同じ [sudeni, mou / mata / onaji]
also - も、また [mo, mata]
always - 常に、いつも [tsuneni, itsumo]
amazing - 素晴らしい [subarashii]
American woman - アメリカ女性 [amerikajosei]
and - そして、と [soshite, to]
annual - 一年の、年間 [ichinenno, nenkan]
answer (*Verb*) - 答える (動詞) [kotaeru (doushi)]
antivirus software - アンチウィルスソフトウェア [anchi uirusu sofutouea]

269

anxiously - 心配して [shinpaishite]
apart, separately - 離れて、別々に [hanarete, betsubetsuni]
apologize (Verb) - 謝る (動詞)、謝罪する
appear (Verb) - 出現する (動詞) [shutsugensuru (doushi)]
application, use - アプリケーション、使う [apurike-shon, tsukau]
appoint (Verb) - 指名する (動詞)、任命する、指定する [shimeisuru (douishi), ninmeisuru, shiteisuru]
appointed - 指名した、任命した、指定した [shimeishita, ninmeishita, shiteishita]
approach (Verb) - アプローチ (動詞) [apuro-chi (doushi)]
appropriate - 相応している、適している、適切な [souou shiteiru, tekishiteiru, tekisetsuna]
approve (Verb) - 認める (動詞) [mitomeru (doushi)]
architectural - 建築上の [kenchikujouno]
architecture - 建築物 [kenchikubutsu]
area (of specialization), profile - (専門)領域、プロフィール [(senmon)ryouiki, purofi-ru]
area, region - エリア、領域、地域 [eria, ryouiki, chiiki]
arrival - 到着 [touchaku]
arrive (Verb) - 到着する (動詞) [touchakusuru (doushi)]
article - 記事、論文 [kiji, ronbun]
ask (Verb) - 尋ねる、聞く (動詞) [tazuneru, kiku (doushi)]
assert (Verb), to confirm, to approve - 断言する (動詞) [dangensuru (doushi)]
assess (Verb) - 評価する (動詞) [hyoukasuru (doushi)]
assign (Verb) - 割り当てる (動詞) [wariateru (doushi)]
assure (Verb) - 保証する (動詞) [hoshousuru (doushi)]
at / when - で /いつ [de /itsu]
at once, right away, promptly - 一度に、すぐに、てきぱきして [ichidoni, suguni, tekipakishite]

attraction - 魅力 [miryoku]
automatic - 自動の [jidouno]
automatically - 自動的に [jidoutekini]
back - 戻る [modoru]
badly, poorly - 悪く、不十分に [waruku, fujuubunni]
balance (sheet) - バランス (シート) [baransushi-to]
bank - 銀行 [ginkou]
banking - 銀行業 [ginkougyou]
basic - 基本 [kihon]
batch (of goods) - (商品の)バッチ、一部 [(shouhin no) bacchi, ichibu]
be (Verb) - 〜なる (動詞) [〜naru (doushi)]
beautiful - 美しい [utsukushii]
became (Verb) - 〜になった (動詞) [〜ni natta (doushi)]
because - なぜなら [nazenara]
become (Verb) - 〜になる (動詞) [〜ni naru (doushi)]
before - 〜の前 [〜no mae]
Beijing - 北京 [pekin]
best - 最良の、最高、最も [sairyouno, saikou, mottomo]
better - より良い [yoriyoi]
between - 〜の間 [〜no aida]
big, large - 大きい、巨大 [ookii, kyodai]
block (Verb) - ブロックする (動詞) [burokkusuru (doushi)]
book (Verb) - 予約する (動詞) [yoyaku suru (doushi)]
booked - 予約した [yoyakushita]
box - 箱 [hako]
branch - 支店 [shiten]
break - 壊す [kowasu]
briefly, in short - 手短に、要するに [temijikani, yousuruni]
bring (Verb) - 持ってくる (動詞) [mottekuru (doushi)]
British, English - 英語、イギリスの、イギリス人 [eigo, igirisuno, igirisujinno]
British woman - イギリス女性 [igirisujosei]
budget - 予算 [yosan]

build (*Verb*) - 建てる (動詞) [tateru (doushi)]
building - 建物 [tatemono]
built - 建てられた、建設された [taterareta, kensetsusareta]
business, enterprise - ビジネス、企業 [bijinesu, kigyou]
business card - ビジネスカード [bijinesuka-do]
business-center - ビジネスセンター [bijinesusenta-]
busy - 忙しい [isogashii]
but / though - しかし、けれども / けれども [shikashi, keredomo / keredomo]
buy / sell - 買う (動詞) / 売る (動詞) [kau (doushi)]
buyer - バイヤー、買い手 [baiya-, kaite]
by / on - で / の上 / 〜によって [de / no ue / 〜ni yotte]
cafe - カフェ [kafe]
call (*Verb*), to name - 電話する (動詞)、名前をつける [denwasuru (doushi), namae wo tsukeru]
call, ring - 電話する [denwa suru]
call back - 電話し直す [denwashinaosu]
candy - アメ [ame]
car - 車 [kuruma]
card - カード [ka-do]
carefully - 慎重に [shinchouni]
cargo - 貨物 [kamotsu]
carry (*Verb*) - 運ぶ (動詞)、抱える (動詞) [hakobu (doushi), kakeru (doushi)]
case - 事例 [jirei]
catalog - カタログ [katarogu]
category - カテゴリー [kategori-]
celebrate (*Verb*) - 祝う (動詞) [iwau (doushi)]
cell, box - セル、箱 [seru, hako]
center - 中央 [chuuou]
central - 中央 [chuuou]
certain, predefined - 確信して、あらかじめ決められた [kakushinshite, arakajime kimerareta]
change - 変化 [henka]

change (*Verb*) - 変更する (動詞) [henkousuru (doushi)]
cheap - 安い [yasui]
cheaper - より安い [yori yasui]
check (*Verb*), to examine - 確認する (動詞)、調査する [kakuninsuru (doushi), chousasuru]
checking (account) - 当座預金 (口座) [touzayokin (kouza)]
cheer (*Verb*) - 励ます (動詞) [hagemasu (doushi)]
China - 中国 [chuugoku]
Chinese - 中国語、中国の、中国人 [chuugokugo, chuugokuno, chuugokujin]
Chinese woman - 中国女性 [chuugokujosei]
city - 町 [machi]
clean - きれい [kirei]
clean (*Verb*) - 掃除する (動詞) [soujisuru (doushi)]
cleaning / clearing - 掃除 / 清掃 [souji, seisou]
clear, understandable - はっきり、明確、理解できる [hakkiri, meikaku, rikaidekiru]
clearly - はっきりと、明らかに [hakkirito, akirakani]
client, customer - クライアント、顧客 [kuraianto, kokyaku]
climb (*Verb*) - 登る (動詞) [noboru (doushi)]
close (*Verb*) - 閉じる (動詞) [toziru (doushi)]
coffee - コーヒー [ko-hi-]
collaboration, cooperation - 協力、提携 [kyouryoku, teikyou]
collect (*Verb*) - 集める (動詞) [atsumeru (doushi)]
color - 色 [iro]
column - 欄、コラム [ran, koramu]
come (*Verb*), to arrive - 来る (動詞)、到着する [kuru (doushi), touchakusuru]
come by - 〜で来る [〜de kuru]
comfortable - 心地が良い [kokochi ga ii]
commercial - 商業の、コマーシャル [shougyouno, koma-sharu]

commercial advertising - コマーシャル広告 [koma-sharu koukoku]
company, enterprise - 会社、企業 [kaisha, kigyou]
comparing - 比較する [hikakusuru]
competitor - 競争者 [kyousousha]
complete (Verb) - 完了する (動詞) [kanryou suru (doushi)]
complex - 複雑 [fukuzatsu]
computer - コンピューター [konpu-ta-]
conclude (Verb) / to enter / to sign (a contract) - 終わる (動詞) /～に入る / (契約書に)サインする [owaru (doushi) / ～ni hairu / (keiyakushi ni) sain suru]
condition, term - 状況、状態、期間 [joukyou, joutai, kikan]
conduct (Verb), to lead - 指揮する (動詞)、導く [shikisuru (doushi), michibiku]
conference - カンファレンス、会議 [kanferensu, kaigi]
conference room - 会議室 [kaigishitsu]
confidential - 極秘の [gokuhino]
confidently - 自信をもって [jishin wo motte]
confirm (Verb) - 合意する (動詞) [gouisuru]
confirmation - 確認 [kakunin]
conflict - 争い [arasoi]
confuse (Verb), to mix - 混乱する (動詞)、混合する [konran suru, kongou suru]
congratulate (Verb) - 祝う (動詞) [iwau (doushi)]
connect - 繋ぐ、接続 [tsunagu, setsuzoku]
connect (Verb) / to transfer / to switch - 接続する (動詞) / 移行する / 取り換える [setsuzoku suru / ikousuru / torikaeru]
consider (Verb) - 考える (動詞)、考慮する [kangaeru (doushi), kouryosuru]
consist of / be equal to - ～から構成される /～と同等の [～kara kouseisareru /～to doutouno]
constant - 一定の、絶えず続く [itteino, taezu tuzuku]
construction, structure - 建設、建物、構造 [kensetsu, tatemono, kouzou]

consult (Verb) - 相談する (動詞) [soudansuru (doushi)]
contact (Verb) - 連絡を取る (動詞) [renraku wo toru (doushi)]
contain (Verb) - 含む (動詞) [fukuu (douhsi)]
content - 内容 [naiyou]
continue (Verb) - 続く (動詞) [tuzuku (doushi)]
contract - 契約、契約書 [keiyaku, keiyakusho]
control, supervision - 管理、制御、監督 [kanri, seigyo, kantoku]
controversial - 議論の [gironno]
convenient - 便利な、好都合な [benrina, koutsugouna]
conversation - 会話 [kaiwa]
convincing - 説得力のある [settokuryoku no aru]
cooperate (Verb) - 協力する (動詞) [kyouroku suru (doushi)]
copy /sample - コピー /サンプル [kopi-/sanpuru]
copy machine, Xerox, copier - コピー機 [kopi-ki]
corporate - 会社の、組織の、法人 [kaishano, soshikino, houjin]
corporation - 法人 [houji]
correct (Verb) - 直す (動詞) [naosu (doushi)]
correctly - 正しく [tadashiku]
cost (Verb) - かかる (動詞) [kakaru (doushi)]
cost effective - 費用効果のある [hiyoukouka no aru]
council, board (of directors) - 評議会、委員会 (監督の) [hyougikai, iinkai (kantokuno)]
count (Verb) - 当てにする (動詞) [ateni suru (douhsi)]
count for (Verb) / to consider - 計算する (動詞)、数える / 考慮する [keisansuru, kazoeru / kouryosuru]
country - 国 [kuni]
coworker, employee - 同僚、従業員 [douryou, jyuugyouin]

create (*Verb*) - 作成する (動詞) [sakuseisuru (doushi)]
custom built / individual - カスタム作成 / 個別、個人 [kasutamu seisaku / kobetsu, kojin]
damage - ダメージ [dame-ji]
danger - 危険 [kiken]
day - 日 [hi]
deal, transaction - 取引、売買 [torihiki, baibai]
debug (*Verb*) - デバッグする (動詞)、取り除く [debaggu suru (doushi), torinozoku]
decide (*Verb*) - 決定する (動詞) [kettei suru (doushi)]
defective - 欠点のある [ketten no aru]
defend (*Verb*) - 守る (動詞) [mamoru (doushi)]
defense, protection - 守備、保護 [shubi, hogo]
delegate, member, representative - 代表、メンバー [daihyou, menba-]
deliver (*Verb*) - 配達する (動詞) [haitatsusuru (doushi)]
delivery, supply - 配達、供給 [haitatsu, kyoukyuu]
demand - 要求、需要、要求する [youkyuu, juyou, youkyuusuru]
department, division - 部門、部 [bumon, bu]
depend (*Verb*) - 頼る (動詞) [tayoru (doushi)]
described - 記述された [kijutsu sareta]
description - 記述 [kijutsu]
design, development - デザイン、開発 [dezain, kaihatsu]
detail / item / thoroughly - 詳細 / アイテム / じっくり、徹底的に [shousai / aitemu / jikkuri, tetteitekini]
detailed - 詳細な [shousaina]
details, requisites - 詳細、必要な [shousai, shitsuyouna]
determine (*Verb*), to define - 決意する (動詞)、定義する [ketsuisuru (doushi), teigisuru]

develop (*Verb*) - 開発する (動詞) [kaihatsusuru (doushi)]
developer - 開発者 [kaihatsusha]
development - 発展 [hatten]
difference - 違い [chigai]
different - 違う [chigau]
difficult, complicated - 難しい、複雑な [muzukashii, fukuzatsuna]
diligent, studious - 勤勉な、熱心な、勉強好きな [kinbenna, nesshinna, benkyouzukina]
dine (*Verb*) - 食事する (動詞) [shokujisuru (doushi)]
directory - ディレクトリー [direkutori-]
disagreement - 反対意見、意見の不一致 [hantai iken, iken no fuicchi]
discount - 割引 [waribiki]
discuss (*Verb*) - 議論する (動詞)、話し合う [gironsuru (doushi), hanashiau]
discussion - 議論、話し合い [giron, hanashiai]
disk - ディスク [disuku]
display (*Verb*) - 展示する (動詞) [tenjisuru (doushi)]
distribute - 分配する、配る [bunpaisuru, kubaru]
distribution - 配分 [haibun]
district - 地方、地域 [chihou, chiiki]
do (something) in time - 時間内に (何かを) 行う [jikannai ni (nanika wo) okonau]
do, to perform, to make, to engage - する (動詞)、行う (動詞)、作る、携わる [～suru (doushi), okonau (doushi), tsukuru, tazusawaru]
document - 書類、文書 [shoryi, bunsho]
dollar - ドル [doru]
door - ドア [doa]
download (*Verb*) / to load - ダウンロードする (動詞) / ロードする [daunro-do- suru / ro-dosuru]
drawback, disadvantage - 障害、不利 [shougai, furi]
drawing - 製図 [seizu]
during - ～の間 [～no aida]

each, everybody - それぞれ、皆 [sorezore, mina]
early - 早い [hayai]
economist - 経済学者 [keizaigakusha]
efficient, effective - 効率的、効力 [kouritsuteki, kouryoku]
eight - 8、八 [hachi]
electronic - 電子の [denshino]
elevator - エレベーター [erebe-ta-]
eleven - 11、十一 [juuichi]
eliminate (Verb) - 取り除く (動詞) [torinozoku (doushi)]
end - 終わり [owari]
engage (Verb) (in an activity) - 携わる (動詞) [tazusawaru (doushi)]
engineer - エンジニア [enjinia]
engineering - 工学、エンジニアリング [kougaku, enjiniaringu]
Englishman, British - イギリス人、英国人 [igirisujin, eikokujin]
enough - 十分 [juubun]
enter (Verb), to go in, to get into - 入る (動詞)、〜に入る [hairu (doushi), 〜ni hairu]
enterprise - 企業 [kigyou]
entrance - 入口 [iriguchi]
Entrepreneur - 事業家 [jigyouka]
entrepreneurship - 事業欲 [jigyouyoku]
equipment - 機材、設備 [kizai, setsubi]
error - エラー [era-]
escort (Verb) - 案内する (動詞) [annaisuru (doushi)]
establish (Verb) - 創立する (動詞) [souritsu suru (doushi)]
evening - 夜 [yoru]
eventually, at last - 結局は、最後は [kekkyoku ha, saigo ha]
exact, precise - 正確な、精密な [saikakuna, seimitsuna]
examine (Verb), to view - 調査する (動詞)、見る [chousasuru (doushi), miru]
excellent - 素晴らしい、優秀な、大変良い [subarashii, yuushuuna, taihen yoi]
except, besides, but - 〜以外、〜を除いて [〜igai, 〜wo nozoite]

exchange - 交換 [koukan]
excuse (Verb) - 許す (動詞)、言い訳をする [yurusu (doushi), iiwake wo suru]
execute (Verb) - 遂行する (動詞)、実行する
execution - 実行 [zikkou]
exhibition - 展覧会 [tenrankai]
exit (Verb), to leave - 出る (動詞)、去る [deru (doushi), saru]
expand (Verb) - 拡大する (動詞) [kakudaisuru (doushi)]
expend (Verb), to spend - 消費する (動詞)、費やす [shouhisuru (doushi), tsuiyasu]
expenditure - 支出、消費、費用 [shishutsu, shouhi, hiyou]
expense - 支出、費用 [shishutsu, hiyou]
expensive - 高価、(値段が) 高い [kouka, (nedan ga) takai]
experience - 経験 [keiken]
experienced - 経験した、経験のある [keikenshita, keiken no aru]
explain (Verb) - 説明する (動詞) [setsumeisuru (doushi)]
express (Verb) - 表現する (動詞) [hyougensuru (doushi)]
extension - 延長 [enchou]
external - 外部の [gaibuno]
extra - 余分の [yobunno]
factory, plant - 工場、施設 [koujou, shisetsu]
failure, crash - 失敗、衝突 [shippai, shoutotsu]
fame - 名声 [meisei]
fast - 速い、早い [hayai, hayai]
faster - より速い、より早い [yorihayai, yorihayai]
fax - ファックス [fakkusu]
feature - 機能、特徴 [kinou, tokuchou]
fifteen - 15、十五 [juugo]
fifty - 50、五十 [gojuu]
figure out - 解決する、理解する [kaiketsusuru, rikaisuru]
file (Verb) - ファイルにまとめる (動詞) [fairu ni matomeru]

file /folder - ファイル /フォルダ [fairu /foruda-]
fill out - 埋める [umeru]
finally - やっと、最後に [yatto, saigoni]
finance (Verb) - 融資する (動詞) [yuushisuru (doushi)]
financial - 財務 [zaimu]
find (Verb) - 発見する (動詞) [hakkensuru (doushi)]
find out / to clarify - 発見する、確認する / 明確にする [hakken sur, kakunin suru / meikakunisuru]
finish (Verb) - 終わる (動詞) [owaru (doushi)]
firm - 会社 [kisha]
first - 最初、始め、1番 [saisho, hajime, ichiban]
five - 5、五 [go]
flight - フライト [furaito]
floor - 階 [kai]
fly (Verb) - 飛ぶ (動詞) [tobu (doushi)]
for - 〜のため [〜no tame]
for a while, for a short time - しばらくの間、短い間 [shibaraku no aida, mijikaiaida]
force (Verb) - させる (動詞) [saseru (doushi)]
forced - 強いられる [shiirareru]
foreign - 外国 [gaikoku]
forget (Verb) - 忘れる [wasureru (doushi)]
form (Verb) - 形づける (動詞) [katachi zukeru (doushi)]
format, form - フォーマット、フォーム [fo-matto, fo-mu]
formation - 変形 [henkei]
forty - 40、四十 [yonjuu]
found - 発見された [hakkensareta]
four - 4、四 [yon]
free - 自由 [jiyuu]
free (of charge) - (料金が)無料 [(ryoukin ga) muryou]
French, Frenchman - フランス語、フランスの、フランス人 [furansugo,furansuno, furansujin]
French woman - フランス女性 [furansujosei]
Friday - 金曜日 [kinyoubi]
friend - 友達 [tomodachi]
from - 〜から [〜kara]
from the start, from the beginning, first - 開始から、始めから [kaishikara, hajimekara]
full - 全て、全体 [suubete, zentai]
function - 機能 [kinou]
funds, means - 資産、財産 [shisan, zaisan]
future - 未来 [mirai]
gather (Verb) - 集める (動詞)、収集する [atsumeru (doushi), shuushuu suru]
general - 一般の、一般的 [ippanno, ippanteki]
general manager, director - 総支配人、取締役、指導者 [soushihainin, torishimariyaku, shidousha]
German - ドイツ語、ドイツの、ドイツ人 [doitsugo, doitsuno, doitsujin]
Germany - ドイツ [doitsu]
get (be) interested / to interest - (〜に)興味を持つ / 興味を持たせる [kyoumi wo motsu / kyoumi wo motaseru]
get down to, to start - 取り掛かる、開始する [torikakaru, kaishisuru]
get rid of - を取り除く [wo torinozoku]
give (Verb) - あげる (動詞)、与える、渡す (動詞) [ageru (doushi), ataeru, watasu (doushi)]
glad, happy, joyful - 安心、嬉しい、喜ばしい [anshin, ureshii, yorokobashii]
go (Verb), to head - 行く (動詞)、へ向かう [iku (doushi), he mukau]
go out, to leave - 出る、出発する [deru, shuppatsusuru]
goal, target - ゴール、目標 [go-ru, mokuhyou]
good - 優れた、良い、元気 [sugureta, yoi, genki]
Goodbye! - さようなら！[sayounara!]
goods, products - 商品、製品 [shouhinn, seihin]

Greek - ギリシャの、ギリシャ人 [girishano, girishajin]
green - 緑 [midori]
group - グループ [guru-pu]
growth - 成長 [seichou]
guarantee (*Verb*) - 保証する (動詞) [hoshousuru]
guest - 客、ゲスト [kyaku, gesuto]
guys - 皆 [minna]
hacker - ハッカー [hakka-]
half an hour - 30 分 [sanjuppun]
handle (*Verb*), to cope - 扱う (動詞)、うまく処理する [atsukau (doushi), umakushorisuru]
hang (*Verb*), to crash - つるす (動詞) [tsurusu]
happen (*Verb*), to occur - 起こる (動詞)、発生する [okoru (doushi), hassei suru]
hard - 硬い [katai]
have (*Verb*) - 持っている、所有する (動詞)、手に取る (動詞)、持つ [motteiru, shoyuusuru (doushi), tenitoru (doushi), motsu]
he - 彼 [kare]
headquarter - 統括会社、ヘッドクオーター [toukatsugaisha, heddokuo-ta-]
hear (*Verb*), listen (*Verb*) - 聞く (動詞) [kiku (doushi)]
Hello! - こんにちは！ [konnichiha!]
help (*Verb*) - 助ける (動詞)、役立つ [tasukeru (doushi), yakudatsu]
hence / from here - したがって、ここから [shitagatte, kokokara]
here - ここ [koko]
here is - これは〜です [kore ha 〜 desu.]
high - 高い [takai]
high speed / fast - 高速 / 早い [kousoku, hayai]
higher / above - より高い / の上 [yori takai / no ue]
highrise - 高層建築 [kousoukenchiku]
history - 履歴、ヒストリー [rireki, hisutori-]

hold (*Verb*) / to escort - 持つ (動詞) / エスコート [motsu (doushi) / esuko-to]
hope (*Verb*) / to expect - 希望する (動詞)、願う、期待する [kibou suru (doushi), negau, kitaisuru]
hot - 暑い [atsui]
hotel - ホテル [hoteru]
hour, time - 時間 [jikan]
how - どうやって [douyatte]
how much (many) - いくら (いくつ) [ikutsu (ikura)]
huge - 大きな、巨大な [ookina, kyodaina]
human / man - 人間 / 人 [ningen / hito]
hurry (*Verb*), to rush - 急ぐ (動詞) [isogu (doushi)]
I - 私 [watashi]
idea - アイデア [aidea]
if - もし [moshi]
ill, to be sick - 気分悪くなる、病気になる [kibun ga warukunaru, byouki ni naru]
impatience - 短気 [tanki]
important - 重要 [juuyou]
in - 〜の中 [〜 no naka]
inaccuracy - 不正確 [fuseikaku]
incompatibility - 両立しがたい、合わない [ryouritsu shigatai, awanai]
inconvenience - 不便 [fuben]
incorrectly - 間違って [machigatte]
increase (*Verb*), to grow - 増加する (動詞)、増える、育つ [zoukasuru (doushi), fueru, sodatsu]
indicator - 指標、指示するもの [shihyou, shijisurumono]
inexpensive - 費用のかからない / 高くない [hiyou no kakaranai / takakunai]
influence (*Verb*) - 影響する (動詞) [eikyousuru (douhshi)]
inform - 通知する [tsuuchisuru]
information - 情報 [jyouhou]
initially, first - 最初は、始め [saisho ha, hajimeni]
innovation - 革新 [kakushin]
innovative - 革新的な [kakushintekina]

inquiry - 質問、問い合わせ [shitsumon, toiawase]
insignificant, minor - ささいな、マイナーな [sasaina, maina-na]
installation - 設置 [secchi]
instead, in return, as a replacement - よりも、その代わりに、見返りに、代わりとして [yorimo, sono kawarini, mikaerini, kawari toshite]
interest - 興味 [kyoumi]
interesting - 興味深い、面白い [kyoumibukai, omoshiroi]
interface - インターフェース [inta-fe-su]
international - 国際的な [kokusaitekina]
Internet - インターネット [inta-netto]
interpreter - 通訳 [tsuuyaku]
introduce (Verb) - 紹介する (動詞) [shoukaisuru (doushi)]
inventory - インベントリ、目録 [inbentori-, mokuroku]
invite (Verb) - 招待する (動詞) shoutaisuru (doushi)
issue (Verb), to place - 発行する (動詞)、置く [hakkousuru (doushi), oku]
it - それ [sore]
Italian - イタリアの、イタリア人 [itariano, itariajin]
IT-specialist, IT-professional - IT スペシャリスト、IT 専門家 [IT supesharisuto, IT senmonka]
Japan - 日本 [nihon]
Japanese - 日本語 [nihongo]
joint - 統合 [tougou]
joke (Verb) - 冗談を言う (動詞) [jyoudan wo iu (doushi)]
journalist - 記者 [kisha]
key - 鍵 [kagi]
keyboard - キーボード [ki-bo-do]
kilometer - キロメートル [kirome-toru]
kind, good - 親切、良い [shinsetsu, yoi]
know (Verb) - 知る (動詞) [shiru (doushi)]
known - 知られている [shirareteiru]
land (Verb) - 着陸する (動詞) [chakurikusuru (doushi)]

language - 言語 [gengo]
large, voluminous - 大きい、大きな、豊富な [ookii, ookina, houfuna]
last - 最後 [saigo]
later / after - 後で / 後 [atode / ato]
launch, startup - 発売、開始 [hatsubai, kaishi]
lawyer, attorney - 法律家、弁護士 [houritsuka, bengoshi]
lay down / to go to bed - 横になる / ベッドに入る、寝る [yokoni naru / beddo ni hairu, neru]
lead (Verb), to conduct / to bring / to control - 導く (動詞)、リードする / 持ってくる / 指揮を執る [michibiku (doushi), ri-dosuru / mottekuru, shiki wo toru]
leader, head - リーダー、社長 [ri-da-, shachou]
leadership - リーダーシップ [ri-da-shippu]
learn (Verb), to get to know, to study - 学ぶ (動詞)、知るようになる、勉強する [manabu (doushi), shiruyouni naru, benkyousuru]
leave (Verb) - 残す (動詞) [nokosu (doushi)]
left - 左の、左に [hidarino, hidarini]
legal - 合法 [gouhou]
less - より少ない、少ない [yorisukunai, sukuna]
letter - 手紙 [tegami]
license - 免許、ライセンス [menkyo, raisensu]
licensed, certified - ライセンスのある、認証された [raisensu no aru, nintei sareta]
like (Verb) - 好き [suki (doushi)]
line - ライン、線 [rain, sen]
linger (Verb), to be late - 後に残る (動詞)、遅くなる [ato ni nokoru (doushi), osokunaru]
list (Verb) - 表にする (動詞) [hyounisuru]
listen (Verb) - 聞く (動詞) [kiku (doushi)]
little - 少し [sukoshi]
located, located - 位置する [ichisuru]
located, is - 位置する、〜にある [ichisuru, 〜ni aru]

long - 長い [nagai]
long ago / for long - ずいぶん前、昔 / 長く [zuibun mae, mukashi / nagaku]
look (Verb) / to scan - 見る (動詞) / スキャンする [miru (doushi) / sukyansuru]
love (Verb) - 愛する [aisuru (doushi)]
low - 低い [hikui]
lower / below - より低い / 低い、下 [yori hikui / hikui, shita]
lunch, dinner - 昼食、夕食 [chuushoku, yuushoku]
made, done - 作られた、終わった [tsukurareta, owatta]
magazine - 雑誌 [zasshi]
magnificent, gorgeous - 壮大な、豪華な [soudaina, goukana]
mail - メール [me-ru]
main, major - 中心、主要な [chuushin, shuyou na]
maintenance - メンテナンス [mentenansu]
malfunction, trouble - 故障、問題 [koshou, mondai]
malicious - 悪意のある [akui no aru]
man - 男性 [dansei]
manage (Verb), to lead - 管理する (動詞)、リードする [kanrisuru (doushi), ri-dosuru]
manager - マネージャー、管理者 [mane-jya-, kanrisha]
manufacturing, production - 製造、生産 [seizou, seisan]
manufacturing facilities, production lines - 製造設備、製造ライン [seizousetsubi, seizourain]
many, a lot of - 沢山、多くの [takusan, ookuno]
map - 地図、マップ [chizu, mappu]
margin / stock - マージン / 在庫 [ma-jin / zaiko]
marked, registered - 印をつけた、登録された [shirushi wo tsuketa, touroku sareta]
market - マーケット [ma-ketto]
match (Verb), to correspond - 一致する (動詞) [icchisuru (doushi)]
material - 資料 [shiryou]

may, can - してもよい [〜shitemoyoi]
meanwhile / until - その間に / 〜まで [sonoaidani / 〜made]
meet (Verb) / to introduce - 会う (動詞) / 紹介する [au (doushi) / shoukaisuru]
meeting - 会議、ミーティング [kaigi, mitingu]
message - メッセージ [messe-ji]
metallic - 金属の [kinzokuno]
method - 方法 [houhou]
mine, my - 私の [watashi no]
minute - 分 [fun]
mistake, flaw - 間違え、欠点 [machigae, ketten]
model - モデル [moderu]
modern - モダン、現代の [modan, gendaino]
modified / improved - 修正された / 改良された [shuuseisareta / kairyousareta]
modify (Verb) - 修正する (動詞) [shuuseisuru (doushi)]
Monday ['mʌndei] - 月曜日 [getsuyoubi]
money - お金 [okane]
monitor - モニター [monita-]
monitor (Verb), to watch - モニターする (動詞)、監視する [monita-suru (doushi), kanshisuru]
month - 月 [tsuki]
monthly - 毎月の [maitsukino]
mood - ムード [mu-do]
more - 更に、より [sarani, yori]
more complex / difficult - 更に複雑な / 難しい [sarani fukuzatsuna, muzukashii]
more confidently - より自信を持って [yori jishin wo motte]
more convenient - より便利に [yori benrini]
more convincing - より説得力のある [yori settokuryoku no aru]
more detailed - より詳細に [yorishousaini]
more expensive - より高価な [yori koukana]
more profitable - より有益な [yori yuuekina]
morning - 朝 [asa]

most - 最も [mottomo]
motivate (Verb) - 動機付ける (動詞) 、やる気になる [doukizukeru (doushi), yarukininaru]
mouse - マウス [mauseu]
move (Verb) - 動かす 、動く (動詞) [ugokasu, ugoku (doushi)]
movement - 動き [ugoki]
much more - さらにもっと [saranimotto]
multiple - 複数 [fukusuu]
must, to have to - 〜する必要がある 、〜しなければならない [〜suru hitsuyou ga aru, 〜shinakereba naranai]
mutually beneficial, win-win - 相互利益 、ウィンウィン [sougorieki, uinuin]
name - 名づける 、名前をあげる [nazukeru, namae wo ageru]
near, close - 近い [chikai]
necessarily, unavoidably - 必ずしも 、やむをえず 、避けられない [kanarazushimo, yamuoezu, sakerarenai]
need - を必要とする [hitsuyouto suru]
need, necessary - 必要 、必須 [hitsuyou, hissu]
negotiations - 交渉 [koushou]
neighboring - 近所の [kinjyono]
network - ネットワーク [nettowa-ku]
new, novel - 新しい 、目新しい [atarashii, metarashii]
newest - 最新の [saishinno]
news - ニュース [nyu-su]
next - 次 [tsugi]
nice - 良い 、素敵 [yoi, suteki]
night - 夜 [yoru]
nine - 9 、九 [kyuu]
no - いいえ [iie]
no one - 誰も [daremo]
node - ノード [no-do]
noon - 正午 [shougo]
normal - 普通 、標準 [futsuu, hyoujun]
not - 〜でない [〜de nai]
not big, small - 大きくない 、小さい [ookikunai, chiisai]
not enough - 十分でない [juubun de nai]

note - メモ 、ノート [memo, no-to]
note (Verb), to notice - 書きとめる (動詞) 、気づく [kakitomeru (doushi), kizuku]
nothing - 何もない [nanimo nai]
notice (Verb) - 気づく (動詞) [kizuku (doushi)]
novelty - ノベルティ [noberuti-]
now - 今 [ima]
number - 数字 、番号 [suuji, bangou]
obedient - 従順な [juujunna]
obligation - 義務 [gimu]
obligatory - 義務的な [gimutekina]
obliged - せざるおえない [sezaruoenai]
obtain - 手に入れる [te ni ireru]
occasion - 状況
occur (Verb) - 起こる (動詞) [okoru (doushi)]
of course - もちろん [mochiron]
of the office - 事務所の [jimusho]
offer (Verb) - 提供する (動詞) 、申し出る [teikyousuru, moushideru]
office - オフィス 、事務所 [ofisu, jimusho]
often - よく [yoku]
old - 古い [furui]
on - 〜の上 [〜no ue]
one - 1 、一 [ichi]
one hundred - 100 、百 [hyaku]
only - 〜だけ [〜dake]
open (Verb) - 開ける (動詞) [akeru (dosuhi)]
openly - オープンに [o-punnni]
optimism - 楽天主義 [rakutenshugi]
optional / additional - オプションの / 追加の [opushonno / tsuikano]
or - または [mataha]
order - オーダー 、注文 [o-da-, chuumon]
order (Verb), to book - 注文する (動詞) 、予約する [chuumonsuru, yoyakusuru]
other - 他の [hoka no]
our - 私たちの [watashitachi no]
over, above - 〜を超えて 、〜の上 [〜wo koete, 〜no ue]
own - 所有する [shoyuu suru]

package, parcel, batch - パッケージ、包み、バッチ [pakke-ji, tsutsumi, bacchi]
paid - 支払われた [shiharawareta]
panoramic - パノラマ式の [panoramashikino]
paper - 紙 [kami]
parameters - パラメーター [parame-ta-]
part - 一部 [ichibu]
participant, member - 参加者、メンバー [sankasha, menba-]
participate (Verb), to take part - 参加する (動詞) [sankasuru (doushi)]
participation - 参加 [sanka]
partner - パートナー、仲間、協力者 [pa-tona-, nakama, kyouryokusha]
pass (Verb) - パスする (動詞) /経過する (動詞) [pasusuru (doushi) / tsuukasuru]
past / last - 過ぎた /最後の [suugita /saigono]
path - 道 [michi]
pay (Verb) - 払う (動詞) [harau (doushi)]
pay extra - 余分に払う [yobun ni harau]
payment - 支払い [shiharai]
people - 人々 [hitobito]
percent - 率、パーセンテージ [ritsu, pa-sente-ji]
perform (Verb) - 実行する (動詞) [jikkou suru (doushi)]
period, time, phase - 期間、時間、フェーズ [kikan, jikan, fr-zu]
periodical - 定期刊行の [teikikankouno]
persuade (Verb) - 説得する (動詞) [settoku suru (doushi)]
persuasively - 説得力を持って [settokuryoku wo motte]
phone - 電話 [denwa]
piece, unit - 断片、破片 [danpen, hahen]
place - 場所 [basho]
plan - 予定、計画 [yotei, keikaku]
plan (Verb) - 計画する (動詞) [keikakusuru (doushi)]
plane, airplane - 飛行機 [hikouki]
planning - 計画 [keikaku]
plastic - プラスチック [purasuchikku]

pleasant - 満足できる、楽しい [manzokudekiru, tanoshii]
please - お願い、どうぞ [onegai, douzo]
pleased - 満足して、喜んで [manzokushite, yorokonde]
pleasure - 喜び、楽しみ [yorokobi, tanoshimi]
point, moment - 点、その時 [ten, sonotoki]
popular - 有名 [yuumei]
position, post - 役職、地位 [yakushoku]
positive - ポジティブ [pojitibu]
possible, perhaps - 可能である、もしかしたら [kanou dearu, moshikashitara]
prefer (Verb) - 〜をより好む (動詞)、〜をより望む [〜 wo yori konomu (doushi), 〜 wo yori nozomu]
preliminarily - 予備的に [yobitekini]
preparation, training - 準備、訓練 [junbi, kunren]
prepare (Verb) - 用意する (動詞) [youisuru (doushi)]
present - 出席する [shussekisuru]
presentation - プレゼンテーション [purezente-shon]
preventative maintenance - 予防メンテナンス [yobou mentenansu]
preview, review - プレビュー、レビュー [purebyu-, rebyu-]
previous - 前の、前回の [maeno, zenkaino]
price, rate - 値段、レート [nedan, re-to]
price list - 値段表、値段のリスト [nedanhyou, nedan no risuto]
print (Verb) - 印刷する (動詞)、プリント [insatsu suru (doushi), purinto suru]
printed - 印刷した [printoshita]
printer - プリンター [purinta-]
probably - 恐らく [osoraku]
problem - 問題 [mondai]
process - 処理 [shori]
process (Verb) - 処理する (動詞) [shorisuru (doushi)]
processing, clearance - 処理する、一掃 [shori suru, issou]

processing / accounting - 処理 / 会計 [shori / kaikei]
producer, maker, manufacturer - プロデューサー、メーカー、製造業者 [purodu-sa-]
product, products - 製品 [seihin]
profession, occupation - 職業、業務 [shokugyou, gyoumu]
profit, benefit - 利益、もうけ [rieki, mouke]
profitable, advantageous, lucrative - 有益な、有利な、もうかる [yuuekia, yurina, moukaru]
program - プログラム [puroguramu]
programmer - プログラマー [purogurama-]
project - プロジェクト、企画 [purojekuto, kikaku]
promising, perspective - 約束された、有望な、期待できる、考え方 [yakusokusareta, yuunouna, kangaekata]
prompt (Verb) - 駆り立てる (動詞) [karitateru (douhsi)]
prospect, perspective - 予想、予測、視点 [yosou, yosoku, shiten]
provide (Verb), to include - 提供する (動詞)、〜を含める [teikyousuru (doushi), 〜 wo fukumeru]
public - 公共の場、公共の [koukyou no ba, koukyou no]
punctual - 時間に正確な [jikan ni seikakuna]
purchase, buy - 購入、買う [kounyuu, kau]
quality - 質、品質、クオリティ [shitsu, hinshitsu, kuoriti-]
quantity - 量 [ryou]
question - 疑問 [gimon]
quickly - 急いで [isoide]
rain - 雨 [ame]
raise (Verb) - 上げる (動詞) / 持ち上げる、増加する (動詞) [ageru (doushi) / mochiageru, zoukasuru (doushi)]
rather / faster / likely - むしろ / より早く / きっと〜でありそうな [mushiro / yori hayaku / kitto 〜 de arisouna]

ratio - レート、割合 [re-to, wariai]
rational - 合理的な [gouritekina]
read (Verb) - 読む (動詞) [yomu (doushi)]
ready - 準備する、用意する、用意、準備 [junbisuru, youisuru, youi, jyunnbi]
realization - 認識 [ninshiki]
really - 本当、本当に、とても [hontou, hontouni, totemo]
reason - 理由 [riyuu]
receive (Verb) / to perceive - 受け取る (動詞) / 了解する [uketoru (doushi) / ryoukaisuru]
reduce (Verb), to cut - 削減する (動詞)、切る [sakugensuru (doushi), kiru]
refer (Verb) / to turn to - 参照する (動詞)、仕事をする [sanshou suru (doushi), shigoto wo suru]
reference, review - 参照、調査する、評判 [sanshou, chousasuru, hyouban]
refinement - 洗練 [senen]
reflected - 反映された、反射された [haneisareta, hanshasareta]
regional - 地域の [chiikino]
regular, normal - 通常、普通、普段 [tsuujyou, futsuu, fudan]
relation, feedback - 関係、フィードバック [kankei, fi-dobakk]
reliable - 頼りになる [tayorininaru]
remainder / balance - 残り / 残高 [nokori / zandaka]
remove (Verb), to delete, to take off - 取り除く (動詞) [torinozoku (doushi)]
renewal - リニューアル [rinyu-aru]
replace (Verb) - 置き換える [okikaeru (doushi)]
report - レポート、報告 [repo-to, houkoku]
report (Verb) - 報告する (動詞) [houkoku suru (doushi)]
represent (Verb) - 象徴する (動詞)、代表する [shouchou suru, daihyou suru]
reputation - 評判 [hyouban]
request - 頼む、要求 [tanomu, youkyuu]

281

require (*Verb*) - 要求する、求める (動詞) [youkyuu suru, motomeru (doushi)]
requirement - 要求 [youkyuu]
resource - 源、リソース [minamoto, reso-su]
respond (*Verb*) - 応答する (動詞) [outousuru (doushi)]
responsibility, duty - 責任、責務 [sekinin, sekimu]
responsible, liable - 責任のある [sekinin no aru]
rest - 残り [nookri]
rest (*Verb*), to recreate, to relax - 休む、休養、休憩する (動詞)、リラックスする [yasumu, kyuuyou, kyuukeisuru, rirakkusu suru]
restart (*Verb*), to reboot - 再起動する (動詞)、リブートする [saikidousuru (douhsi), ribu-tosuru]
restriction / limit - 制限 / 上限 [seigen / jougen]
result, bottom line - 結果、最低値 [kekka, saiteichi]
return - 返金、リターン [henkin, rita-n]
return (*Verb*) - 帰る、戻る (動詞) [kaeru, modoru (doushi)]
revenue, income - 総収入、収入 [soushuunyuu, shuunyuu]
reverse - 反対にする [hantai ni suru]
right - 右の、右に [migino, migini]
right / guarantee - 正しい / 保証 [tadashii, hoshou]
ring (*Verb*), to call - 鳴らす (動詞)、呼ぶ [narasu, yobu]
road - 道路 [douro]
room - 部屋 [heya]
route, direction - ルート、方向 [ru-to, houkou]
run (*Verb*) - 走る (動詞) [hashiru (doushi)]
Russian - ロシア語、ロシアの、ロシア人 [roshiago, roshiano, roshiajin]
safely / reliably - 安全に / 頼りになるように、壊れることなく [anznni, tayorininaru youni, kowarerukoto naku]
sale - 売る [uru]
sales - 売れ行き [ureyuki]
salesman, dealer - 営業マン、ディーラー [eigyouman, di-ra-]
sample - サンプル [sanpuru]
save (*Verb*) / to keep / to store - 保存する (動詞) / 保つ / 保管する [hozonsuru (doushi) / tamotsu / hokansuru]
saving, preservation - 預金、保存 [yokin, hozon]
scan (*Verb*) - スキャンする (動詞) [sukyan suru (doushi)]
schedule, regimen - 予定、摂生 [yotei, sessei]
scheme - 計画 [keikaku]
second - 2番 [niban]
secondary - 2番目の [nibanmeno]
secretary - 秘書 [hisho]
section / block - セクション / ブロック [sekushon / burokku]
secure (*Verb*), to set down - 守る、保証する (動詞)、固定する [mamoru, hoshousuru (doushi), koteisuru]
see (*Verb*), look (*Verb*) - 見る (動詞)、会う [miru (doushi), aru]
sell (*Verb*) - 売る (動詞) [uru (doushi)]
send (*Verb*) - 送る、送信する (動詞) [okuru, soushinsuru (doushi)]
separate - 離す [hanasu]
serious - 真面目な、重要な [majimena, juuyouna]
server - サーバー [sa-ba-]
service - サービス [sa-bisu]
set up, to install, to put, to place - 設定、セットアップ、インストール、設置する、置く [settei, setto appu, insuto-ru, secchisuru, oku]
setting, tuning - 設定する、チューニング [setteisuru, chu-ningusuru]
seven - 7、七 [nana]
seventh - 7日、七日 [nanoka]
she - 彼女 [kanojyo]
sheet / list - シート / 表、一覧、リスト [shi-to / hyou, ichiran, risuto]
shelve - 棚 [tana]

shield - シールド [shi-rudo]
shipment - 発送 [hassou]
shortage / loss - 不足 / 損失 [fusoku, sonshitsu]
show (Verb) - 見せる (動詞) [miseru (doushi)]
side - 横、側 [yoko, soba]
sign (Verb) - 署名する (動詞)、サインする [shomeisuru (doushi), sainsuru]
significant - 重要な、著しく [juuyouna, ichijirushiku]
significantly, considerably, much - 著しく、ずいぶん、とても [ichijirushiku, zuibun, totemo]
simple - シンプル [shinpuru]
simpler, easier - よりシンプルな、より簡単な [yori shinpuruna, yori kantanna]
situation - 状況 [joukyou]
size - 大きさ、サイズ [ookisa, saizu]
skill - 能力 [nouryoku]
sleep (Verb) - 眠る (動詞) [nemuru (doushi)]
slightly, a bit, a little bit - 少々、少し、ちょっと [shoushou, sukoshi, chotto]
slow - 遅い [osoi]
small - 小さい [chiisai]
so, that - それでは、そのため、あれ [sore deha sonotame, are]
so, then - つまり、そして [tsumari, soshite]
software, program - ソフトウェア、プログラム [sofutouea, puroguramu]
sold - 売った [utta]
solution - 解決策 [kaiketsusaku]
some - いくつか [ikutsuka]
someone / some - 誰か / いくつか [dareka / ikutsuka]
sometimes - 時々 [tokidoki]
soon - すぐ [sugu]
Sorry - 申し訳ありません [moushiwake arimasen]
southern - 南の [minamino]
spacious, roomy - 広い、広々とした [hiroi, hirobirotoshita]

Spain - スペインの [supeinno]
Spanish woman - スペイン女性 [supeinjosei]
speak (Verb), to present - 話す (動詞)、発表する [hanasu (doushi), happyou suru]
special - 特別 [tokubetsu]
specialist - 専門家 [senmonka]
specific - 明確な [meikakuna]
specify (Verb), to itemize, to point out - 明示する (動詞)、はっきりする (動詞)、指し示す [meijisuru, hakkiri suru (douhsi), sashishimesu]
speech, presentation - スピーチ、プレゼンテーション [supi-chi, purezente-shon]
spirit - 心、精神 [kokoro, seishin]
staff, personnel - スタッフ、社員 [sutaffu, shainn]
start (Verb) / to get to / to begin - 開始する (動詞) / をやり始める / 始める [kaishisuru (doushi) / wo yarihajimeru / hajimeru]
station - 駅 [eki]
stay (Verb) - 残る (動詞) [nokru (douhsi)]
stop (Verb) / to stay - 止まる (動詞)、留まる [tomaru (doushi), todomaru]
store (Verb) - 保管する (動詞) [hokansuru (doushi)]
strategy - 戦略 [senryaku]
street, outside - 道、道路、外 [michi, douro, soto]
strict - 厳しい [kibishii]
strong - 強い [tsuyoi]
strongly - 力強く [chikarazuyoku]
subject - 主題 [shudai]
subscription - 予約購読、定期購入 [yoyaku kounyuu, teiki kounyuu]
substantial - 実体のある、かなりの [jittai no aru, kanarino]
succeed (Verb) / to manage - 成功する (動詞) / 管理する [seikousuru (doushi) / kanrisuru]
successful, lucky - 成功した、ラッキーな [seikoushita, rakki-na]
successfully - 上手く、成功して [umaku, sekoushite]

such / so - このような / こんな [konoyouna / konna]
sugar - 砂糖 [satou]
suggest (Verb), to offer - 提案する (動詞) [teiansuru (doushi)]
suit (Verb) / to arrange - はまる (動詞)、合う / アレンジする [hamaru (doushi), au / arenjisuru]
suitable (about terms or conditions) - 〜に適している (期間や状況に) [〜ni tekishiteiru (kikan ya joukyouni)]
sum (Verb) - 合計する (動詞) [goukeisuru (doushi)]
sure - 確かである [tashika dearu]
system - システム [shisutemu]
table - テーブル [te-buru]
tactfully - 上手に [jyouzuni]
take (Verb) - 持つ、持っていく (動詞)、取る (動詞) [motsu, motteiku (doushi), toru (doushi)]
take into account, to consider - 考慮した上で、考える [kouryoshita uede, kangaeru]
take place, to pass - 開催する、行われる、通り過ぎる [kaisai suru, okonawareru, toorisugiru]
talk (Verb) / to reflect - 話す (動詞) [hanasu (doushi)]
tall, high - 背の高い、高い [se no takai, takai]
task - タスク、仕事 [tasuku, shigoto]
taxi, cab - タクシー [takushi-]
tea - 紅茶 [koucha]
teach (Verb) - 教える (動詞) [oshieru (doushi)]
technology - テクノロジー [tekunoroji-]
tell (Verb) - 言う (動詞)、教える [iu (doushi), oshieru]
ten - 10、十 [juu]
tested, proven - 試験された、証明された [shikensareta, shoumeisareta]
testing - 試験 [shiken]
thank (Verb) - 感謝する (動詞) [kansha suru (doushi)]

thank you - ありがとうございます [arigatougozaimasu]
thanks to - 〜のおかげで [〜no okagede]
that - あれ [are]
then - そして、それから [soshite, sorekara]
there - そこ [soko]
they - 彼ら、彼女ら、それら [karera, kanojyora, sorera]
thing - 物 [mono]
think (Verb), to contemplate - 考える (動詞)、〜だと思う、熟考する [kangaeru (doushi), 〜dato omou, jyukkosuru]
third - 3番 [sanban]
thirty - 30、三十 [sanjuu]
this - これ [kore]
thoughtful - よく考え抜いた
thousand - 1000、千 [sen]
three - 3、三 [san]
through, in (a certain time) - 通して、徹底して、後に (一定時間) [toushite, tetteishite, goni (itteijikan)]
Thursday - 木曜日 [mokuyoubi]
ticket - チケット [chiketto]
time - 時間通りに、時間内に [jikandoorini, jikannai ni]
time, due date - 時間、締め切り日 [jikan, shimekiribi]
tire (Verb) - 疲れさせる (動詞) [tsukaresaseru (doushi)]
title, name - 題名、名前 [daimei, namae]
to / so that / in order - 〜に、〜〜のために / 〜となるように / 〜するために [〜ni, 〜no tameni / 〜tonaruyouni / 〜surutameni]
today - 今日 [kyou]
together - 一緒に [isshoni]
tomorrow - 明日 [asu]
trade - 商業 [shougyou]
trade (Verb) - 取引する (動詞) [torihiki suru (doushi)]
trading, commercial - 取引、広告、宣伝 [torihiki, koukou, senden]
traditional - 伝統的な [dentoutekina]

transfer (*Verb*) - 移動する (動詞) [idousuru]
transportation - 輸送 [yusou]
trip - 出張、旅 [shucchou, tabi]
true, correct - 本当、訂正 [hontou, teisei]
try (*Verb*) - 挑戦する (動詞)、試す、試す (動詞) [chousen suru (doushi), kokoromiru, tamesu (doushi)]
Tuesday - 火曜日 [kayoubi]
turn (*Verb*), to rotate - 回転する (動詞) [kaitensuru (doushi)]
turn (*Verb*) to / to return - 仕事を始める (動詞) [shigoto wo hajimeru (doushi) / modoru]
turn out - 〜になる [〜ni naru]
turnover - 回転率 [kaitenritsu]
twelve - 12、十二 [juuni]
twenty - 20、二十 [nijuu]
two - 2、二 [ni]
unclaimed - 要求されていない [youkyuu sareteinai]
under - の下 [no shita]
understand (*Verb*) - 理解する (動詞) [rikaisuru (douhsi)]
undesirable - 望ましくない [nozomashikunai]
unit - ユニット、単位 [yunitto, tani]
unplanned - 予定していない [yotei shiteinai]
unprofitable - 利益の無い [rieki no nai]
up to date - 最新式の [saishin no]
update, renew - アップデート、リニュー [appude-to, rinyuu]
updated - アップデート [appude-to]
urgently - 緊急に [kinkyuuni]
use (*Verb*) - 使う (動詞) [tsukau (doushi)]
useful - 役に立つ [yakunitatsu]
user - ユーザー / 利用者 [yu-za- / riyosha]
usual / familiar - 普段 / 良く知っている [fudan, yokushittiru]
usually - 普段 [fudan]
value (*Verb*), to appreciate - 評価する、尊重する (動詞)、感謝する [hyoukasuru, souchou suru (doushi), kansha suru]

value, significance - 価値、重要性 [juuyousei]
various - さまざまな [samazamana]
version - バージョン [ba-jon]
very - とても [totemo]
view - 視界、景色 [shikai, keshiki]
view (*Verb*), to watch, to look - 見る (動詞) [miru (doushi)]
viral - ウィルスの [uirusuno]
visible, seen - 目に見える、見える [meni mieru, mieru]
visit - 訪ねる [tazumeru]
visitor - 訪問者 [houmonsha]
volume - 量 [ryou]
wait (*Verb*) - 待つ (動詞) [matsu (doushi)]
waiting, anticipation, expectation - 待っている、予想、予期、期待 [matteiru, yosou, yoki, kitai]
waiting room - 待合室 [machiaishitsu]
walk (*Verb*) - 歩く (動詞) [aruku]
want (*Verb*) - 欲しい (動詞) [hoshii (doushi)]
warehouse - 倉庫 [souko]
warm - 暖かい [atatakai]
was - 〜だった [〜datta]
watch (*Verb*), to look - 見る (動詞) [miru (doushi)]
way - 方法 [houhou]
we - 私たち [watashitachi]
weather - 天気 [tenki]
Web designer - ウェブデザイン [uebudezain]
Wednesday - 水曜日 [suiyoubi]
week - 週 [shuu]
welcome (*Verb*), to greet - 迎える (動詞) [mukaeru (doushi)]
well - 上手に、うまく [jyouzuni, umaku]
wellknown, famous - 良く知られた、有名な [yokushirareta, yuumeina]
what / that / which - 何 / あれ / どれ [nani / are / dore]
when - いつ [itsu]
where / from where - どこ / どこから [doko / doko kara]

285

whether - 天気 [tenki]
which - どれ [dore]
who - 誰 [dare]
wholesale - 卸売り [oroshiuri]
whose - 誰の [dareno]
why - どうして [douhsite]
will be - 〜になる、来る [〜ni naru, kuru]
window - 窓 [mado]
wired, connected - 有線の、接続した、繋がった [yuusen no, setuzokushita, tsunagatta]
with / at - 〜と /〜で [〜to / 〜de]
without - 〜を除いて [〜wo nozoite]
woman - 女性 [josei]
wonder (*Verb*), to be surprised - 驚く (動詞)、不思議に思う、驚く [odorok (doushi), fushigi ni omou, odoroku]
word - 言葉 [kotoba]

work (*Verb*) - 働く (動詞) [hataraku (doushi)]
worker - 働く人、従業員 [hataraku hito, juugyouin]
worry (*Verb*) - 心配する (動詞) [shinpaisuru (doushi)]
write (*Verb*) - 書く (動詞) [kaku (doushi)]
write-off, cancellation - 取り消し、キャンセル [torikeshi, kyanseru]
year - 年 [nen]
yes - はい [hai]
yesterday - 昨日 [kinou]
yet - まだ [mada]
you - あなた [anata]
young - 若い [wakai]
your - あなたの [anatano]

Recommended books

First Japanese Reader for Beginners
Bilingual for Speakers of English
Beginner and Elementary (A1 A2)

This book starts the series of Japanese Graded Readers. The book consists of Beginner and Elementary courses with parallel Japanese-English texts. The author maintains learners' motivation with funny stories about real life situations such as meeting people, studying, job searches, working etc. The method utilizes the natural human ability to remember words used in texts repeatedly and systematically. The second and the following chapters of the Beginner course have only about thirty new words each. The texts are provided with the phonetic transcriptions Furigana and Romaji. The audio tracks are available inclusive online.

First Japanese Reader for Students
Bilingual for Speakers of English
Beginner Elementary (A1 A2)

Each chapter is filled with words that are organized by topic, then used in a story in Japanese. Questions and answers rephrase information and text is repeated in English to aid comprehension. The quick and easy-to-use format organizes many of life's situations from knowing your way around the house, studying at university, or getting a job. The method utilizes the natural human ability to remember words used in texts repeatedly and systematically. The audio tracks are available inclusive on www.lppbooks.com/Japanese/

Learn Japanese Language Through Dialogue
Bilingual for Speakers of English
Beginner Elementary (A1 A2)

The textbook gives you a lot of examples on how questions in Japanese should be formed. It is easy to see the difference between Japanese and English using parallel translation. Common questions and answers used in everyday situations are explained simply enough even for beginners. The audio tracks are available inclusive on www.lppbooks.com/Japanese/

First Japanese Reader for Business
Bilingual for Speakers of English
Beginner Elementary (A1 A2)

First Japanese Reader for Business is a resource that guides readers with the Japanese vocabulary, phrases, and questions that are relevant to many situations in the workplace. With twenty-five chapters on topics from the office to software and supplementary resources including the Japanese/English and English/Japanese dictionaries, it is the book to help the businessperson take their Japanese language knowledge to the professional level. The audio tracks are available inclusive on www.lppbooks.com/Japanese/

First Japanese Medical Reader for Health Professions and Nursing
Bilingual for Speakers of English
Beginner Elementary (A1 A2)

First Japanese Medical Reader for Health Professions and Nursing will give you the words and phrases necessary for helping patients making appointments, informing them of their diagnosis, and their treatment options. Medical specialties range from ENT to dentistry. Supplementary resources include the Japanese/English and English/Japanese dictionaries. Use this book to take your Japanese knowledge to the health professional's level. The audio tracks are available inclusive on www.lppbooks.com/Japanese/

www.ingramcontent.com/pod-product-compliance
Lightning Source LLC
Chambersburg PA
CBHW080636170426
43200CB00015B/2861